The Necessary Past

The Necessary Past

Revising History in Contemporary African American Poetry

✦

Annette Debo

NORTHWESTERN UNIVERSITY PRESS
EVANSTON, ILLINOIS

Northwestern University Press
www.nupress.northwestern.edu

Printed in the United States of America

10 9 8 7 6 5 4 3 2 1

Library of Congress Cataloging-in-Publication Data

Names: Debo, Annette, 1964– author.
Title: The necessary past : revising history in contemporary African American poetry / Annette Debo.
Description: Evanston : Northwestern University Press, 2024. | Includes bibliographical references and index.
Identifiers: LCCN 2023049390 | ISBN 9780810146877 (paperback) | ISBN 9780810146884 (cloth) | ISBN 9780810146891 (ebook)
Subjects: LCSH: American poetry—African American authors—20th century—History and criticism. | American poetry—African American authors—21st century—History and criticism. | Historical poetry, American—20th century—History and criticism. | Historical poetry, American—21st century—History and criticism. | Literature and history—United States. | History in literature.
Classification: LCC PS153.B53 D43 2024 | DDC 811.509896073—dc23/eng/20240105
LC record available at https://lccn.loc.gov/2023049390

For Steve

CONTENTS

ACKNOWLEDGMENTS

I started writing a book quite different from this one, but this is the book that needed to be written. Its origin point was a class on African American literature and history that I teach with the historian Elizabeth Gillespie McRae. The interchange between literature and history has always fascinated me, but teaching that class over the last decade deepened my understanding of how these two fields interact. Early on, as I struggled to discover where my writing was headed, I sat in my study crowded by towering piles of poetry volumes, so many that they covered the floor and spilled off the shelves. So many focused on the historical poem. And there it was, the heart of my book.

It is also there that the thanks must begin: to Libby McRae, who sets a high standard. True team teaching—when the joint lectures, readings, assignments, and discussions are intertwined—is demanding, and I have enjoyed every minute of the classes we've taught together.

I also want to thank all of the poets who graciously gave of their time and attention in long conversations with me. It has been such a pleasure to talk with Elizabeth Alexander, Camille Dungy, Major Jackson, A. Van Jordan, Mendi Obadike, Evie Shockley, Natasha Trethewey, Frank X Walker, and Kevin Young. For conversations at conferences, over panels, during dinners and visits, thanks are due to dear friends Meta DuEwa Jones, Keith Leonard, Mary Helen Washington, Jean-Philippe Marcoux, Suzanne Churchill, Linda Kinnahan, Bill Maxwell, Tyrone Williams, and Aldon Nielsen, as well as more friends, fellow panelists, and organizers at the American Literature Association, Modernist Studies Association, and Penn State Celebrating African American Literature conferences.

At Western Carolina University, I'd like to thank former department heads Brent Kinser and Laura Wright, Dean David Kinner, and Provost Richard Starnes, all of whom supported this project enthusiastically. Heidi Buchanan and Dan Wendell at Hunter Library always deserve thanks, especially for the obscure sources used here. The Scholarly Development Assignment at WCU gave me time for research and writing, as did the Short-Term Fellowship at Emory University's Stuart A. Rose Manuscript, Archives, and Rare Book Library.

At Northwestern University Press, senior acquisitions editor Faith Wilson Stein and project editor Maia Rigas have been such a pleasure to work with, from the beginning, when readers were tough to find because COVID was stealing our collective energy, through the revision process, and on to this very book I can now hold in my hands. I'd also like to thank the generous and exacting readers who stepped forward despite the pandemic energy drain. Their readings made this book more precise, more insightful, and much better concluded.

And thanks are always due to my family who patiently listen to my ideas on rivers, hikes, and yoga mats in the Blue Ridge Mountains where we live. For Steve, this book has seen its own share of national and personal history. Here's to finishing it, persevering through COVID, and heading out into a world we are all in the process of redefining.

PREFACE

As I sat writing the opening chapter of this book during the summer of 2020, when mass protests roiled American cities following the murder of yet another African American man, George Floyd, by a Minneapolis police officer on May 25, 2020—coupled with a raging worldwide pandemic disproportionately impacting the African American community—the significance and weight of history made itself felt. Floyd's death is one on a continuum that is much too long: Breonna Taylor, Botham Jean, Philando Castile, Sandra Bland, Freddie Gray, Tamir Rice, Michael Brown, Eric Garner, Trayvon Martin, and so many more. A 2019 study by the National Academy of Sciences concludes that "police violence is a leading cause of death for young men, and young men of color face exceptionally high risk of being killed by police." Most at risk are African American men, who are "about 2.5 times more likely to be killed by police over the life course than are white men," but African American women also share the risk since they are "about 1.4 times more likely to be killed by police than are white women."[1] How did we get to a moment where Black men call out "I can't breathe" and then die at the hands of people whose primary responsibility is to protect the community?

At least part of the answer is wrapped up in how people choose to perceive the past. Even though the way history was told changed radically around 1970, as I will argue in the upcoming introduction, those newer, more accurate versions of the past are not necessarily well-known or accepted by all. Historian Eric Foner emphasizes:

> Slavery is a case in point. Nowhere is the gap between scholarly inquiry and public perceptions of history more stark. It is probably safe to say that the finest body of American historical writing to appear during the past thirty years has been produced by scholars of slavery and emancipation. This literature has not only established beyond question the centrality of slavery to the history of the United States but has refashioned our understanding of subjects ranging from colonial settlement to the American Revolution and the origins and consequences of the Civil War.[2]

A romanticized version of what is called Southern heritage as told by some white Southerners may now rarely describe the Civil War as the war of Northern aggression, but that version still has traction fifty years after the study of history began debunking those deeply held beliefs—and we see this discord in the way histories are told, heard, and accepted.

In my small city of Asheville, North Carolina, an obelisk bearing the name of Zebulon Baird Vance, a Confederate officer who served as governor and in the US Senate, was erected in 1896 by the United Daughters of the Confederacy and until recently dominated Pack Square, likely a location for the sale of enslaved people during antebellum times. We also had two other Confederate monuments, one next to the Vance Monument honoring Robert E. Lee and the other located by the Buncombe County courthouse, all prominent locations. A resolution by the City of Asheville and Buncombe County to remove or modify these monuments passed during what is coming to be called the long year of 2020, and two Confederate monuments were taken down. The Vance Monument was first shrouded while its fate was debated, and in 2021 the city decided to remove it. By that fall, it sat, reduced to a few blocks, waiting for the lawsuits contesting its removal to be settled in the courts. The courts originally came down on the side of removal, but in late 2022, the case was picked up by the North Carolina Supreme Court, stymieing efforts to replace it.

Confederate monuments around the country have been receiving equal censure. Silent Sam was toppled in Chapel Hill, statues of Confederate leaders were removed from Monument Avenue in Richmond, Virginia, and NASCAR banned the Confederate battle flag from its events—but the lawsuits are ongoing, in part because some states like North Carolina passed laws prohibiting the removal of monuments from public property, a law whose primary intent was to protect Confederate monuments. In nearby Sylva, a statue of a Confederate soldier—erected in 1915, the year the notorious film *The Birth of a Nation* was released—stands in front of what was once the county courthouse, now a library. Protests there have allegedly featured armed men attending a "vigil" around the statue and nearby protestors carrying Black Lives Matter signs and speaking out against police violence. But why have these wildly inaccurate versions of "Southern heritage" lasted so long and been defended so vehemently? Why haven't the histories written around 1970, far from new now fifty years later, made more inroads into all public beliefs about the past?

The answer is about the power in controlling history or, to quote Natasha Trethewey, who quotes George Orwell, "Who controls the past controls the future; who controls the present controls the past."[3] What contemporary African American historical poetry ultimately achieves is teaching history beyond the academy, reinstating African American history into popular memory. These poems shift the power dialectic in revising who speaks, whose stories are told, and who controls the past, present, and future. Art has the power to change people and even nations, and poetry is uniquely situated to handle the many ambiguities in history. And times do change: witness the spectacular National Museum of African American History and Culture prominently located on the mall in Washington, DC—which opened in 2016 and to which tickets remain hard to come by—and the 2018 opening of the expansive National Memorial for Peace and Justice in Montgomery, Alabama, with its focus on the history of lynching, as well as civil rights museums in Atlanta, Memphis, Birmingham, and Greensboro. Similarly, the Black historical poem writes African American history into public memory, reaching new audiences, creating monuments in words that honor figures like Sara Baartman, the Native Guard, MacNolia Cox, Jack Johnson and Jean-Michel Basquiat, Medgar Evers, and free and enslaved Blacks from the mid-nineteenth century.

While historical fiction by African American writers, primarily the neo-slave narrative, has received substantial critical attention, this study is the first book-length scholarly work to consider the Black historical poem. In critical studies like this one, we always build on the work of those who have written before us, and I am honored to offer a shout-out to the scholars who wrote the work that brought me to this point, this subject, this book. My work joins the following distinguished book chapters and articles on history and poetry: Trudier Harris's "History as Fact and Fiction" in the *Cambridge History of African American Literature*, Evie Shockley's "Going Overboard: African American Poetic Innovation and the Middle Passage," Olga Dugan's "Renegade Poetics, Southscapes, and the Poetry of History in Natasha Trethewey's *Thrall*," Pat Righelato's "Rita Dove and the Art of History," Wendy W. Walters's "Elizabeth Alexander's *Amistad*: Reading the Black History Poem through the Archive," Howard Rambsy II's "Catching Holy Ghosts: The Diverse Manifestations of Black Persona Poetry," and Joel Brouwer, who in 2001 issued a general call for more historical, and less confessional, poetry in "Clio Rising." Furthermore, in 2020 scholars Joanne V. Gabbin and Lauren K. Alleyne, of the influential Furious Flower Poetry Center, emphasized that critical studies of African American poetry have not kept up with the "dynamic blooming" of this field[4]—and so my study extends the critical attention dedicated to a genre flourishing in the twenty-first century.

Among the many noteworthy books written by the scholarly community working on African American poetry, I am particularly indebted to the work in Evie Shockley's *Renegade Poetics: Black Aesthetics and Formal Innovations in African American Poetry*, Meta DuEwa Jones's *The Muse Is Music: Jazz Poetry from the Harlem Renaissance to Spoken Word*, Keith Leonard's *Fettered Genius: The African American Bardic Poet from Slavery to Civil Rights*, Aldon Nielsen's *Black Chant: Languages of African-American Postmodernism* and *Integral Music: Languages of African-American Innovation*, Lorenzo Thomas's *Extraordinary Measures: Afrocentric Modernism and Twentieth-Century American Poetry*, Jean-Philippe Marcoux's *Jazz Griots: Music as History in the 1960s African American Poem*, Howard Rambsy II's *The Black Arts Enterprise and the Production of African American Poetry*, Hillary Holladay's *Wild Blessings: The Poetry of Lucille Clifton*, and Joanne V. Gabbin's three monumental *Furious Flower* collections, as well as volumes by Lauri Ramey, William J. Harris, and many more.

Introduction

The Contemporary Wave of Historical Poetry

"Poets are lyric historians," proclaimed Langston Hughes.[1] Today, the historical poem is an increasingly important genre in contemporary African American poetry. To be sure, the historical impulse is shared between literary generations and across genres. Many significant historical poems have been written by earlier writers like the three who most influenced the poets covered here—Robert Hayden, Michael S. Harper, and Rita Dove—and the drive to address history is shared by fiction writers in the flourishing neo-slave narrative genre—think of such novelists as Toni Morrison and Colson Whitehead—as well as in drama by playwrights like August Wilson and Suzan-Lori Parks. And yet, something new is happening in African American poetry in the sheer volume of poems tackling historical subjects. We are witnessing an outpouring of historical poetry by poets born in the 1960s and 1970s, a generation born as the Black Arts Movement was peaking and who benefited from the achievements of the civil rights years and newly created Black studies programs. The contemporary Black historical poem has important work to do in and beyond the academy. It is revising the past, transforming the present, and leading us toward a more just future.

The chapters that follow this introduction first look back at how Hayden, Harper, and Dove's combined influence created fertile ground for this flood of historical poetry and then explore the use of the historical poem by writers born after 1960, a generation Kevin Young positions as not the tail end of the Black Arts generation "but rather at the start of another 'new thing.' . . . We are the front lines of a new century."[2] The current wave of historical poetry began with Elizabeth Alexander's 1990 *The Venus Hottentot* about Sara Baartman, the African woman who was put on display in Europe from 1810 to 1815 and dissected after her early death, a figure whom Alexander recovers and to whom she bequeaths agency and interiority—and so I start there in considering the impulse to reinvent historical subjects, both famous and forgotten. In *Native Guard*, Natasha Trethewey embarks on a quest for social justice by connecting the victims of domestic violence to African American troops who fought and died during the Civil War to racial identity in the twenty-first-century South, the volume's structure physically enacting these three issues in its sections whose edges blur and bleed across one another. A. Van Jordan's *M-A-C-N-O-L-I-A* reimagines the life of an ordinary person who did something extraordinary, thirteen-year-old MacNolia Cox, who in 1936 advanced to the national spelling competition, vanquished only when the white judges dredged up "nemesis," a word absent from the approved list—her story one of African American resistance and achievement. In the multilayered *To Repel Ghosts: The Remix*, Kevin Young writes an extended sequence about heavyweight champion Jack Johnson within a book ostensibly about Jean-Michel Basquiat, a literary use of the visual art technique pentimento. Johnson's image is the underlayer that shows through, American history resurging into the present, illuminating the range and limits imposed upon Black male talent and celebrity. Frank X Walker wades into the civil rights years, writing about the assassination of Medgar Evers from multiple points of view in *Turn Me Loose*, a polyvocality that forces its disparate speakers to reckon with their actions in the spirit of truth and reconciliation. In *Suck on the Marrow*, Camille T. Dungy speculates on lives that could have been lived during the decades between the end of the international slave trade and the 1850 Fugitive Slave Law—years left unaddressed by most writers—and the forced migration of free and enslaved African Americans from the mid-Atlantic states to the Deep South. The conclusion addresses single poems by Major Jackson, Mendi + Keith Obadike, Dawn Lundy Martin, Quraysh Ali Lansana, Evie Shockley, and Tracy K. Smith, contemplating where this wave of historical poetry is headed now in the first decades of the twenty-first century.

Not only does this generation of writers have unprecedented access to archival material—previously forgotten and ignored—but the way histories are told and the focus of those histories changed radically around 1970, as their formal education would have begun. Negro History Week was created in 1926 by historian Carter G. Woodson and the Association for the Study of Negro Life and History, and it was placed during the second week of February to coincide with the birthday of Frederick Douglass on February 14 and Abraham Lincoln on February 12. Leaders of the Black United Students at Kent State University proposed that the week be expanded to Black History Month, which was first celebrated in February 1970 and officially recognized by the US government as part of the 1976 Bicentennial. Similarly, Kwanza was created in 1966 by Maulana Karenga. *Jet* magazine, begun in 1951, was "a newsmagazine, a gossip rag, a grapevine, a trumpet," a publication of "race-pride" that every Black American read, according to Elizabeth Alexander.[3] It garnered national attention through its coverage of the lynching of Emmett Till, and it offered extensive coverage of civil rights events. *Ebony*, another influential publication of the Black-owned Johnson Publishing Company, began publishing in 1945 and was modeled after the "big picture" magazine *Life*. Its executive editor, historian Lerone Bennett Jr. of *Before the Mayflower* (1962) and other influential history books, edited the multivolume *Ebony Pictorial History of Black America*, which recounted

African American history from the African past through the civil rights movement and Black Power revolution to his present in the 1970s, and his work at *Jet* and *Ebony* allowed him to reach a much broader audience than he would through academic publications. The first Black Studies Department was famously formed at San Francisco State University in 1968, and by 1971, over five hundred programs had been created at four-year colleges and universities.[4] Historian Thomas C. Holt describes the shift in the 1970s and '80s to "understanding black history as black people experienced it," a change he credited, in part, to Ralph Ellison's review (unpublished until 1964) of Gunnar Myrdal's *An American Dilemma*.[5] Thus, the histories contemporary poets grew up reading focused on fuller representations of African American life, the issue of objectivity in history came under question, and postmodernism impacted history as well as literary studies. Theorists like Hayden White and Stephen Greenblatt probed the relationship between literature and history, historians like Nell Irvin Painter and James Goodman told histories in new ways, and Eric Foner, in his book by the same name, contemplated the question, Who owns history?

The poets themselves have weighed in on why their generation is producing such a large volume of historical poetry. Kevin Young likens the contemporary use of history to hip-hop's borrowing from older music: "History is ever-present, the past easily taken from ('sampled'), repeated ('looped'), collaged together, unified often only by voice and by the rhythm of day-to-day life ('flow' and 'beat')."[6] Elizabeth Alexander echoes Arthur Schomburg in "The Negro Digs Up Her Past," repeating his title with only "his" changed to "her" and reiterating his first line: "The American Negro must remake his past in order to make his future." She comments, "That's what the old folks say, and I think it is still true. Never have we had more material to work with, more archival sources and resources with which to explore and then imagine the past."[7] Camille T. Dungy maintains that "we are the first generation of black Americans with broad access to education, publication and many other tools necessary to and expected of the progressive thinker and writer."[8] Major Jackson credits holidays like Black History Month and Kwanza, a fuller representation of African Americans on television, and parents who kept *Jet* and the *Ebony Pictorial History of Black America* in the house.[9] Growing up, Evie Shockley watched *Eyes on the Prize*, voraciously read the 704-page *Roots*, and in college carried a paperback edition of Lerone Bennett Jr.'s *Before the Mayflower*. Because she grew up in a family of educators—her grandparents were teachers, her aunt and uncle taught at Meharry Medical College, and her mother and father taught in public schools—she grew up with W. E. B. Du Bois, in a house full of books, and with parents deeply involved in the newly desegregating Tennessee public schools she began attending in 1970.[10] Tyehimba Jess believes that "there are more people than ever with access to US history and to the history of US poetry; and we can use those tools to plumb the subtleties of these systems."[11] Douglas Kearney says that "when your history has been compromised . . . there is a point where you want to simplify it. Then you complicate it again,"[12] and Natasha Trethewey's pronouncement speaks to much of her generation writing historical poetry: "I take up the burden of history."[13]

However, historical subjects are chosen because they not only speak to the past, but their concerns reverberate into the present as well. The poets choose carefully, targeting topics that allow them to stand, Janus-faced, in spaces of duality, facing both the past and the present. Trethewey articulates this sentiment: "Even when I'm writing about events that have taken place in the past I am always writing about the present."[14] And Jackson convincingly argues that "poets who write about history are engaged in fundamental political activity."[15] Jackson also predicts historical poetry's significance: "Against postmodern conceptions of a present lacking historic roots or any single, linear narrative of existence but containing a muddle of images from the past that are recycled and compete for supremacy with no understanding of their original context, American poets believe that history is a continued presence that should find shape in our literary works."[16] These poets challenge the status quo in the treatment of African Americans just as certainly as the Black Arts generation did before them, asking for fundamental changes in the quest for social justice.

Because there is such a wealth of historical poetry to draw upon, I have had to draw clear parameters to make this study manageable. I have chosen to define the generation of poets under consideration as those born after 1960.[17] This border, as tenuous as it is, separates writers who came of age during the civil rights years from those who were growing up during that time. For example, Rita Dove, the youngest of the writers I have designated as influencing this generation, was born in 1952 and so turned eighteen, college age, in 1970. She participated in the initial recovery movement—still ongoing—one busy constructing the literary canon to which the later generation had access. In an interview she describes that moment: "Black literary writers were not yet part of the curriculum, so we dug them up on our own. . . . We Black students in the early 1970s, and also a few white ones, discovered an Afro-American literature shunned by most of academia, and that was very affirmative and constructive."[18] On the other side of the 1960 divide is Natasha Trethewey, who describes herself as being born "on the heels of the Civil Rights Movement" in 1966.[19] She benefited from the literature unearthed by Dove and her contemporaries, as well as from the experiences lived by her own parents who met at Kentucky State College, marrying in the midst of the changes being wrought by the civil rights years. While this generational differentiation feels logical, I remain quite aware that it excludes many significant writers publishing important historical poetry but who were born before 1960 such as Ai, Cornelius Eady, Thylias Moss, Marilyn Nelson, M. NourbeSe Philip, Patricia Smith, and Yusef Komunyakaa—and I hope that this study spurs critical interest in their historical poetry as well.[20]

Furthermore, I define the historical poem as one written about events in the past, rather than about the current events through which the poets are living. In considering influence, then, this stipulation eliminates poets like the towering Gwendolyn Brooks, so very influential but who largely wrote about subjects that were our history but her current events. Similarly, this definition excludes post-1960 writers like Claudia Rankine and her powerful *Citizen* with its impressive analysis of current events but generally not the past. Moreover, I limited the poets considered in the following six chapters to only those writing extended historical sequences, which are not necessarily book length (as only four covered here are), but each sequence had to go well beyond a single poem. Many contemporary writers pen beautiful solo poems, a selection of which are addressed in the conclusion. In choosing the six poets to cover in full chapters, I also had to make hard choices among a plethora of gifted writers for the sake of balance—in gender, content, and style—and I opted for variety in subjects and their time frames, backgrounds of the poets, and approaches to structure and form.

However, before those chapters begin, this one continues with a consideration of the relationship between history and poetry.

"History, as nearly no one seems to know, is not merely something to be read. And it does not refer merely, or even principally, to the past. On the contrary, the great force of history comes from the fact that we carry it within us, are unconsciously controlled by it in many ways, and history is literally *present* in all that we do. It could scarcely be otherwise, since it is to history that we owe our frames of reference, our identities, and our aspirations," wrote James Baldwin for *Ebony* in 1965.[21] Baldwin's oft-quoted statement emphasizes the great heft of history in people's lives, how it affects identities and futures, that it is truly about the present and what is to come, documenting, reflecting, and creating lives. In conceptualizing the relationship between history and literature, both Lionel Grossman and Hayden White describe them as types of discourse, branches of rhetoric, until around 1800, when history shifted toward the empirical, aspiring to accurately document the past, and literature became not just a linguistic discourse to be used by all but a sacred space saved for the artistic elite.[22] White describes the shift as history moving "from its status as a discourse to its status as a (putative) science."[23] Instead, he argues, "properly understood, histories ought never to be read as unambiguous signs of the events they report, but rather as symbolic structures, extended metaphors, that 'liken' the events reported in them to some form with which we have already become familiar in our literary culture."[24] This philosophical stance, which has become increasingly less controversial since he first introduced it in the 1970s, opens up a space of play that facilitates exploring the relationship between history and literature, discourses separated for a mere two centuries, a separation more constructed than actual.

However, before, this theoretical space opened up in the late twentieth century, African American history was being written by powerful thinkers like William Wells Brown, George Washington Williams, W. E. B. Du Bois, Arthur Schomburg, A. A. Taylor, Carter G. Woodson, Charles H. Wesley, William Leo Hansberry, Benjamin Quarles, John Hope Franklin, and Lerone Bennett Jr., to mention only a few of the most celebrated historians. Historians C. Vann Woodward and Herbert Aptheker were also writing about Black resistance and civil rights, but often the academy was dominated by histories in which African Americans were ignored or relegated to positions where they were being acted upon, placed in the object rather than the subject position. Thomas C. Holt claims that white Americans knew little about African American history until 1944, when Gunnar Myrdal's *American Dilemma* was published, a work that indicted white racism but limited Black experience to reacting to oppression, and he applauds Ralph Ellison's objections to Myrdal's representation of their community.[25] In a review written in 1944 but unpublished until its inclusion in Ellison's 1964 *Shadow and Act*—it was determined too combative by the *Antioch Review*, which had arranged for his review but demurred after reading it—Ellison objected to Myrdal's positioning of African American people as simply recipients of racism: "But can a people . . . live and develop for over three hundred years simply by *reacting*? Are American Negroes simply the creation of white men, or have they at least helped to create themselves out of what they found around them? Men have made a way of life in caves and upon cliffs; why cannot Negroes have made a life upon the horns of the white man's dilemma?"[26] By 1964 this review could be published, and it is now one of the markers of the definitive turn in how African American history, and indeed all American history, was told.

Around 1970, the way history was told made a radical shift to representing African Americans as actors, subjects in the American story. Holt describes the change:

> Consequently, in sharp contract with the century of scholarship that preceded it, that of the 1970s and 1980s gave its attention almost exclusively to the problem of understanding black history as black people experienced it. No longer would black history be simply the history of relations between the races or of black contributions to the nation's life and progress. It would be the history of black communities, churches, schools, businesses, families, and folk culture. In that history blacks would no longer be relegated to nonspeaking roles, the passive victims of white hostility or beneficiaries of white benevolence. They would be actors with top billing, creating institutions, sustaining communal values, and passing on a legacy of struggle and creativity to their posterity.[27]

This shift was the result of tumultuous social change: the Vietnam War, the second-wave feminist movement, African independence wars, the 1960s urban uprisings, and, above all, the civil rights struggle, itself a product of decades, even centuries, of protest work. The civil rights years are often dated by specific historical events, beginning in 1954 with *Brown v Board of Education*, which declared that the doctrine of separate but equal in public education was unconstitutional, and ending with the 1964 Civil Rights Act and 1965 Voting Rights Act. This legislation outlawed discrimination based on race (as well as religion, sex, or national origin); it eliminated voter discrimination (like the literacy test or the poll tax); and it declared unconstitutional segregation in schools, the workplace, or public accommodations.[28] This delineation has come to be known as the classic civil rights movement (with a focus on the nonviolence practiced by Dr. Martin Luther King Jr.), vying with alternate conceptions of the era like the Black Liberation Movement (a Pan-Africanist name that aligns the US movement with contemporaneous African independence struggles against colonialism) or the Black freedom struggle (more general terminology that stretches farther into the past and future). Furthermore, the classic dates of 1954 to 1965 represent the narrowest construction of the era, with many historians like Glenda Elizabeth Gilmore, Adriane D. Lentz-Smith, and Timothy B. Tyson extending its reach. Historian Jacquelyn Dowd Hall coined the term "the Long Civil Rights Movement," and she delineates expansive borders, positing its origins in radical 1930s labor politics and the events of World War II, borders that went far beyond the South, and a longevity well beyond the 1970s.[29] Ultimately, the civil rights years were a very American revolt, and they happened on a continuum of Black resistance stretching back to Africans rebelling during the Middle Passage and the revolts of enslaved people during antebellum times.[30]

Vincent Harding, one of the historians entering the field in this time of change, confirmed the shift in the representation of African American people. In a 1970 article, he offered a call to arms: "We who write Black History cannot track our 'bleeding countrymen through the widely scattered documents of American history' and still believe in America. We cannot see luster when we must glimpse it through oceans of tears. We cannot—do not wish to—write with detachment from the agonies of our people. We are not satisfied to have our story accepted into the American saga. We deal in redefinitions, in taking over, in moving to set our own vision upon the blindness of American historiography."[31] He emphasized that this refocus will impact the entirety of American history; it will bring an entirely new way to see the country's past: "Rather our emphasis is on exposure, disclosure, on reinterpretation of the entire American past. We want to *know* America at its depths, now that invitations to its life are besieging us. And it is clear even now that the black past cannot be remade and clearly known without America's larger past being shaken at the foundations."[32]

Historian Nell Irvin Painter reflected on the years around 1970, years in which she was part of the "first relatively large group of African Americans to enter the nation's leading graduate schools, large in comparison to the one or so blacks per history department every three or four years before."[33] She summarized her generation's goals:

> Having read what historians and social scientists had written about African Americans and grown indignant, we resolved to disprove racist lies. We would sweep away mid-20th-century white historiography, in which blacks were invisible or were present in United States history only in the roles of contented darkey or immobilized victim. When blacks had appeared, their actions were invariably connected to the judgment of some sort of failure, as in Reconstruction after the Civil War. Groping toward new ways of thinking about black people (and not just race relations), we would show black people as we knew we really were, self-reliant and reasonable. We were not always aware of older historians whose thinking paralleled our own.[34]

Historian Robert L. Harris Jr., in writing about the shift in American history that he too places around 1970, documented the increasing interest in African American history from book publishers, the National Endowment for the Arts (which sponsored seven workshops in African American history in 1968), and the state school systems that incorporated African American history into their curricula.[35] Moreover, in his 1970 *The Politics of History*, Howard Zinn titles his chapter on Black studies programs, which he clocks as being established about 1969, "What Is Radical History?," yet one more indication that the shift in how history was told happened around 1970.[36] Moreover, in 1988, Benjamin Quarles reflected on the tremendous changes in his discipline, describing the proliferation of Black studies in all universities as not only healing for the African American community but also as a shift that makes it "impossible for American society to be properly appraised if blacks are left out of the picture."[37]

Particularly representative of this shift was the treatment of the institution of slavery. Most historical accounts had relied on the documents created by the enslavers, but a new consideration of the significance of slave narratives—taking them seriously as narratives of enslaved life rather than folklore—and the archival documents surrounding them fundamentally changed the historical estimation of the institution of slavery. Historian Norman R. Yetman describes these changes:

> The new model of slavery that emerged in the early 1970s stressed the creative, independent dimension of black culture. Black culture was not merely an abject, passive reaction to or "pathological" imitation of white culture. Black culture, which blacks themselves had created, was different from white culture, it reflected an active and creative process. This emphasis on the creative, not reactive, dimension of the black experience and the importance of black culture and

> social institutions in sustaining the essential humanity of those who had been enslaved became the primary focus of the research on slavery in the 1970s.[38]

The major figure in this change was John W. Blassingame and his 1972 *The Slave Community*, in which he plumbed *Slave Narratives: A Folk History of Slavery in the United States from Interviews with Former Slaves* produced by the Works Projects Administration (WPA), as well as other primary sources to analyze the institution of slavery through the eyes of the enslaved people rather than the enslavers. He sought to present how they experienced being enslaved as individuals and the rich lives they created within such an oppressive institution. In the same year and with the same focus on slave narratives and archival materials, George P. Rawick introduced a nineteen-volume series of slave narratives with the volume *From Sundown to Sunup*. He drew a detailed portrait of the institution of slavery, focusing on the integrity of the family and the centrality of religion. Three other studies are also often mentioned in this vanguard of histories: Eugene D. Genovese's *Roll, Jordan, Roll* (1972) traced Black resistance in enslaved communities, particularly considering how religion functioned to provide values and strength; Herbert G. Gutman focused on the nuclear family in *The Black Family in Slavery and Freedom* (1976); and the secular culture created by enslaved people was delineated in *Black Culture and Black Consciousness* (1977) by Lawrence W. Levine. (The entire collection of WPA Slave Narratives, along with photographs and other materials, has now been digitized and is available online through the Library of Congress.)[39]

Close on the heels of these new assessments of the institution of slavery—which primarily addressed men and their cultural roles—came histories about African American women, beginning in the late 1970s and '80s. Sharon Harley and Rosalyn Terborg-Penn's 1978 *The Afro-American Woman: Struggles and Images* is credited as being the first book of historical essays on African American women. It was followed in 1982 by the well-known and wide-reaching *All the Women Are White, All the Blacks Are Men, but Some of Us Are Brave*, which featured historians, literary critics, activists, theologians, sociologists, artists, and writers. Gloria T. Hull, Patricia Bell-Scott, and Barbara Smith's groundbreaking collection of Black feminist scholarship helped establish Black women's studies and shifted the trajectory of feminism from a limited focus on white, middle-class, heteronormative women to a feminism that applied an intersectional lens, or at least one that began heading in that direction. In 1984 Paula Giddings published *When and Where I Enter: The Impact of Black Women on Race and Sex in America* in which she traced the influence of African American women on American history, focusing on their achievements and activism for equality. The following year, 1985, saw the publication of *Labor of Love, Labor of Sorrow: Black Women, Work, and the Family, from Slavery to the Present*, Jacqueline Jones's study of the work done by Black women, as well as their aspirations for their families and themselves. Also in 1985, Deborah Gray White published *Ar'n't I a Woman: Female Slaves in the Plantation South*, in which she objected to the previous historical studies on the institution of slavery, which were limited to studying men, and instead she wrote about enslaved women's roles. White's book topic was so new that the Library of Congress had no subject heading to describe it and so—in that same year and because of White's book—created the official Library of Congress subject heading "Women Slaves."[40] Darlene Clark Hine joined White in 1986 with her influential essay "Lifting the Veil, Shattering the Silence: Black Women's History in Slavery and Freedom" in the volume she also edited, *The State of Afro-American History: Past, Present, and Future*. On the literary side, collections of new and recovered texts were poised to pour forth. One of the earliest anthologies to appear was *The Black Woman*, edited by Toni Cade (before she was Toni Cade Bambara). She wrote that this work grew out of "impatience," impatience with too few periodicals addressing African American women, who were not addressed by the white women's feminist movement or by academic or governmental studies.[41] Her collection was also part of the process of filling those spaces with representation of African American women by African American women, as was the work appearing in the 1970s by Toni Morrison, Alice Walker, and Maya Angelou.

The radical shift in how African American history was told—around 1970—was part of momentous changes in the field of history as a whole. Objectivity, as the hallmark of professional historians established during the years between 1880 and World War I, what Peter Novick marks as the beginning of the profession, came under fire by New Left historians in the early 1960s.[42] Moreover, the consensus approach embraced by the post–World War II generation of historians was rejected. Novick clocks a significant marker of these changes as the 1968 student takeover of buildings at Columbia University, specifically the occupation of Fayerweather Hall, which housed graduate studies and the office of influential historian Richard Hofstadter. As the burgeoning social movements forced more points of view to be recognized, in those years and the decades following them, "historical objectivity has become more problematic than ever before," Novick argues.[43] Another contributing factor was the arrival of postmodernism, a potent influence on history and literature. Postmodernism destabilizes surety, renounces the existence of a center or foundation, upends genre conventions, illuminates contradictions and uncertainties, and denaturalizes the seemingly known and established.

Developments in the field of literature—in both theoretical approaches and the basic makeup of the canon—paralleled the shifts in history. Criticism, in the 1960s, began to turn away from the New Critics and to reflect the social movements happening then. History had long been used as an authoritative backdrop against which to read literature, but Stephen Greenblatt and the field of New Historicism fundamentally altered that relationship. This approach equalized historical and literary texts, treating them as co-texts. In its early days, critics might take a historical text like the Emancipation Proclamation, pair it with a literary text like *The Autobiography of Frederick Douglass*, and read them with an eye toward what each illuminated in the other, or like Greenblatt, trace the perambulations of artifacts such as his famed cardinal's hat, working from the premise that both literature and historical accounts impacted culture and offered insights into their historical moment. Stories that had been previously untold like the lives of people of color, the working class, women, LGBTQ+ figures, or children were considered, and a particular focus was placed on the use of primary documents, valuing firsthand sources over previously synthesized secondary sources—although practitioners were expected to be well versed in conventional history as well. New Historicism also drew attention to the critics' position in history and their inability to step outside their culture. All writers and critics have an unassailable bias in this critical lens; none can achieve objectivity because all are positioned in history, culture, and time.

Greenblatt shied away from defining New Historicism, declining to prescribe a process its critics should follow in general or even to lay out precepts that could define its parameters. He and Catherine Gallagher wrote in their book titled *Practicing New Historicism*—which, oddly enough given its title, circles ambiguously about what that practice might look like—that "the task of understanding then depends not on the extraction of an abstract set of principles, and still less on the application of a theoretical model, but rather on an encounter with the singular, the specific, and the individual."[44] They continued, offering at least a vague sketch of the landscape of New Historicism, which they describe as "a history of possibilities: while deeply interested in the collective, it remains committed to the value of the single voice, the isolated scandal, the idiosyncratic vision, the transient sketch." These possibilities expose "the tension between certain artifacts (including many of the works that have been regarded as canonical works of art) and their cultures. . . . Accordingly, we mine what are sometimes called counter-histories that make apparent the slippages, cracks, fault lines, and surprising absences in the monumental structures that dominated a more traditional historicism."[45] The plethora of possibilities offered by this critical approach appealed to many literary critics, and as its popularity grew, its application became more diffuse, but its practitioners retained the fundamental belief in history and literature as equal co-texts with powerful relationships to culture, what Louis A. Montrose succinctly and famously termed "the historicity of texts and the textuality of history."[46]

Prominent within the New Historicism sections in anthologies and readers is the towering presence of Hayden White and, in particular, his 1978 essay "The Historical Text as Literary Artifact." As literary theorists have argued that language has power rather than relegating it to the role of a passive transmitter that people simply use to communicate, White argued that the narrative form into which historical events are placed has power rather than being merely a transparent vehicle for knowledge. He wrote, "But in general there has been a reluctance to consider historical narratives as what they most manifestly are: verbal fictions, the contents of which are as much *invented as found* and the forms of which have more in common with their counterparts in literature than they have with those in the sciences."[47] White positioned history as more art and less science because of its dependency on "the techniques of *figurative language* both for our *characterization* of the objects of our narrative representations and for the *strategies* by which to constitute narrative accounts of the transformations of those objects in time. And this is because history has no stipulatable subject matter uniquely its own; it is always written as part of a contest between contending poetic figurations of what the past *might* consist of."[48] History, like literature, is invested in understanding the world, and that understanding is dependent on the form in which it is told. The form itself must be familiar to be understood, and that familiar structure then exerts a power of its own over the content placed in it. Despite the many early and continuing challenges to his theory, White deviated little throughout his career and in 2014—four years before his death—reiterated and clarified his contention that "the term 'history' is the signifier of a concept rather than a reference to a thing or domain of being having material presence."[49] Because history is told through literary forms, readers understand that "the story told is intended to be taken as a description which explains by the emplotment of events as *recognizable* as a story of a particular kind: tragic, comedic, romantic, epical, farcical, and so on, as the case may be."[50] Thus, historical and literary texts often have more in common than not.

White offers Toni Morrison's character Sethe in *Beloved* as an example of the ambiguous line separating historical and literary writing. He proposes that since Sethe fits the historical facts known about the historical figure Margaret Garner, then "what kind of fiction—a fiction that is in no way at odds with the known facts—would that be?"[51] Morrison herself describes her goals in creating Sethe as "fill[ing] in the blanks that the slave narrative left" because she uses the historical facts known about Garner but then gifts Sethe an interior life, the consciousness that could not be recorded in newspaper accounts or antebellum slave narratives. What results is a fictional character and novel that apply what historians have discovered about the institution of slavery but do so through fully rounded characters, figures impossible for mere data or dates to capture. Morrison's need to create a character to embody that knowledge is a need to transform the historical facts into truth because, she claims, "facts can exist without human intelligence, but truth cannot."[52] White supports Morrison's efforts since the issue addresses such significant issues about humanity that "the writer interested in facing directly the ethical issues (the question: what should I do?) involved in the consideration of such phenomena might well take on the role of performing *in* writing the kind of action being presented as event." Even though imagining Sethe's thoughts and mindset steps beyond the edges of the historical record, he argues, her character captures pivotal truths that often remain out of reach of historians to imagine.[53] The necessity of this truth is also emphasized by James Baldwin, only seven years Morrison's junior, who in 1980 delivered a speech at Wayne State University in which he argued that "history is not the past. It is the present. We carry our history with us. We *are* our history."[54] Just as recovering early and forgotten texts has been primary to the development of the African American literary tradition, inscribing historically accurate truths into literary texts—seen, through White's theories, as little distanced from the narratives written by historians—became an increasing imperative for writers in the 1980s, directly following the 1970 shift in how African American history was told.

By the 1980s, not only had their perspective on history itself changed, but historians themselves began to write more in the style of what is typically identified as literary, the border between the two fields blurring even further. In "The Call of Stories," David Samuels examines the writing of historians who sound awfully like novelists by writing history that privileged narrative rather than coldly referenced facts—there being mixed opinions on what those were any more. This shift was also noted by Lee Gutkind, one of the foundational thinkers in the field of creative nonfiction. In "History into Nonfiction Narrative," that decade is identified as the moment when historians shifted to employing more narrative and fewer charts, graphs, and lists to the point that nonfiction writing classes became part of the graduate coursework in history.[55] Historian James Goodman is one prominent representative of this next wave of historians, with his groundbreaking 1994 *Stories of Scottsboro*, a finalist for the Pulitzer, which told the Scottsboro Boys' stories from multiple perspectives, as well as his years as the US editor of the journal *Rethinking History*. For this journal, which emphasized experimental historical writing, he edited special issues that emphasized creative historical writing. Goodman describes his goals: "What I meant by creative writing, as I said from the first, was pieces in which writers took writing and form seriously,"[56] a shift into what feels much like the creative nonfiction Gutkind was writing and teaching.

In that same decade, as the historians shifted closer to writing literature, a similar impulse percolated into African American literature, and writers began writing more historically. This change can be clocked to Rita Dove's 1986 *Thomas and Beulah* and Morrison's 1987 Pulitzer Prize–winning *Beloved*, according to Major Jackson.[57] Moreover, Elizabeth Alexander marks the 1980s as the moment when August Wilson "began his un-trendy but radical project of looking to the past. It took vision to recognize, as he did, that until we examine our history we will not be able to look or move forward."[58] Critic Thadious M. Davis also posits the 1980s as a turning point in historical writing, arguing that "the 1980s marked a decided shift among African American writers who considered 'history' and the past and its relationship to the present moment."[59] These 1980s writers engender the historical impulse that flourishes in the post-1960 generation, one facilitated by all of the changes in how history was written as well as by a new focus in universities on African American history, literature, and culture initiated by Black studies programs, creating an educational foundation for the post-1960 generation that emphasized knowledge, theoretical perspectives, and historical and archival materials unavailable to earlier writers.

Simultaneously, poetic form took on a new significance for the entire post-1960 generation of poets. Some closely follow in the footsteps of Rita Dove, who innovatively combined narrative and lyric poetry in *Thomas and Beulah*; others borrow and transform poetic forms from Europe, the Americas, Africa, Asia, and the Middle East; and still others create new complex and playful forms ideally structured to fit their new content. Critic Keith D. Leonard uses the term "fettered" to describe the relationship between African American poets and European American poetic conventions. He argues that it is in 1967, the year of the Second Black Writers' Conference at Fisk University, that the tension shifts. The civil rights movement with its talented, revolutionary poets breaks the chains anchoring poets to forms in which the burden to prove their worth is implicit, leaving contemporary poets free to use form without fear of entanglement. Trethewey, herself a recognized virtuoso in her manipulation of form, answered the question of why she writes poetry by emphasizing form. She said,

> Because of those elegant envelopes of form that poems are. Because of the music and lyricism and density and compression, poems can be memorable in a way that a long piece of fiction isn't. Not that the language of the novel or story isn't memorable, but the ease with which we might memorize a poem and carry it with us in our heads is appealing to me. The way a poem has a smaller space to fit into, and because that density and compression of a poem crystallizes and intensifies image, emotion, idea, sound.[60]

Jordan concurs that "every art form needs some restriction or pattern to either work within or to push against," and he finds the sonnet—which he describes as "an incredibly flexible form in the 21st Century"—a particularly appealing form.[61] Besides adapting established forms, Jordan created the definitional poem, Terrance Hayes invented the golden shovel (which Major Jackson doubled), Patricia Smith resurrected the abecedary, and Natasha Trethewey modified the palindrome and the crown of sonnets. Other poets use the tanka, ghazals, sestinas, villanelles, pantoums, hinge poems, contrapuntal poems, found poems, and so many more, the proliferation and creation of form inexorably marking their generation.

By far the dominant approach in historical poetry is the persona poem. Persona poems—which Tony Medina calls an "extension of the artist"[62]—offer poets the latitude to speak through a historical figure, to embody their experiences, to use this assumed voice to interpret, reshape, reconfigure the past, while simultaneously writing about their contemporary present. Alexander emphasizes that persona poems are always, wittingly or unwittingly, about the writer as well as their ostensible subject,[63] and Trethewey calls the masks donned in persona poems "somehow thicker. I think you are allowed to investigate the self a little bit more comfortably behind the thicker mask, the distant historical mask of a persona."[64] In notes in her archive, Trethewey pondered "the imaginative possibilities of combining the poet's language with that of the characters' language, the poet's figurative interpretation of the character's lived/known experience. The blending of psyches that goes deep into the as yet uncharted areas of the human heart."[65] Thus, the poetic voice combines that of the historical speaker, now recovered and brought to life, and the poet, the contemporary lens through which that history is viewed. Critic Howard Rambsy II insightfully describes this approach as "catching holy ghosts or embodying the spirits of others,"[66] injecting a sense of the mystical into Trethewey's articulation of the persona as "the blending of psyches." This form, in which copious research is fused with the speaker position, offers poets a space to combine the facts and their informed imagination, to create an experience for readers unavailable in documents and lists. Mendi Obadike offers an explanation that may account for the form's popularity: at Cave Canem—the professional organization so instrumental in nurturing and shaping this generation of poets—in 2001, Cornelius Eady called for more persona poems, encouraging poets to explore through that form, many of which were workshopped that year.[67] But whether that moment is the origin point or not, the persona poem has become overwhelmingly popular, and its form has become ideal for speaking to the past and about the present simultaneously.

Into all of these poetic forms, the post-1960 generation writes history. Trethewey even goes so far as to postulate that "poetry can be a genre of history."[68] Like Morrison, Trethewey slices a thin line between historical facts and truth. She documents her deep dives into historical accounts and primary sources, looking for what hasn't been emphasized, noticed, or bothered with before, following the trend Greenblatt initiated in criticism. The challenge faced by the poets, then, is to present the history faithfully while at the same time creating art, a not inconsiderable task. Trethewey describes her role as a historian: "If an audience wonders if the poems are true and asks, 'Did it happen?,' I say, 'Maybe (pauses).' 'Is it true?' 'Yes.' Because I'm interested in historical memory, I don't feel like I can contribute to that by being historically inaccurate. I want to get as close to what is plausible or what could have been."[69] Just as Hayden White supports Morrison's creation of Sethe based on the historical Margaret Garner, the same can be said for the historic truths Trethewey—and these other poets—are creating. Elizabeth Alexander may have said it best: "And the imagination, in the history poem, can take up where written history stops. . . . It is the unique potential of poetry to be able to locate and activate what is in the imagination. Art takes us to knowing that may have no other way of being found, and that is one of the very things we need to know in order to move more intelligently forward."[70] The historical poem merges the capabilities of poetry with the newly known and documented in history to produce a way to create a new kind of future, informed by the past and the present. Are these poets reaching the truth about history? As Greenblatt stipulates, every generation is located in their historical moment and bound to inescapable biases. They are reaching a truth, and as historian Eric Foner emphasizes, "there is nothing unusual or sinister in the fact that each generation rewrites history to suit its own needs."[71] This group of poets writes a history that reflects the cultural and academic advances made during their lifetimes, one that is as truthful to the present as possible in any historical moment, and one that writes into public memory a necessary past.

Chapter 1

✦

Praising the Seers

Celebrating the Historical Influence of Robert Hayden, Michael S. Harper, and Rita Dove

Elizabeth Alexander praises the "seers" who bequeathed their interest in history to her generation,[1] and Kevin Young writes that "there is a long line of folks for us to acknowledge, to praise, to owe our current literary lives to. I see it as the writer's job, especially the African American writer's job, not to 'kill the literary father' but rather to celebrate our ancestry."[2] In historical poetry, this celebration of writers invokes poets whose careers span much of the twentieth century: Robert Hayden (1913–1980), Michael S. Harper (1938–2016), and Rita Dove (born 1952). Hayden refused to identify as a specifically Black poet, instead arguing that his racial identity did not take precedence over his identity as a poet. In the past, this refusal meant his exclusion from critical constructions of the Black Arts Movement (BAM), but critics like Evie Shockley argue for a broader definition of the Black aesthetic and the poetry scene, writers, and trends in the mid- to late twentieth century. About poets like Hayden and Harper, she writes, "To create a rigid separation between these poets' work and that of their BAM counterparts would be to reify black nationalist politics as the only recognizable antiracist politics and to perpetuate the notion of *a* Black Aesthetic in the face of the wide variety of ways in which poets explore matters of race and 'blackness.'"[3] Similarly, Alexander argues for altering the trajectory of BAM to include Harper, a shift in critical perspective that resituates these poets and their significance and influence.[4] Dove, born in 1952, a college student by the 1970s but still too young to have been fully involved in BAM, becomes a dominant figure connecting these earlier poets to those following her just a decade later. The paths these three writers forged create the space where historical poetry flourishes today.

When the post-1960 generation discusses the poets who influenced their decision to write about history, Robert Hayden is mentioned most often. A late modernist, Hayden is a member of the midcentury generation that includes Gwendolyn Brooks, and his interest in history can be traced to his college days at Detroit City College (later Wayne State University), his 1930s work for the Federal Writers' Project in Michigan, his 1941 research at the Schomburg Collection in New York City, and his research while pursuing graduate training at the University of Michigan.[5] Hayden often referred to his interest in history and in a 1975 interview called himself "history oriented."[6] In other interviews, he described himself as "fascinated" by histories of the Civil War, the African presence, and the institution of slavery, and he repeatedly maintained that he "hoped to correct the false impressions of our past, to reveal something of its heroic and human aspects." He viewed history as "a long, tortuous, and often bloody process of becoming," a reference to the changes he saw in the ways, for example, enslaved people, Native Americans, and women were treated from the eighteenth century onward. For Hayden, these shifts in how history was told was a "process of redefinition," a process in which he participated through his historical poems, poems that had the power to redefine the role of African Americans in history.[7] Wilburn Williams Jr. interprets Hayden's idea of constant redefinition as a claim that "the past . . . need not be past at all. His speakers confront their history as active participants in its making, and not as distant onlookers bemoaning their isolation; the past is carried into the present,"[8] what Vilma Raskin Potter calls "a continuing journey both communal and private."[9] Thus, the poet can remake history, connecting it more fully to the present moment. Edward Hirsch emphasizes the "long, fragmentary, collage-like history poem" as one of the dominant modes in Hayden's oeuvre,[10] and Charles T. Davis underscores that "history has haunted Robert Hayden from the beginning of his career as a poet."[11] Fred Fetrow, in his exploration of Hayden's many historical personae, makes the case that Hayden "was and probably continues to be regarded as a poet almost preoccupied with the past, one who took a special interest in Black history in particular."[12] Hayden's body of work offers poems about significant figures from his lifetime like Malcolm X, Martin Luther King Jr., Robert Kennedy, and Paul Robeson, as well as poems about important figures from the past like Nat Turner, Harriet Tubman, Frederick Douglass, Crispus Attucks, Phillis Wheatley, John Brown, and Paul Laurence Dunbar. While a few of these poems are purely elegiac, others center on a historical figure and speak to the larger historical contexts of slave rebellions, the Underground Railroad, and the Civil War, but none is referenced as often as a poetic influence as his "Middle Passage."

"Middle Passage" began as part of a collection Hayden called *The Black Spear*, in response to Stephen Vincent Benét's *John Brown's Body*, a historical epic about the Civil War that won the Pulitzer in 1929. Benét called for a poet able to "sing" the "blackskinned epic, epic with the black spear / I cannot sing you, having too white a heart."[13] Hayden answered his call, writing that "I dared to hope that I might be that poet," and he began writing on the institution of slavery and the Civil War from an African American perspective.[14] Even though *The Black Spear* won the University of Michigan's 1942

Hopwood Major Poetry Award, the volume was not published as such, and its poems evolved as Hayden's expertise grew, some appearing in his later volumes.[15] "Middle Passage," which Hayden had meant to open that collection, was not completed in time to be included and so first appeared in *Phylon* in 1945, a publication then edited by W. E. B. Du Bois. After revisions, which included excising its prologue and entire stanzas, the poem was published in Edwin Seaver's collection *Cross Section 1945*. A second set of revisions prepared the poem for Hayden's 1962 volume *A Ballad of Remembrance*—the version critics consider to represent his final wishes—and it is this "Middle Passage" (albeit with some limited changes in font, capitalization, and spacing) that is in his *Collected Poems*.

"Middle Passage" is divided into three sections, a structure described in detail by Hayden. The first section reveals, he explains, "the dreadful conditions aboard the slavers, the brutal and inhuman treatment of the slaves" in scenes cut together in a mode he calls "cinematic," shifting from one scene to the next without expository transitions, a form emphasizing fragmentation like T. S. Eliot's "The Waste Land."[16] Countering plantation literature and accounts of slavery still inclined to present it as a benevolent institution—Hayden was writing before history changed in 1970 and thus before slave narratives were generally accepted as historical documents rather than political propaganda—"Middle Passage" opens with the ships leaving Africa carrying captives. The ships' names are ironically invoked, from the religious *Jesús* to the ineptly named *Mercy* to the more accurately designated *Desire*. Interspersed are the descriptions of the sharks following the ships, lines from prayers to a Christian god, stories of Davy Jones's locker, a captain's journal entries, and diary entries of the enslavers documenting the laments of the Africans, the diseases inflicting them, the horrific conditions below deck, the women who are repeatedly raped, and a fire that kills many of the Africans. This first section establishes what Hayden names as the poem's themes: "man's cruelty to man [and] the Negro's heroic struggle to be free."[17]

The second section, the shortest, is told through the persona of a trader who is reminiscing about the wealth he accumulated over twenty years of trading. Hayden explains that this section, using the ballad form, implicates not only the traders but also the African leaders who sold their own into slavery. The trader, lamenting the ill health that keeps him away from Africa, tells the story of what he considers his triumphs, the Africans he transported to the Americas. He names the places in West Africa from which enslaved people came, the ethnic groups captured by other Africans and sold to him, and the African leaders who became wealthy from the trade by providing women for sex and neighboring villagers for labor, leading their neighbors to the factories on the coast. The account told by this single persona, Hayden wrote, was a "composite" based on various first-person accounts.[18]

The longest section, the third, is primarily based on the 1839 *Amistad* slave rebellion, in which fifty-four Africans from Sierra Leone revolted against their Spanish captors, taking control of the ship between Cuba and the Caribbean islands. The Mende, led by Cinquez (Joseph Cinqué, whose African name was Sengbe Pieh), left two of the crew alive with orders to take the ship back to Africa, but the crew would turn the ship back to the Americas at night and eventually sailors from the United States discovered the ship near Connecticut. Because the African people had been kidnapped after the legal end of the international slave trade, their case for freedom went to court, and in 1841 the US Supreme Court ruled in the *United States v. The Amistad* that the Mende be freed. By choosing to focus on the *Amistad* triumph rather than a less successful rebellion in this third section, Hayden concludes the poem with an instance in which traders have been mastered and Africans liberated. The voyage from Africa comes full circle in "a rebellion in which the cargo, the tenor, seizes the vehicle and redirects it homeward," argues critic Aldon Nielsen.[19] In 1842, the surviving thirty-nine Mende were returned to Sierra Leone: "Voyage through death / to life upon these shores," a triumph Hayden could cite. He describes this third section as a climatic culmination of the first two, "meant to recapitulate all the themes introduced earlier and focuses on the heroic resistance to slavery introduced at the very beginning."[20]

Hayden's "Middle Passage" offers the poets who followed him a model for writing the historical poem through his development of personas, his intention to correct the historical record, and his use of historical archives. Major Jackson posits that this poem "is probably most exemplary in its example of parsing time over a sequence and creating a persona by which to mediate history."[21] The persona poem allows Hayden to transport his audience to another time and place, and he gains authenticity by, for the space of the poem, becoming his subject. He extravagantly uses a myriad of personas here, among them the captain on a slave ship, crew members and ship officers, a person giving a deposition, voices in prayer and song, an old trader, and a crew member from the *Amistad*, all controlled by the poet's external voice. Hayden describes his use of a persona in his poem "The Ballad of Nat Turner" as an opportunity to "reveal [Turner] more dramatically and with greater economy. I could create a stronger illusion of a living presence,"[22] and the same holds true for "Middle Passage," as well as for the contemporary writers' persona poems.

Just as he models using the persona poem, Hayden influences the next generation through his goal to "contribute toward an understanding of what our past had really been like. I set out to correct the misconceptions and to destroy some of the stereotypes and clichés which surrounded Negro history."[23] Inspired by his example, Natasha Trethewey says she felt "compelled to do the same thing."[24] History has long been marred by untruths and forgotten truths like leaving the 1921 Tulsa riots out of the history books until the twenty-first century or the absence of African American soldiers on Ship Island's plaque of remembrance that Trethewey writes about in *Native*

Guard. All of the poets addressed in this study seek to represent the truth, a lofty goal that Hayden bequeaths to them. They tell new stories about, for instance, Sara Baartman, Jean-Michel Basquiat, and Medgar Evers, resurrect the histories of people like MacNolia Cox, or create figures from the Civil War or Philadelphia's Free Black community to figure in forgotten histories.

This truth telling is often accomplished not only by research but also by incorporating historical records and documentary sources into poetry. In a 1972 interview, Hayden clarified the years of research that contributed to his knowledge of the institution of slavery and the Middle Passage: "I read all sorts of books, including a famous account of the slave trade entitled *Adventures of an African Slaver*. I read histories, journals, notebooks, ships' logs"—discourses that end up in his "Middle Passage."[25] Elizabeth Alexander credits "Middle Passage" as a "predecessor" of her own "Amistad" sequence, and she writes that Hayden's poem "calls on archival materials to imagine life aboard those slave ships during the Middle Passage and features the character Cinquez."[26] One of her poems in *Crave Radiance*, "Hayden in the Archive," pictures Hayden at his research, probing records, efforts that result in lyric poetry, "crystalline ironies," and "repetition rampant."[27] The poem is insistent, drawing his attention in perhaps the same way the archival records drew hers. Natasha Trethewey uses direct quotes from sources, many elucidated in her notes, which become a crucial part of the work of reading her poetry, as do Frank X Walker and Camille T. Dungy. In *To Repel Ghosts: The Remix*, Kevin Young repeatedly samples from history, offering a similarly collage-like historical poem. Into his volume, Young incorporates titles and text from Jean-Michel Basquiat's paintings, as well as quotes from voices ranging from newspaper reporters to novelists to intellectuals to song lyricists to professors.

In a 1972 interview, Hayden offered advice to younger poets writing historical poems. Hayden recommended reading as much as possible about the subject and examining images from the period, both tools that aid in creating an understanding and a subsequent vision of a historical time. For him, however, this background information, while vital, was like "scaffolding," that is, a basis on which to build poetry. Once the scaffolding is established, he maintained that the poet's imagination shapes the information into poetry, imagination fueled by the poet's "emotional response to the material." His concluding recommendation was that the poetry strive to tell the truth: "And, finally, I think one has to be careful not to permit his biases to distort the material he has set out to use. Truth—at least as much truth as one is capable of discerning and expressing—and accuracy are desirable goals."[28] All of the contemporary poets addressed here share Hayden's project to tell historical truths, truths that create a poetry that can cause social change, for, as Hayden wrote, "poetry *does* make something happen, for it changes sensibility."[29]

Michael S. Harper already shared Robert Hayden's sentiment that poetry makes things happen when they met for the first time in 1970. Harper recounts:

> I met Robert Hayden at the University of Michigan (Ann Arbor) at a poetry reading I was giving, one of several in the area as a part of a circuit; I had spotted him seated toward the rear, near the exit, and when I concluded I walked up to him and said, "Mr. Hayden, it's a great honor to meet you, to have you come to my reading. You're a great poet—would you sign WORDS IN THE MOURNING TIME for me?" Taking his WORDS in hand, and smiling, he said, "I was all prepared not to like you."[30]

That rather inauspicious beginning led to a relationship so close that Harper referred to Hayden as "kin," a word of special significance for him, marking a familial relationship stretching beyond blood: "We'll think of you around Xmas especially, kinship time, and you're kin to us."[31] Robert B. Stepto notes that "a primary tradition in Afro-American letters is, then, the honoring of kin, particularly kin who share the goal of artistic excellence. . . . Harper might be a special case, as his six volumes of verse constitute an orchestrated litany between past and present, kin and non-kin, creating historical landscapes on which heroes and types meet across time-line and cultural boundaries."[32]

Hayden returned the compliment, remarking that he felt "blessed that I have you as a friend—as kin."[33] The kinship of these two writers, based on their shared goal of poetic excellence, developed through correspondence that began two years after they met, stretching from 1972 to Hayden's death in 1980. The letters reveal a growing closeness between the two men with so much in common: writers continuing conversations they began in person, offering feedback, placement of poems, speaking engagements, and emotional sustenance. Twenty-five years younger than Hayden, Harper clearly admired the older poet and wrote insightfully about Hayden's poetry, eventually eulogizing him as "a consummate storyteller who had the pace, coloration and detailed finish of a romantic, with an iconoclastic air."[34] In a 1981 interview with James Randall, Harper commented on Hayden's use of history and how it influenced him:

> Hayden was a great historian, as well as a symbolist poet; I learned a great deal from him. He paid me the ultimate compliment when he said he'd wished he'd written some of the poems in my John Brown sequence; he'd written on the same theme, but with different artistic intent. The icons of much of the heroism and resistance to oppression by Black Americans are implicit in all of my work—which is to say, I have a certain perspective on events, on America, on the language, on

> culture, and on cross-fertilization. . . . I did not see many voices from my own ancestors ably represented in our literature, and I wanted to do my part, to testify to their efforts and achievements, and the values implicit in the making of this country and its character.[35]

Almost twenty years later, in a 2000 interview, when Michael Antonucci asked Harper if he cared "to elaborate on the idea of poets as historians," Harper responded by quoting from Hayden's "American Journal," the title poem from Hayden's volume of the same name, which Harper published in 1978:

> america   as much a problem in metaphysics as
> it is a nation earthly entity an iota in our
> galaxy   an organism that changes even as i
> examine it   fact and fantasy never twice the
> same   so many variables[36]

Harper furthered the project of poet as historian begun by Hayden, which for Harper became an opportunity to testify to African American achievements, and to recover a lost and misinterpreted past.

When talking about the writers who influenced him, Harper paid tribute with his assertion that "we stand on the shoulders of our elders," and, in turn, contemporary poets consider him, in addition to Hayden, one of their greatest influences. Elizabeth Alexander, in *The Black Interior*, pays homage by emphasizing his wide reach through his engagement with "black identity, black pride, jazz and jazz musicians as subject and metaphor, black masculinity, and black history."[37] Moreover, Major Jackson emphasizes Harper's use of history, positing that the current interest in the historical poem has roots in Harper's poetry,[38] and poet Joel Brouwer claims that Harper is "a living, breathing encyclopedia of the African American experience."[39] Harper himself discussed his interest in history in interviews, such as his interview with Aldon Nielsen in which he talks about the "unwritten, undiagnosed history," all that was not known and that he had to discover on his own, and his role in teaching "the first black literature and black history courses" at universities in the 1960s.[40]

Harper's very first book, *Dear John, Dear Coltrane* (1970), offers the poem "American History," the opening salvo in Harper's many poems incorporating historical fragments that inform the entirety of the poem, history permeating the present. This nine-line poem begins with the 1963 bombing of the Sixteenth Street Baptist Church and reaches backward to an incident in which five hundred captives newly arrived from Africa are hidden from British soldiers underwater in Charleston Harbor, where one has to assume they drown. The poem ends with the lines "Can't find what you can't see / can you?," marking the United States' blindness toward its history of slavery, which was changing at the very moment, 1970, when this volume was published.[41] Other poems in Harper's extensive body of work use similar historical fragments like "Bristol: Bicentenary Remembrances of Trade,"[42] which, after opening with Hayden's words from "Middle Passage," connects the United States, Great Britain, and South Africa through the transatlantic slave trade, and "The Battle of Saratoga (Springs) Revisited," in which Harper traces his own stay at Yaddo in the space that was once Katrina Trask's study to her African servant Etienne and her view of his "*cannibal ancestry.*"[43] "The Body Polity" incorporates the Scottsboro Boys, the Tuskegee flyers, and the last remaining formerly enslaved person;[44] "Prayer: Mt. Hood and Environs" juxtaposes images of the Klan next to Native Americans as well as Lewis, Clark, and their guide, the enslaved York; and "History as Bandages: Polka Dots and Moonbeams" references Gabriel Prosser's 1800 slave revolt in Richmond, Virginia.[45] Furthermore, Harper's repetition of the word "history" in book titles, poem titles, and poetic lines becomes an invocation, a motif, a constant remembrance of the African American past, most pronounced in the volume *History Is Your Own Heartbeat*.

It is only in *Debridement*, however, that Harper offers sustained attention to a single historical subject.[46] This volume opens with "History as Cap'n Brown," a sequence of twenty poems about the nineteenth-century radical John Brown, whose quest to eliminate the enslavement of people ended with his failed raid on Harper's Ferry and subsequent hanging in December 1859—a topic that Hayden confessed to Harper he had "beaten him to. . . . This was subject matter he loved, the Civil War, and the agonies loosed on the nation, so much yet unresolved."[47] Like Hayden, Harper relies heavily on poetic personae—primarily Brown, but a few lines are voiced by Shields Green, Sojourner Truth, and Frederick Douglass—a strategy that clearly influences the post-1960 generation, as does his penchant to venerate a historic figure with a then questionable reputation. Twelve of these poems were first published in distinguished historian Benjamin Quarles's 1972 *Blacks on John Brown* as interest in Brown was rekindled by Stephen B. Oates's 1970 *A Biography of John Brown*. James W. Loewen confirms, in his study of high school textbooks, that the textbook industry's discussions of Brown also shifted in 1970: "For Brown's actions made no sense to textbook writers between 1890 and about 1970. To make no sense is to be crazy."[48] Harper's verse recounts Brown's life between the years of the 1854 Kansas-Nebraska Act and the 1859 raid on Harper's Ferry, years known as Bleeding Kansas. His John Brown becomes a major figure in African American history, significant for the actions that destabilized the institution of slavery, a martyr to the goal of equality, and a figure worthy of renewed attention during the civil rights years.

In poetry as dense and lyrical as he describes Hayden's "Middle Passage," Harper's twenty poems engage history not in chronological sequence but instead by seizing on the events in Brown's life that were most significant to the African American community, presenting a Brown who was not crazy because he was willing to die to free enslaved people but who was revered as a martyr and a hero, albeit flawed. These poems eschew a logical march through the events Harper incorporates, instead offering unexpected juxtapositions, elliptical references, and a circular momentum, in which all avenues lead to Harper's Ferry. The epigraph would be a spoiler if the events were not so well-known because it quotes what Brown said to Virginia's governor as he lay wounded after his attack on the Harper's Ferry armory: he tried to take the guns to arm enslaved people for a rebellion but failed. The poem that begins the sequence shifts from that final defeat, in what would be a flashback in narrative, to the story of how Brown arrived there, and that story begins with the 1854 Kansas-Nebraska Act. "Kansas and America" introduces the issue: because Kansas was established as a state whose status as free or slave would be decided by popular sovereignty, white people, both abolitionist and proslavery, rushed to move to the state. Pitted against the proslavery supporters, many of which were moving across the border from the slave state Missouri, was the group that came to be known as free state settlers or Free Staters, who, despite their name, were not necessarily abolitionists like Brown. Some simply wanted land and not to compete with the unpaid labor of enslaved people. With the dominant time frame and situation established, many of the poems feature Brown's most notorious battles: the Pottawatomie Massacre, in which five proslavery figures were killed by Brown's orders as revenge for the May 21, 1856, Sacking of Lawrence; the August 30, 1856, Battle of Osawatomie from which Brown emerged as a skillful tactician despite losing his son Frederick and other men; and the 1858 Hamilton Massacre, or Marais des Cygnes Massacre, in which eleven Free Staters were shot, five of whom died, and the proslavery fighters largely went unpunished, underscoring which side the politicians supported. Also included are the caning of Massachusetts Senator Charles Sumner by Representative Preston Brooks over an antislavery speech Sumner delivered, the attacks on Brown's entire family including when his two sons John and Jason were held as prisoners, the 1855 skirmish known as the Wakarusa War, and the 1856 Battle of Black Jack. By the time the sequence reaches only the fourth poem, "Dreams: American," however, the focus returns to the raid on Harper's Ferry, the dominant event, which insistently reappears throughout Harper's entire poetic sequence, a repetition that reinforces its significance, a refrain to all the other poems. Brown's final raid informs the rest of the sequence because it is his consummate act to free enslaved people, the most significant decision of his life from Harper's point of view. "Dreams: American" opens at the Harper's Ferry armory, engine house, and rifle factory, in the midst of the battle in which Brown and his men refused to kill hostages and decided not to use people as human shields. The final stanza portrays Brown during the forty days between his sentencing and hanging, the length of time Jesus spends in the desert during the Temptation described in the Gospels. The poem's final lines, "insanity is like a very / pleasant dream to me," quote Du Bois's biography of Brown, which, in turn, was quoting a November 28, 1859, letter from Brown to D. R. Tilden, again emphasizing a Brown who died for an important cause, not a man who was "crazy" to die to free enslaved people.[49]

Harper provides a model for recovering less well-known figures significant to African American history, writing what is considered found poetry, and emphasizing the multilayered nature of history. Besides Brown, Harper makes sure that those fighting with Brown—especially lesser-known African Americans like MacNolia Cox, whom A. Van Jordan recovers—take center stage as heroic figures and are brought to public attention, particularly through carefully naming the leading members of Free Black communities, the naming itself an invocation. It is the last poem in the sequence, "Manuel for the Patriotic Volunteer," that offers a catalog of people fighting the institution of slavery. The use of this technique simultaneously elevates the fight against the institution of slavery into the epic tradition and offers an invocation to those who fought oppression. The great size of the list recognizes figures largely forgotten and impresses through sheer numbers in opposition to national memory, which recognizes only a few, token rebels. Listed are followers of Brown, fighters who participated in the raid, the followers of Douglass who could be swayed by Brown: the white John Henry Kagi, who died at Harper's Ferry; Richard Richardson, who fought there; the white Aaron D. Stevens, who gave his life there; the white Charles W. Moffett, who survived; and Shields Green. Harper's second stanza lists free nineteenth-century Northern Blacks achieving professional distinction and combating white opposition through organizations like the Odd Fellows, which offered insurance-like benefits to its members suffering from illness, disability, or family deaths: John van Salee de Grasse, a doctor with a practice in Boston; James McCune Smith, a prominent New York physician; the Philadelphian abolitionist Robert Purvis; the New York lawyer George B. Vashon, who helped establish Howard University's Law School, originally from Pennsylvania, where he was not allowed to take the bar; the AME minister Lewis Woodson, one of the original trustees who founded Wilberforce University, the first historically Black college run by African Americans; the abolitionists, educators, and politicians Gideon Langston (later Quarles), Charles Henry Langston, and John Mercer Langston, all educated at Oberlin College; Harriet Tubman; the formerly enslaved Josiah Henson, who penned *The Life of Josiah Henson, Formerly a Slave, Now an Inhabitant of Canada, as Narrated by Himself*; Frederick Douglass; the abolitionist, AME bishop, and author Jermain Wesley Loguen; Daniel Payne, AME bishop and president of Wilberforce University; Peter Ogden, a ship's steward instrumental in the creation of the Odd Fellows Philomathean Lodge; abolitionist, self-emancipated person, minister, and writer Samuel Ringgold Ward; the gifted orator, minister, and abolitionist Henry Highland Garnet; Charles Lenox Remond, a leading abolitionist speaker; and Henry Bibb, a self-emancipated person and founder of the abolitionist newspaper *The Voice of the Fugitive*—"black heroes all" and ones well-known to Brown, people whom Du Bois credits with giving Brown his belief that enslaving people was wrong through their individual achievements and their growing organizations.[50]

Harper's sequence relies extensively, almost exclusively, on Du Bois's 1909 biography *John Brown*, a layering that quotes Du Bois—and through him, his sources—so thoroughly that it bears much in common with the found poetry popular with contemporary poets like Camille T. Dungy and Tracy K. Smith. Harper turned to one of the greatest African American historians, borrowing not only his vision of Brown's significance to the Black community but also his very words, transforming them into poetry. This poetry offers a tribute or homage—rather than revision—because in order to understand Brown's significance to the African American community, Harper implies that readers must understand Du Bois's early twentieth-century view of Brown as a hero, untinged by the then popular promotion of Brown's insanity.[51] Harper uses many exact quotes, like his opening epigram, which begins, "MY NAME IS JOHN BROWN," but he also incorporates Du Bois's words by reversing, slightly revising, abbreviating, condensing, and piecing together words, phrases, and sections from Du Bois to create his poems. To cite a very few examples, Du Bois's phrase "the cost of liberty is less than the price of repression" becomes Harper's "the price of repression is greater than the cost of liberty."[52] In describing the Free Staters, Du Bois writes that there were "a few who hated slavery, more who hated Negroes, and many who hated slaves," which Harper revises into "*Some hated slavery / Some hated Blacks / Some hated slaves*," but "All loved land."[53] For "'Emperor': Shields Green: Fugitives," Shields Green's words are taken from Du Bois, beginning with the sentence "I b'lieve I'll go wid de ole man." The following two lines borrow lines offered later in Du Bois's book, as the urgency of the situation accelerates Green's response. The emphasis on the shifting verbs increases the poem's insistence from "I b'lieve I'll go" to "I guess I'll go" and finally "I must go," the shift reflecting the urgency of the coming battle and Green's dedication to the cause.[54] The final fourteen lines of the sequence describe Brown's arrival at the Harper's Ferry armory, his futile attempt to move the arms, Robert E. Lee's arrival, the impending Civil War, and Brown's last stand on the literal "powder magazine" of the armory. Key words and phrases in these lines originate in Du Bois's book, condensed from at least fifteen pages into just a few lines, but lines that capture Brown's essential significance.

Not only are Harper's poems composed through Du Bois's outlook and his very words, but the eleventh poem, positioned in the exact middle of the twenty-poem sequence, is "Four Worthies: Souls of Black Folk," a poem rooted in Du Bois's biography but one that speaks more to Du Bois than to Brown. Du Bois's assertion that "four things make life worthy to most men: to move, to know, to love, to aspire"[55] becomes Harper's four-line verse, just as "souls of black folk" becomes half of the poem's title. Harper expands on each of Du Bois's four qualities of life; for example, line 3 is "to *Love*, woman, child, land, trees."[56] By delineating what it really means to live through Du Bois's eyes—a life he has but that enslaved people were denied—Harper makes clear that his poetry is about both John Brown and Du Bois, Du Bois as significant as the named subject. This statement about the human condition speaks to Harper's lifetime as well, in the twentieth century and in the struggle for civil rights. Harper has limited himself to the vision of Brown presented by Du Bois, and that vision is heavily layered since a substantial part of Du Bois's study consists of direct quotes from his own sources like John Brown's letters edited by Franklin Benjamin Sanborn, James Redpath's biography of John Brown, and William Elsey Connelley, whose book on John Brown focused on his time in Kansas. Within this layered representation—a technique with much in common with Trethewey's three circling and overlapping sections in *Native Guard* and Young's work on Jack Johnson presented through the lens of Basquiat—Harper stakes out his own John Brown.

In a 1964 essay, renowned historian Lerone Bennett Jr. embraced John Brown, who, he wrote, "*was* a Negro," more dedicated to the cause of freedom than even Frederick Douglass, and a person who "made of himself an act of transcendence."[57] Brown impressed a range of African American leaders during the Black Power years, including Robert F. Williams, Eldridge Cleaver, H. Rap Brown, Floyd McKissick, and even Malcolm X.[58] For Harper, John Brown was a hero who accepted defeat and welcomed death, chose to be a martyr for the abolitionist cause, was a white man who relinquished much of his privilege, fought injustice throughout his life, and sacrificed himself and his family for the cause of freedom for all men. By remembering the history of Brown and his contributions to the African American community, the nation, for Harper, could choose to see clearly, to build a solid future rather than foundering on lies and ruins. It could embrace its past and in so doing build a nation of which Brown, Du Bois, and Harper would be proud.[59]

In 1994, Harper, along with coeditor Anthony Walton, published the anthology *Every Shut Eye Ain't Asleep*, which presented African American poets born between 1913 and 1962, an anthology that not only connects Harper to Hayden, whose lengthy selection opens the volume, but also offers many poems from Rita Dove, who had already been awarded the Pulitzer Prize and was the current national poet laureate (two poems by Elizabeth Alexander concluded the volume).[60] Dove, the third and final poetic ancestor covered here, was born in 1952, not even two decades after Harper and less than a decade before the 1960 generational border used in this study, but her work provides the bridge from Hayden and Harper to the poets born after 1960. In an interview with Charles H. Rowell, Dove explains that she first read Hayden in graduate school and that "he's one of my idols,"[61] and as the third African American poet laureate of the United States, she follows in Hayden's footsteps—he was the first and Gwendolyn Brooks the second.

Critics closely align her with Harper, whom she knew, and with whom she shared the stage at events like Furious Flower and who was often listed as one of her influences. In her volume *Grace Notes* (1989), she dedicated "Canary" to Harper, a poem about jazz, Billie Holiday, and tragedy, with its evocative final line: "If you can't be free, be a mystery."[62] In addition to her poetic response to Harper's use of music, she said in an interview that "Michael Harper, by the way, often uses blues and jazz idioms, and he uses them very, very deftly—what a difference to the would-be poets of the black struggle and their contemporary successors! Harper is proof that one can write cogently and compellingly in those idioms. You have to know what you're doing."[63] Furthermore, she wrote a similar analysis focusing on his use of music for the *Washington Post* in 2000 and commented on Harper's ability for "clear-eyed and compassionate dealings with the hard news of life." She wrote, "No other poet has embodied the riffs and modalities of jazz and blues more exquisitely than Michael S. Harper; sometimes the ellipses are so deep, the multiple meanings keep hitting long after you've turned the page. A Harper poem teaches how to think on many different levels, to hold one thought like a pianist holds a chord while the other hand goes about its business. He's a master of the double-take."[64]

While Dove's own work is less focused on music in content and technique, the multiple meanings and the double take are techniques often visible in her poetry, which refuses transparency and riffs on memory, biography, and national history. For her part in further establishing generational connections to Hayden and Harper, Dove edited the *Penguin Anthology of Twentieth-Century American Poetry* (2013), in which she included poems by both Hayden and Harper.

Like Hayden and Harper, Dove writes about history, a response to realizing she had been excluded, as she explained in an interview with Steven Ratiner:

> Well, it really begins with two feelings I had as a child: first, that *I* wasn't represented in History . . . neither as a female or as a Black person. And second, the nagging sense that ordinary people were not represented in history, that history gives you the tales of heroes, basically—and not what happens to "ordinary" people who live through the events. You are right that the twin poles of history and memory have certainly not only fascinated me—I'd almost say haunted me all these years. Because I think history is a very powerful weapon. If you can edit someone out of history, then the next generation—those who do not have a personal memory of certain events anymore—won't have anything to go on.[65]

Thus, her poetry becomes a space where she writes "ordinary" people back into history. She told Steven Bellin that when she was in junior high, she realized that the Civil War had ended only one hundred years earlier, a realization that brought the end of the institution of slavery closer to her life than simply the date of 1865. She explained,

> so that's when it hit home for me. I began to understand that history isn't merely facts and isolated events to be memorized, but that it is lived through people. Trying to fit my own history, and the history of my race and gender, into the Grand Chronicle—History with a capital H—led me to the realization that the underside of History, as it were, was infinitely more interesting. So in my work I make a conscious effort to treat History and history equally.[66]

In her poetry, Dove humanizes history, writing ordinary people's lives into national context, the little *h* into the big *H*.

Since she turned eighteen in 1970, the moment of sweeping change in how history was told, Dove enjoyed advantages earlier poets like Hayden and Harper did not such as access to lost and forgotten African American texts as her generation worked to recover them. Too young to be a peer with the writers creating Black studies programs, Dove nonetheless came of age in the midst of the sweeping curricular changes and helped further the recovery movement, in part through the historical subjects of much of her poetry. Furthermore, as a writer, Dove arrived at a moment when critical judgment of a poet's use of form was shifting, according to critic Keith D. Leonard. BAM loosened the demand to use formalism to prove oneself, and Dove arrives on the literary scene at the moment when Black writers are becoming unfettered and developing the freedom to use form in new ways, ways she pioneered in her method of fusing the lyric poem with narrative poetry.

Each of the six primary poets covered in this study lists Dove as an important influence on their work—for both her historical poems and her innovative form—and Elizabeth Alexander particularly emphasizes the impact "Parsley," the final poem in *Museum* (1983), had on her work.[67] The poem's title establishes the historical references in the poem, what has come to be called the "Parsley Massacre." In October 1937, the dictator Rafael Trujillo of the Dominican Republic ordered the deaths of Haitians living on the border of his country in an act of ethnic cleansing in which thousands of people, perhaps as many as twenty thousand, were massacred. The anecdotal litmus test of citizenship was how people pronounced the word "parsley," *perejil* in Spanish. Native Spanish speakers rolled their *r*, which marked them as Dominicans, while Haitians' French or Creole pronunciation marked them with a death sentence based on linguistic differences. The men, women, and children who could not pronounce the shibboleth were brutally murdered and almost fifty years later enshrined in this poem about the misuses of power, which Dove read at the White House. Critic Pat Righelato argues that in *Museum* Dove "developed a historical mode with confidence," the volume's title suggesting that "the past is a collection of artefacts to be scrutinized, but the historicizing imagination of the poet is also alive to the idea that the past is the collection of images and stories made and made up about it, that these are visitable and usable, to be revived and revised."[68] Dove visits the past for the rest of her career, reviving and revising history.

"Parsley" marks Dove's early interest in historical poems, but it is the 1986 volume *Thomas and Beulah* that decisively influences the next poetic generation.[69] Describing himself as one of Dove's fans, Frank X Walker places her as one of the key figures (with Natasha Trethewey and Patricia Smith) in the "crown" of poets writing today.[70] Trethewey, who has many ties to Dove, testified to the influence of *Thomas and Beulah*: "My father gave me a copy of *Thomas and Beulah* by Rita Dove. I read it and thought, so you can write poems about this, your family history? I immediately started carrying it around with me everywhere I went. I began emulating it and learning from it, so I really think that it was life-changing in that way. It's the book that gave me direction or at least showed me into a beginning of what it was that I was interested in doing."[71] Kevin Young, similarly, found in this volume "a beginning" for his own work, particularly through its focus on family: "I remember vividly reading Rita Dove's *Thomas and Beulah* a long time ago now, and just realizing I could write about *my* family. Before then I felt like I had to do something grander in a more shallow sense, that surface sense of the sea or some large theme which block—and I thought determined—what I was trying to say." Young emphasizes that Dove provided a model through which he could write about family in a national historical setting, something he achieves in his first book, *Most Way Home*: "But, for me, people like [Yusef] Komunyakaa and Dove who are very influential, especially on my first book, were able to write about something personal but make it part of history and recognize history as a personal process—whether the Vietnam War or the March on Washington or the Great Migration."[72] In 2005, Camille T. Dungy interviewed Dove, and she commented on Dove's ability to "reimagine what might have been the story of that story, or the story behind the story," to speak for "those who have not had their histories on record."[73] Dungy has also emphasized how much Dove has been a primary influence in her use of form and of the vernacular, techniques that contemporary poets have applied widely. Finally, A. Van Jordan—who, like Dove, is from Akron and even attended the same John R. Buchtel High School—posited *Thomas and Beulah* as the primary influence on his generation and the volume with which they all compared their work when he borrowed Harold Bloom's language, explaining that he could write his own work "once I got beyond the Anxiety of Influence of *Thomas and Beulah*."[74]

As the post-1960 generation describes, Dove influenced them by offering new models of historical content and poetic form. Her content fuses autobiography with poetic imagination and complements those with a historical backbone. Her story, told through Thomas and Beulah, who offer "two sides of a story" that are "meant to be read in sequence," as directed on the volume's dedication page, uses "the personal history of your family and set[s] it against the backdrop of the public history of the Great Migration that has been recorded as part of American history," according to Charles H. Rowell.[75] The two speakers are based on Dove's maternal grandparents, and Dove emphasized the sources for her content: her memories of her grandparents coupled with extended conversations with her mother. She also underscores that not all of the content is based on family memory. She purposefully created some of the events and altered details as basic as her grandmother's name, choosing Beulah over her actual name of Georgianna.[76] As she told Earl G. Ingersoll,

> Yes, there are definitely autobiographical elements in my poems, especially the ones based on my grandparents; obviously those are based on some facts, but some of those facts came from my grandparents' lives, some came from my mother's life or my father's life; some came emotionally from my own experience—everything having to do with pregnancy and motherhood in the Beulah section, for instance. I mixed and matched things up and that's why, in my mother's copy of *Thomas and Beulah* I wrote the dedication, "To Mom, the only one who knows which stories are true." Sure enough, I didn't know anymore! But she could sort them out.[77]

Helen Vendler describes this merging of the historical and the imaginative as Dove's ability to "make a biographical fact the buried base of an imagined edifice,"[78] and Dove herself situates the imaginative work her poetry does as "a way, I think, of connecting our almost inarticulated emotions, all of our guilts, all of our fears and joys, as a way of articulating them so that we can recognize them."[79]

Undergirding the autobiographical and imaginative in *Thomas and Beulah* are local and national history. Dove emphasizes Akron's significance as an industrial hub, a city reshaped by the rubber industry and the Great Migration, an act of resistance on the part of millions of people who voted with their feet. She originally intended to write a third section on Akron, but her impulse to chronicle this midwestern industrial city's significance was diverted into both the chronology at the volume's end and Akron's ubiquitous presence. Akron was an important stop on the Underground Railroad, where Sojourner Truth delivered her 1851 "Ain't I a Woman?" speech, Booker T. Washington addressed a Christian Endeavor convention in 1904, Marcus Garvey founded the United Negro Improvement Association in 1914, and W. E. B. Du Bois delivered major speeches in 1920. Akron was a city of newcomers whose population jumped from 69,067 in 1910 to 208,435 in 1920 and whose African American population increased from 657 to 5,580 over the same decade, despite the punitive Jim Crow laws and customs inflicted upon them.[80] Dove's volume incorporates major events like the innovative half-mile, $1,227,859 viaduct built to span the Little Cuyahoga River in 1922; the construction of the Goodyear Zeppelin Airdock in 1929; the 1932 USS *Akron* accident in which a mooring mishap with the blimp caused one broken arm and two deaths; the unusual August 30–31 nights in 1943 when the northern lights could be seen as far south as Akron; and Thomas being frustratingly sidelined from active duty during World War II because of his age. Like Hayden and Harper, Dove depended on historical research to draw this Akron, which was distanced from her own upbringing by decades, as she told Steven Schneider: "I had to go to the library and read a whole bunch of stuff I never counted on researching to try to get a sense of that period of time in the industrial Midwest,"[81] her research creating the setting for lives crafted through family reminiscence, memory, and imagination.

While better than the South—which Thomas fled in 1921 and Beulah's family in 1906—Akron, like all of the Northern industrial cities, was riddled with racism and segregation. In their book *Wheels of Fortune* about the rubber industry in Akron, Steve Love and David Giffels document that "in the early years, black workers in the rubber shops were relegated to the lowest jobs. They cleaned spittoons. They scrubbed toilets. They swept floors. During World War I, when blacks arrived from the South to help with the war effort, they found jobs, good ones compared with the low-paying agricultural jobs many had left in Alabama and Tennessee. But the work they had in Akron was still the worst in the rubber plants."[82] Beulah's family suffer a cross burning in their yard while she is too young to fully understand its symbolism, and the Klan was active in 1920s Akron, with over fifty thousand members in Summit County—members who held positions as sheriff, mayor, judges, and county officials. Klan members won majority control of the Akron School Board from 1925 to 1928. A lack of housing in this fast-growing city caused clashes between European immigrants still learning English, white Southern migrants, and African Americans escaping the South. Before marrying, Thomas lived in work barracks, conditions described in *The WPA Guide to Ohio*: "Frequently nine men used the one room, sleeping in eight-hour shifts. Chickens were even evicted to make sleeping rooms for the workers."[83] Finding housing afterward was equally difficult because, in part, although the rubber barons like F. A. Seiberling designed neighborhoods in the 1910s to be affordable for their employees—known as Goodyear Heights and the neighboring Firestone Park—the companies refused to sell to homes to African American employees.[84] Nonetheless, Thomas and Beulah persevere despite the presence of "the white sheet" and redlining. Historic Black neighborhoods developed in then less desirable areas, and on Bishop Street, Thomas and Beulah had European immigrant neighbors, the older generation resisting the integration of the neighborhood while the "youngest and blondest" daughter "slipped by mornings for bacon and grits," the glimmer of future change.[85]

Despite the discrimination, people flowed in from the South because of the benefits from the Midwest's industrial job opportunities. Wage work in the factories brought a freedom no industry in the South could match. In "Nothing Down," Thomas and Beulah purchase a new car, and Thomas had already been featured in a Nash when he was courting her. Beulah passes by the Peerless—a brand that produced high-quality luxury automobiles from 1900 to 1931—and chooses a "sky blue Chandler."[86] Chandler produced quality automobiles for middle-class Americans, and in the early 1920s, one of their new cars would have cost between $19,000 and $30,000 in today's dollars, an indication of the high wages Thomas was drawing in the prosperous twenties. The poem's title marks the precarious nature of the car's purchase as it is lost during the Depression, when the well-paying jobs evaporated everywhere and most lost more than cars. Thomas has to resort to part-time janitorial work at the ironically named Satisfaction Coal Company in the 1930s but is later employed at Goodyear Aircraft during the World War II industry boom. Beulah steps into the workforce when her youngest is eleven years old at Charlotte's Dress Shoppe and a few years afterward develops the skill of hat making.

Dove has good reason to see Akron as a place of opportunity, even if it came begrudgingly, because her father was part of the generation who integrated Goodyear, the Great Migration opening doors to eventual success. In 1941, Ray Dove operated an elevator at Goodyear, working the night shift so he could go to the University of Akron during the day. According to Dove, as a gifted graduate student, he was chosen for an accelerated program to quickly gain the skills the nation needed for the war effort, a program run at the University of Illinois—a university that then panicked over where to house an African American student.[87] But it was only in 1953 that Goodyear reluctantly hired him as the first African American researcher in the industry. He worked there until 1986, retiring as a senior researcher and section head after a successful and productive career on the forefront of rubber research and the changing racial makeup of American corporations. William R. Miller began working for Goodyear in 1952 and in 1980 was named the company's first African American executive, and in the 1940s workers like Otis Spurling at Goodyear and Clark Smith at Firestone were two of the men who forced their way into not only the better-paying jobs building tires but eating in the cafeteria rather than the locker room.[88] By the time Dove was reflecting on Akron in 1998, she could write, "The Akron I grew up in was a town where class systems were not so rigid that one couldn't make it by dint and savvy and heart; a place where it was possible to purchase your own home and even have a backyard and garden; a city where you could expect a decent education for your children."[89] Nonetheless, as her volume clearly documents, her grandparents did not enjoy those same opportunities.

Akron's alleys, canals, viaducts, vacant lots, smokestacks, streetlamps, pavement, and railroad tracks quietly dominate the volume, decidedly Akron but ultimately a landscape bigger than just a single city. Its often unlovely urban setting influences Thomas and Beulah but is also shaped by them, the local and ordinary directing the course of the nation. Thomas and Beulah—representative of their generation—wield power as they transform the industries and wars reconfiguring the United States into a world power and step into a later twentieth century in which Beulah witnesses the March on Washington, a grandson named Malcolm, the new term "Afro-Americans," and integrated workplaces and company picnics, parks, and lakes, substantive changes from the legally segregated blue pools of only 1940. This volume, thus, not only offers a beautifully choreographed duet but also reaches far beyond individuals, family stories, and autobiography to chart the development of urban African American identity and community during the twentieth century.[90]

Thomas and Beulah also represents a triumph in technique for Dove, a merging of lyric and narrative poetry, an inspiration for the next generation's experimentation with form. Helen Vendler claims that "Dove is principally a poet of dramatic force—a quality found relatively in lyric, a genre by its nature reflective, circling, and static,"[91] and her individual poems live up to that description. For this volume, however, Dove explained that she wanted the poems to enact a narrative strategy as well:

> At that point I did want them narrative; I thought there must be a way to get back into poetry the grandness that narrative can give, plus the sweep of time. Lyric poetry does not have that sweep of time. Lyrics are discrete moments. On the other hand, a lot of narrative poems can tend to bog down in the prosier transitional moments. I didn't see very many long narrative poems that really weren't smaller poems linked together. So one of the things I was trying to do was string moments as beads on a necklace. In other words, I have lyric poems which, when placed one after the other, reconstruct the sweep of time. I wanted it all. I wanted a narrative and I wanted lyric poems, so I tried to do them both.[92]

Her poems are successful individually, and often anthologized as such, but the larger project offers the sweep of the twentieth century, the changes brought about through the Great Migration and into the civil rights years. Dove demands that the genre of poetry fit itself to her needs, and the genre generously opens itself into something new, a new type of narrative for a new moment in history.[93]

By influencing younger poets so broadly and profoundly, *Thomas and Beulah* helped create the energy, the initiative that transformed into the profusion of historical poetry being published today. Dove, herself the legacy of Hayden and Harper, exerted such potent influence not only through modeling new directions in historical content and poetic form but also through sheer timing, with *Thomas and Beulah* being published as many of the younger generation of poets attended college and one year earlier than Toni Morrison's *Beloved*. It opened wide the door of historical poetry, and the post-1960 poets walked through, stepping forward into their generational project of writing the past—and through it the present—in their historical poetry.

Chapter 2

✦

Digging Up the Past

Elizabeth Alexander's *The Venus Hottentot*

Born in 1962, Elizabeth Alexander is one of the most established poets of her generation, having published in excess of eleven books of poetry, three books of nonfiction, an edition of Gwendolyn Brooks's poems, and an exceptional memoir, a body of work that began with her 1990 book *The Venus Hottentot*. This first volume was published three years after Alexander completed her MA in Creative Writing at Boston University and during her PhD work at the University of Pennsylvania. Becoming an established writer so early in her career meant she was, as she phrased it, floating by herself for a few years.[1] Alexander has deep ties to the generation that came before her—she studied with Derek Walcott, developed a friendship and correspondence with Michael S. Harper, grew close to Rita Dove—and Alexander's generation, defined in this study as poets born after 1960, was following her example in their book publications by the late 1990s. Alexander stands out as the forerunner of this group, the poet other writers in this study looked to for inspiration, for one of their own writing innovative historical poetry and being rewarded for her skill and talent. Besides teaching at universities such as Chicago, Smith, Yale, and Columbia—and currently the president of the Andrew W. Mellon Foundation—Alexander has become one of the most celebrated poets of her generation, receiving accolades beginning in the early 1990s: an NEA Fellowship, a Guggenheim Fellowship, the Hurston-Wright Award, and the Schomburg Medal; in addition, she was the inaugural poet for President Barack Obama's first term in office. Awards signal arrival in both the poetry and academic worlds, and Alexander has turned that cultural capital into a space from which she can speak challenging truths to the nation and support the flourishing community of African American poets.

The poetic community is connected by webs of friendships and institutions—connections this study sketches at the beginning of each chapter because the lines of influence within this generation are as important as those linking Hayden, Harper, and Dove to contemporary poets, and the most significant of them is Cave Canem. Alexander refers to herself as a coconspirator in its creation and development, someone who has been there since the beginning, fostering relationships between poets.[2] Cave Canem was founded by Toi Derricotte and Cornelius Eady in 1996. Its core offering is a weeklong retreat, and poets who are accepted are invited back for two additional summer retreats, all in a space of five years. Fellows have the opportunity to hone their craft with eminent faculty mentors like Alexander and create their own writing network, working in a space Eady describes as a home or a haven, "*haven* being defined in this case as a place where you are *seen, understood, challenged*, and *encouraged* at what you are doing as a poet." It is a place of interchange, where poets of different backgrounds, training, and styles influence one another: "The spoken-word poet tries on the skin of the MFA poet; the MFA poet buffs stanzas with a little street noise; a silence is broken; a hurt or dream or dread is aired; chances are taken; traditions are borrowed, broken, claimed, and reworked."[3] Derricotte believed that a specific space for African American poets was needed because these poets were not being taught or cultivated: "I had been writing since I was ten. In all my years of study—from grade school through graduate school—I had never read a black poet. I had never been taught by a black teacher. I was skeptical when I was presented with poems by Langston Hughes when I was sixteen, when I heard the "angry" poems of Haki Madhubuti and Amiri Baraka. There was a suspicion that black people weren't really good enough to be published, to be poets." For her too, Cave Canem is a "kind of heaven," a space for Black poetry to flourish.[4]

Cave Canem's name, Harryette Mullen explains, means "beware the dog," a saying taken from a mosaic of a dog guarding the House of the Tragic Poet in Pompeii. This classically named organization has become, Mullen claims, "not black utopia or a poets' paradise but a plausible and portable literary renaissance that has strengthened connections among black poets while also nurturing an expanding repertoire of black poetry." She credits the BAM's radical aesthetics for making possible her generation's formal and thematic freedom: "What seems to characterize the current conversation is a greater tolerance of difference, uncertainty, and even confusion in our lives and in our work as poets. We can exist as black artists without hermetic definitions of art or blackness."[5] Michael S. Harper testifies to the connections Cave Canem makes between the poetic generations as well:

> I think Cave Canem is a remarkable turn for the better, an advantage to black poets in the digital age; I taught three summers (1998–2000) in their program, and I am inspired by their productivity and vision, not to mention their publication record by alumni(ae). I have taught Natasha Trethewey's *Native Guard* in my Advanced Poetry Writing seminar, even written for her tenure at Emory, though I don't know her personally. In fact I've supported a number of the Cave Canem folks for college and university assignments, and I've been

> happy to do so. Cornelius Eady, Elizabeth Alexander, toi derricote [sic], Michael Weaver, and Thomas Sayers Ellis are all excellent and diverse artists. They represent a fearlessness and zeal I find invigorating, a resource for the American tongue at large.[6]

Alexander agrees about the many possibilities open to contemporary poets and the significance of institutionally supporting poetry: "What has always been vital to me about the space that Cave Canem makes is that I believe we have truly made room for widely divergent spokes of black aesthetics, poetics, and identity. We live, as Lucille Clifton has said, not in 'either/or' but in 'and/but.' "[7] All of the poets addressed in this study are connected through Cave Canem, whose influence stretches across the decades and the country.

Published six years before Cave Canem even began, a marker that truly indicates its position as the origin point for this generation's historical poetry, Alexander's *The Venus Hottentot* opens with a poetic sequence presenting Sara Baartman, a South African woman exploited in London and Paris in the early 1800s. "Consider the charge sent through the poetry community when Elizabeth Alexander released *The Venus Hottentot*," wrote poet Camille T. Dungy. "The title poem, by redefining the terms and lens through which the body and life of Sartje Baartman would be viewed, forecast an emergence of books with similar projects."[8] Major Jackson likewise claims that Alexander's *The Venus Hottentot* and Rita Dove's *Thomas and Beulah*, published three years earlier, "have been so influential to African American poets, both could be argued as ushering in the past two decades worth of historical poems by African Americans."[9] Significantly, Alexander began her career by focusing on history, a decision that underscores the centrality of history in her artistic life. Her recovery and revision of Baartman, a woman about whom information is still scant and fraught, ties her not only to Baartman's African identity but also to the postcolonial rebuttal of European colonialism's racist interpretations of Africans and the diaspora. As part of the generation born during the civil rights era, Alexander benefited from the recovery of African American texts and must have been intrigued by the story of this African person. Her poem features a shadowy historical figure paraded for her physical "otherness" by Europeans, a figure who has become a symbol for colonial oppression as well as postcolonial recovery, a figure to whom Alexander bequeaths agency, determination, and an interior life, something the historical record can never achieve.

Baartman never completely disappeared from historical memory, but she was returned to public attention in the 1980s by scientist Stephen Jay Gould.[10] In his 1981 book *The Mismeasure of Man*, which disputes theories of biological determinism, Gould mentions the Venus Hottentot, whose skeletal measurements disrupted efforts on the part of some scientists to find biological markers of racial superiority. These scientists were intent on proving the superiority of the racial group Caucasians—the term itself a scientific and anthropological error—and one route they promoted was to demonstrate that Caucasians were more evolved by proving they were farther distanced from apes than other racial groups. However, Baartman's skeleton scored much further away from apes in its measurements than did Caucasian skeletons, thus defeating their premise that Caucasians were more advanced, a result they could disown, according to Gould, by abandoning that measurement and looking for another that would more neatly prove the result they sought. The next year, Gould dedicated his October 1982 monthly column in the periodical *Natural History* to Sara Baartman. Beginning his essay with Carl Sagan's *Broca's Brain*, Gould describes the personal tour he was given of the Musée de l'Homme in Paris. The same tour that brought the jar holding Paul Broca's brain to Sagan's attention focused Gould's attention instead on the shelf above the brains, which held, he wrote, "a little exhibit that provided an immediate and chilling insight into nineteenth-century *mentalité* and the history of racism: in three smaller jars, I saw the dissected genitalia of three Third-World women. I found no brains of women, and neither Broca's penis nor any male genitalia grace the collection."[11] This occasion provided Gould with the platform to discuss Baartman's story further, publicity that led to renewed public interest in her in the 1980s in the midst of the South African antiapartheid movement, a formal request from President Nelson Mandela that France return her remains to South Africa, and the repatriation of her remains in 2002, when they were buried on a hilltop in the Gamtoos Valley on August 9. Literary critic Sander L. Gilman addressed Baartman in his influential article "Black Bodies, White Bodies," which was published not only in *Critical Inquiry* in 1985 but also in Henry Louis Gates Jr.'s *"Race," Writing, and Difference* in the same year. Alexander, who studied with Gates, first met Baartman in Gilman's work.[12]

As best could be proven by 2009—an important caveat since historical research on Baartman continues to be done and seemingly authoritative myths about her abound[13]—Sara Baartman, who is also known by her Afrikaner name or the paternalistic diminutive form Saartjie, "little Sara," was a member of the Khoekhoe—whom the Dutch called the Hottentots, a term by now synonymous with ethnic slurs. Baartman's Khoisan name has proven unrecoverable so far, and it now appears that she was born in the Camdeboo, about fifty miles north of the Gamtoos River valley in the 1770s rather than around 1790, as typically cited, which means that in London she was a mature woman rather than a twenty-year-old. After growing up on colonists' farms on the eastern border of South Africa, Baartman was sold to Pieter Cesars in 1795 or 1796, an enslaved person with an uncertain status since the enslavement of people indigenous to an area was forbidden by the Dutch. Pieter brought her to Cape Town, where she remained for more than a decade, forced to do domestic labor and nurse children for him and his employer, which was possible because Baartman bore three children, all of whom died in infancy, before going to London. In 1803, Baartman moved to the household of Hendrik Cesars (Pieter's brother) and his wife, both Free Blacks like Pieter, for whom she was not entirely a servant, not quite enslaved, but not free. To meet his many debts, Hendrik borrowed money, which he was unable to repay, and by 1808 it seems he was already making money by displaying Baartman to Europeans in Cape Town as the Hottentot Venus and possibly forcing her into sex work. Alexander Dunlop, a Scottish military surgeon with financial problems, concocted the plan to display Baartman in London, and he pressured Hendrik to accompany him and Baartman. By the fall of 1810, Baartman was being shown in London at private viewings and in public spectacles, the advertisements and her costume combining the exhibit of scientific specimens, the draw of the sideshow, and the lure of exoticized sexuality. The placards advertising Baartman, and subsequent caricatures, emphasized the size of her buttocks and her unusual dress—markers of otherness used to justify colonization, as the English compared their own bodies to hers, constructing a narrative to make their own superior. Her Khoekhoe language, a language containing clicking sounds that Europeans could rarely learn to pronounce and so denigrated, was also used to exoticize a woman who by then spoke not only her native language, but also English, French, Dutch, and most likely other African languages. Moreover, her genitalia were rumored to be unlike European women's, but she kept the intimate parts of her body carefully out of public view until her death, upon which her elongated labia were placed in a jar as a scientific specimen. Barbara Chase-Riboud, in her well-researched novel about Baartman, implies that large buttocks were a symbol of beauty cultivated by the Khoekhoe through special foods and lotions and that while Baartman's elongated labia might be hereditary, they might also be a result of intentional labia stretching, a type of female genital mutilation.[14] By 1814, her popularity in England having waned, Baartman traveled to Paris with Henry Taylor where she was again advertised as a spectacle to be looked at, a scientific specimen to be studied. In 1815, during a frigid winter, Taylor disappeared, and she began working for S. Reaux, known as an animal trainer. After Baartman died in December 1815, probably from pneumonia, her body was brought to the laboratory of Georges Cuvier, an anatomist and one of most well-known scientists at the time. Cuvier made a plaster cast of her body, saved her skeleton after dissecting her body, and placed her brain and genitals in jars of formaldehyde. His subsequent writings about Baartman's body furthered his claims of Caucasian superiority in what was accepted as science at the time. Artists like Alexander oppose Cuvier's goals and conclusions, using their art to revise Baartman's story.

Alexander's *The Venus Hottentot* is composed of two different sequences. In the first Cuvier speaks, and in the second, much larger section Baartman refutes his positions. The structure is based on Dove's poem "Parsley," Alexander has explained, a poem also organized into two opposing voices,[15] the first section offering the voices of the murdered Haitians and the second section Trujillo's. Dove's complex poem offers a voice to the thousands of Haitians murdered in the 1937 Parsley Massacre and explores the perverted interior of Rafael Trujillo, a dictator intent on ethnic purity but whose own mother was part Haitian. She plumbs the cruelty and irony in Trujillo's actions, just as Alexander explores the psyche of the colonizer and rebuttal of the colonized in her poem. Besides structure, Alexander appreciates Dove's imagination, which she describes as powerful enough not to caricature Trujillo while still roundly condemning him, a stance she adopts with Baartman and Cuvier.

Cuvier speaks in couplets, a principal poetic unit for verse written in European languages and thus appropriate for the voice of the colonizer. He praises the advances of science, asserts that scientific inquiry will explain national character, speaks to the fate of Baartman's dissected body, and closes with his belief that "elegant facts await me. / Small things in this world are mine."[16] The first six couplets, brief as notations in his notebook of scientific findings,[17] describe the wonder of glimpsing minute objects through a microscope—"Colors dazzle insect wings. / A drop of water swirls / like marble"—an opportunity that at the time seemed wondrous and was available only to a select few. As part of his discoveries in the natural world, Cuvier noted that "cranial measurements / crowd my notebook pages, // and I am moving closer, / closer to how these numbers // signify aspects of / national character," shifting the poem to his belief in three world races—Caucasian, Mongolian, and Ethiopian—and his claim that cranial size and shape determined racial identity and the quality of civilizations.[18] As a European, he placed his own group at the top, thus allowing him to discuss the racial inferiority of others as he compared them to Caucasians. The poem then skips forward more than a hundred years to the time when Baartman's genitalia were kept in a jar in the Musée de l'Homme, a future Cuvier could not have foreseen but a direct and damning result of the European colonization he facilitated, a colonization aided and abetted by scientific interpretations of people who were other than European as lesser. A case in point is the term, dressed up in Latin roots, created to describe Baartman's physique, *steatopygia*—defined as a large amount of fat on the buttocks. The *OED* traces the etymology of the word to William John Burchell's 1822 *Travels in the Interior of Southern Africa*. Thus it is an official sounding, quasi-medical Latin term developed to describe an anatomy generally different from what Europeans were accustomed to and specifically to make it appear that the Khoekhoe body was lesser or even diseased. All of these colonizing tools—inventing medical terms, conducting scientific explorations, and writing seemingly authoritative treatises—were for the cause of proving European superiority and therefore establishing the rights of Europeans to oppress people around the globe.

Baartman rebuts Cuvier in the second section, which begins with the number "2" but no name, unlike the first section labeled "1. Cuvier," perhaps because her Khoisan name is unknown or because the identity given to her, the Venus Hottentot, titles the poem. Also offered at the poem's opening is the date 1825, ten years after Baartman's death. Thinking back to her choice of that date, Alexander calls it an unconscious decision, perhaps a desire to borrow Morrison's thinking about Sula who dies before the end of her book: "I wanted Sula to be missed by the reader. That's why she dies early. There's a lot of book after she dies, you know. I wanted them to miss her presence in that book as the town missed her presence."[19] Thus, Baartman surreally speaks from the dead in unrhymed octaves, a stanza length often used in ballads to recount stories as Baartman does. The octaves, far outdoing Cuvier's couplets in length and complexity, emphasize the importance of Baartman's voice and the expansive nature of her section.[20] The entirety of this second section takes place in London and Paris during the time she was exhibited as a spectacle, both for the general public who could pay to see her and for the scientists who felt sure that her body offered the proof they needed to justify their beliefs. Here, however, she is given the subject position—she speaks as she does not historically; she confides her monetary hopes for the exhibition, which are never realized; she objects to the physical and sexual spectacle she has become; she claims her achievements, which fly in the face of her objectification; and she imagines what she would find if she could, instead, dissect Cuvier. In Alexander's poem, Baartman explains the plan she was offered, to share equally in the profits of her exhibition, proceeds that would allow her to live in Cape Town, upon her return, as a wealthy woman. Instead, she finds herself in London displayed in a cage with observers paying to view her body, to consider whether her buttocks consist of muscle, bone, or fat, and even to pinch or prod her: "I am a black cutout against / a captive blue sky, pivoting / nude so that the paying audience / can view my naked buttocks."[21] Baartman wore a skintight, flesh-colored dress, which revealed much of her body when on display so that her audience could imagine her naked. In London of 1810, shows that displayed human or animal "specimens" were popular and appealed to the appetite for what Europeans considered to be exotic, the other, fostered by Britain's colonization of much of the world. Baartman finds herself next to singing mice, a contortionist, and a pig. Because she is placed in the setting of a sideshow, she too is seen as unique but representative, an embodiment of peoples whose oppression is made acceptable to the Europeans who, to her, smell like cabbage and rotting teeth.

In the poem's second half, Baartman comments on Cuvier, who is obsessed with investigating her genitals, expecting them to help him realize his scientific theories of a racial hierarchy. Baartman asserts her own identity in this part of the poem, revealing that she speaks many languages and that the gamble she took in coming to Europe was entrepreneurial, a choice she hoped would be better than her life in South Africa. However, she has instead been made into a "wordless Odalisque,"[22] whose health is failing from the cold weather and poor food. She kept her genitals private while alive—even when Cuvier and other scientists were given three days at the Jardin des Plantes during which to study and draw her nude body, a decision on her part that Clifton Crais and Pamela Scully call "a profound statement of self"—but after her death, Cuvier dissects her body.[23] In the last stanza, Alexander imagines Baartman turning the tables on Cuvier, dissecting him instead for museum exhibition and preserving his heart, which she expects to be "shriveled and hard, / geometric, deformed, unnatural," a physical rendering of the colonialist psyche, which combined oppression, racism, and science.[24]

In choosing Baartman as a poetic persona, Alexander enters an imaginative space, and in a 1996 interview, she encouraged writers and artists to understand Baartman as a woman with "a rich and textured inner life that belies the surface exploitation and presentation."[25] Similarly, in 2010 Alexander again emphasized that "the poet can give the Venus Hottentot voice" and that offering this historical figure a voice "reclaims" her.[26] Toni Morrison, whose celebrated neo-slave narrative *Beloved* was published in 1987, surely influencing Alexander's volume, similarly emphasizes the significance of exploring the interiority of her characters in order to find historical truth:

> Therefore the crucial distinction for me is not the difference between fact and fiction, but the distinction between fact and truth. Because facts can exist without human intelligence, but truth cannot. So if I'm looking to find and expose a truth about the interior life of people who didn't write it (which doesn't mean that they didn't have it); if I'm trying to fill in the blanks that the slave narratives left—to part the veil that was so frequently drawn, to implement the stories that I heard—then the approach that's most productive and most trustworthy for me is the recollection that moves from the image to the text. Not from the text to the image.[27]

Kevin Young likewise underscores the significance of imagining the interior life of past people: "No wonder the black imagination involves much that is hidden, squirreled away, storied. Rather than the madwoman, ours is the cosmology in the attic. Much of that inner life takes its form in what Elizabeth Alexander calls 'the black interior'—for hiding was a tradition not just of the body but of the mind."[28] Alexander's poem uses history as an entry point to the psyche of her subjects, and her interest is in imagining what their selves were like, insights historical documents can never provide. Alexander's Baartman is defiant, ambitious, and smart. She understands Cuvier much better than he will ever understand her, even as closely as he studies and preserves her physical body. As Alexander's readers, we become privy to Baartman's thoughts, which, in this short sequence, create a woman remarkably different from the one recounted in the writings of Cuvier and other Europeans. Through her imagining of that interior, Alexander offers an avenue to the past through the psyche of a historical figure, an avenue we can only engage through art.

Baartman's body has become a symbol used by many creative artists exploring the past and present representation of Black women's bodies.

Alexander frees Baartman from the caricatures published in London newspapers and elsewhere, in which she is drawn as the anatomic opposite of how the British imagined their own physiques. For Alexander, she becomes a speaking subject, a past ancestor, a symbol of colonial resistance, someone who understands her oppressors better than they understand themselves, who can expose how they used science to denigrate her. The titular poem opens the volume, and toward its end, Alexander's "A Poem for Nelson Mandela," who pressured France to return Baartman's remains for almost a decade, claims that "symbols bear power; symbols demand / power," there in reference to Mandela's leadership from prison, a prison from which he was released in 1990 just as this volume of poetry was published.[29] The symbol of Baartman's physical body—since without photographs a true representation of it does not exist—has found power in becoming a symbol of resistance, a repository for the postcolonial imagination, with many possible interpretations because the historical record is so thin. In the wake of Alexander's volume, many other artists and scholars have been inspired by Baartman's story. Suzan-Lori Parks's 1996 play *Venus* uses the bare historical outline of Baartman's life to explore colonization, agency, and objectification, all of which turn on the ability of drama to emphasize spectacle. Parks takes liberties, opens new spaces, and points out the hole in history. In an interview, she emphasizes how little is definitively known about Baartman and says about her own production, "I've left some things out, and I've included other things. Most of it's fabricated, it's questioning the history of history. The play doesn't just swallow the story whole and regurgitate it onto the stage. It embraces the unrecorded truth."[30] In her 2003 *Hottentot Venus*, Barbara Chase-Riboud, like Alexander, imagines Baartman's interior life, as she constructs an entire novel exploring the life of Baartman and the many colonizers who exploited her. A well-researched novel that relies heavily on authorial imagination, it creates a whole person, far beyond what can be documented—as most lives are, especially before the twentieth century—and Chase-Riboud tackles some of the stickier issues like why Baartman would remain with her oppressors in London and Paris. In 2000, visual artist Renée Cox was photographed by Lyle Ashton Harris as the Hottentot Venus, featuring her own body in profile wearing metallic breasts and buttocks, a portrait that disrupts the nineteenth-century drawings, paintings, and engravings of Baartman (2000), and Renee Green created the 1989 installation "Permission" about Baartman at the Studio Museum in Harlem. Intellectual bell hooks mentions Baartman when discussing the objectification of Black women's bodies by European observers who are interested in only certain parts of her body, the sexualized parts that they choose to perceive as diametrically opposed to their own in *Black Looks*,[31] and scholar Deborah Willis's edited collection *Black Venus 2010: They Called Her "Hottentot"* engages the legacy and reclamation of Baartman in creative art. Similarly, Baartman is remembered and revised in South African Diana Ferrus's 1998 poem "I've Come to Take You Home";

the 1998 documentary *The Life and Times of Sarah Baartman*, directed by Zola Maseko, as well as his short film *The Return of Sarah Baartman*; Cathy Park Hong's poem "Hottentot Venus" in her 2002 *Translating Mo'um*; Lydia R. Diamond's play *Voyeurs de Venus*, which premiered in 2006 at Chicago Dramatists; and Douglas Kearney's 2010 poem "Drop It Like It's Hottentot Venus." These varied texts—as well as many more unmentioned here—dismantle the colonial narratives whose truth comes only from repetition.[32] Instead, Baartman, and through her African women and the diaspora, are now imagined in ways that empower them and engage the imagination, offering a new historical view of the past.[33]

Choosing a figure as famous and yet as elusive as Baartman offers particular challenges: Baartman's reentry into public consciousness was furthered by Alexander's volume, but she was a figure who was African rather than African American; she lived almost two hundred years before the publication of Alexander's book; little was definitively known about her, and her compelling story is still shrouded in uncertainty; she is represented by no accurate visual picture; and she spoke minimally in the historical record—a record written by the colonialists. Alexander commented, in a 2001 interview with Natasha Trethewey, that "one of the big challenges was to hold on, especially when the Venus Hottentot herself speaks, because that's a longer part of the poem—to create a voice, and then to hold on to it and keep it consistent when it was not a voice that felt close to my own." Choosing to write about Baartman is fundamentally different from creating a character positioned in the 1910s as Trethewey does in *Bellocq's Ophelia* or writing about an ordinary person denied achievement like A. Van Jordan's MacNolia Cox. Additionally, Alexander's choice to focus on interiority is different from other volumes that will be covered in this study. Alexander's volume is self-contained even with her thorough research: "I did a lot of historical research, though there wasn't a lot to be found about Saartje Bartman at the time. But I read about carnivals and circuses and London in the early nineteenth century, and all kinds of different things that would give me a sense of her world."[34] It explicitly points to no other sources, in contrast to the way that Trethewey leaves a trail of sources in her notes, enticing readers to engage historical accounts by following the bread crumbs. Furthermore, Alexander addresses Baartman's life only in London and Paris rather than her years in Africa, which leaves out perhaps the most important years of Baartman's life but allows Alexander to narrow her focus to the clear exploitation of Baartman's body. She reverses the colonial, quasi-scientific discourse about that body, demonstrating that the negative representations of Black women's sexuality can be traced to specific moments like the presentation of Baartman's body by European men. These men present Baartman's body to a European viewing audience in a carefully constructed scenario that, in turn, reinforces colonial claims of superiority. Alexander's poem seeks a moment of reckoning with the past as her revision of this story begins the process of removing Baartman from these colonial claims. She gives Baartman the high ground and presents Cuvier as disfigured and immoral. Her analysis of how the Black female body is represented through Baartman's experiences speaks also to her present, reimagining the past through new historical knowledge and fundamentally shifting the present discussion of how Black women are represented.

With this volume, Alexander initiated a wave of historical poetry that is very much ongoing, in the work of her fellow poets and in her own writing, particularly in the "Amistad" section of her volume *American Sublime* and in *Miss Crandall's School for Young Ladies and Little Misses of Color*, a book for children that she cowrote with Marilyn Nelson, which focuses on a relatively unknown school for young African American women in Connecticut during the 1830s, a story they tell in twenty-four sonnets. In planning this volume, Alexander and Nelson divided up the research and writing, but no initial agreement was made to write in sonnets. They coordinated their writing after each first wrote alone, perhaps following the path that Walcott suggested to Alexander when she studied with him.[35] Walcott taught her that the form of a poem will suggest itself to the writer, that form makes itself felt as writers work with their content.[36] Form, for Alexander then, emerges organically from the poetic imagination during the researching and writing process.

Alexander's experimentation with form and the historical poem opened spaces, inspiring her peers to continue looking for histories denied or lost and to tell those histories through poetry. She gave Sara Baartman agency and a speaking, rather than object, position, and through her poetry, Baartman takes her rightful position as an elder, an ancestor to be revered, a woman who speaks her mind and claims her body. Alexander's recovery and reconstruction of Baartman is not only about the past but also about the present, about African American women and how they represent their bodies. Alexander takes the first step for her generation of revising the past and reconstructing the present, the origin point of a trajectory that continues to multiply exponentially through a myriad of poets and their proliferating historical subjects.

Chapter 3

✦

Tending the Graves

Natasha Trethewey's *Native Guard*

In an interview, Elizabeth Alexander compares her work to Rita Dove's and Natasha Trethewey's, imagining the three of them as siblings, herself as "the most wildly coiffed of the three sisters" and Trethewey as a writer with "this incredible formal, tight control, but there's a lot that's really raw."[1] By this third decade of the twenty-first century, Alexander and Trethewey have had many moments of contact, both informal and through institutions, including meeting at the inaugural 1994 Furious Flower Conference, a decennial conference celebrating African American poetry. Joanne V. Gabbin, who organized this Furious Flower (and the two subsequent ones in 2004 and 2014), edited a Furious Flower anthology, which included both Alexander and Trethewey, as well as Major Jackson and Kevin Young. Alexander and Trethewey also crossed paths through Cave Canem. Trethewey received the first Cave Canem Prize for *Domestic Work*, spoke at the 2000 award event in honor of that prize, and has returned as a faculty member. Additionally, Trethewey interviewed Alexander for *Southern Spaces* and for *Poets & Writers*, and in a book commemorating the Museum of Modern Art's 2015 exhibition of Jacob Lawrence's *Migration Series* in its entirety, Alexander chose ten poets, one of whom was Trethewey, to write poems inspired by Lawrence's paintings. Their sisterly poetic relationship has its origins in *The Venus Hottentot*, which Trethewey has credited as one of her most important influences and to which she was introduced by scholar Joanne Braxton. In a 2016 interview, Trethewey commented that *The Venus Hottentot* "was the first book by a black woman poet that I was reading when I decided to be a poet," and it showed her how poetry could be combined with history. Alexander's persona poems offered Trethewey a model for how to "inhabit" other voices through the example of Baartman and Cuvier, who "exist side-by-side in this kind of contention with each other, both seeing the same situation in completely different ways," a lesson that influenced Trethewey when writing *Bellocq's Ophelia*, a volume similarly about a single figure and historical truth.[2] Only four years later, Trethewey published *Native Guard*, another volume of historical poetry, this time focused on the Civil War.[3]

Before her involvement in Cave Canem, Trethewey was a member of the Dark Room Collective—another gathering of poets now recognized as one of this generation's key institutions, which began in a Cambridge house shared by poets Sharan Strange and Thomas Sayers Ellis. It predated Cave Canem and motivated Cornelius Eady, who has written about his first introduction to this earlier group:

> Years before Cave Canem began, Tom Ellis and Sharon [*sic*] Strange and others from the Dark Room Collective invited me to come and read for them at their space in Cambridge, Massachusetts. It was like being part of a Sunday revival meeting. A crowd showed up (I couldn't tell who actually lived there and who didn't), some furniture got moved, some chairs unfolded, and Pow! Their living room turned into a salon. I guess I refer to the energy of a revival because that's how they all seemed to take it: with a serious joy and pride in their belief in being black *and* being wordy, which totally disarmed me. Perhaps that was the first time I saw that sort of idea acted on.[4]

Inspired by James Baldwin's death in 1987, Strange and Ellis began the Dark Room Collective, which dated from 1989 to 1998, by building a library of writings by authors they called their "living literary ancestors," creating an extensive reading series, critiquing each other's writing, and growing a group of poets that included not only Trethewey but also Kevin Young, Major Jackson, Tracy K. Smith, and so many more. They knew many established African American poets and other writers of color were in the Boston area and wondered why they saw their role models at so few events: "We wanted to hear them read their words, have conversations with them, clasp their hands. We wanted them to know that their work was appreciated, was inspiring, was changing lives. We wanted to know them and to have them know us." The writers they approached responded enthusiastically, and the list of luminaries appearing at their readings was impressively extensive, including, to name a very few, Derek Walcott, Michael S. Harper, Amiri Baraka, Clarence Major, Alice Walker, Ntozake Shange, Yusef Komunyakaa, Elizabeth Alexander, Nathaniel Mackey, Harryette Mullen, Thylias Moss, Carl Phillips, and Sonia Sanchez. The collective reached out to other parts of the country, making connections with poets in Washington, DC, Philadelphia, and New York, and participating in the inaugural 1994 Furious Flower Conference. Strange emphasizes that the work they did together "began our real apprenticeship—the reading series and our workshops were in a sense our true MFA writing program."[5] This group of poets dedicated to poetic tradition and craft produced so many talented poets, among them Trethewey.

When Trethewey was a graduate student in the MFA program at the University of Massachusetts, Amherst, a friend shared a newspaper article about the Dark Room Collective with her. Soon after, she submitted poems to a special issue on emerging writers coming out in *Agni Magazine*. Ellis, an editor for that special issue, accepted her poems and wrote to her about the Dark Room Collective. Trethewey recalls that "we had a conversation about that and I came down to Boston to a reading where I met all the other members of the Dark room. Apparently, they voted on me and said I could join. So that's how it happened."[6] The Dark Room Collective nurtured its members and its influence, and the relationships between poets that it fostered helped Trethewey develop as a poet who writes about the past, revising the histories told about the United States.

In her poetry, interviews, and public talks, Trethewey often speaks about history and poetry's relationship to it: "I do feel that poets should take on the responsibility of recording or re-recording the cultural memory of a people, and tending the graves is a way of doing this. It means tending to the past, to those things that are not gone or erased or invisible, but are indeed enacting themselves in our daily lives."[7] *Native Guard* tends the graves not only of the Native Guard soldiers—public figures who fought in the national conflict—but also of her own mother, who was murdered in 1985 by her second husband, from whom she had been divorced for about a year. Trethewey used personal memories and history in her first volume, *Domestic Work*, but writing about her mother's murder is far more personal and marks a different level of authorial vulnerability.[8] However, in an interview with Christian Teresi, Trethewey remarked that "*Native Guard* is in no way about my mother's murder. The book is an elegy for forgotten people and lost places. The murder is the backstory in my own life," a seemingly paradoxical claim.[9] I want to suggest that Gwendolyn Ann Turnbough's death anchors the tenor, as well as the movement, of Trethewey's volume to, as she put it, "the backstory" in her own life while simultaneously offering a connection to war, domestic familial violence tying into national familial violence.

To interviewer Joan Wylie Hall, Trethewey said, "My little memories are actually memories of a culture. My experience of race, for example, or even domestic violence has everything to do with the laws at the time, which are a kind of legal history of the nation," and throughout her archive at Emory University, Trethewey's writings reflect the sentiment that she is interested in the intersections between personal and public history, family stories and cultural memory. Thus, Trethewey's mother's death offers a path from the individual history to the national history, and elegies for her become elegies for the many women lost to domestic violence, incidents of larger national violence so that Trethewey can claim, "I'm actually digging deep into historical memory of a nation."[10] While revealing and personal, *Native Guard* is at its core about the United States' past and how that past affects individual lives, the nation, and the South. Trethewey always returns to the absences, the spaces in history, as when she recommends that everyone should read historian David Blight's book on the Civil War *Race and Reunion: The Civil*

War in American Memory: "It's all about the kinds of things that are forgotten, that are left out of the public, cultural memory. He says that certain kinds of remembering and willed forgetting are the stuff of historical memory."[11] Like Blight, Trethewey is interested in how the Civil War is remembered and commemorated, and *Native Guard* adds new stories to the national memory, shifting the focus to the role of African Americans. *Native Guard* tends the graves of the forgotten, connecting the victims of domestic violence to troops who fought and died during the Civil War to racial identity in the twenty-first-century South.

Native Guard, published in 2006 and awarded the Pulitzer Prize, opens with the promise of change. Trethewey offers a journey into history, an engagement with the past that will alter the present:

> . . . . On the dock
>
> where you board the boat for Ship Island,
> someone will take your picture:
>
> the photograph—who you were—
> will be waiting when you return.[12]

The reader's willingness to board the boat marks their readiness for this journey, and the voyage marks a transformation in that the "you" who returns will not be the person who left. That person will transcend the photograph of themself, the picture taken before they set out on what is a quest, a quest for a more accurate rendering of national history and a quest for social justice, the goal that guides much of Trethewey's work.[13]

The volume's structure physically enacts these connections in its three sections. In early drafts, Trethewey used section titles, "Monument," "Document," and "Testament": "The elegies were monuments to my mother, to her memory; they were monuments to my own grief, monuments to that sense of loss that I encountered. The second section 'document,' is called 'Document' because it tries to create an imagined historical document, something we might discover in the archives somewhere or in somebody's attic. And the final section was my own testimony, my testament as native Southerner, as exile, as daughter, who perhaps had not done the work I should have done."[14] In its final form, the section titles disappeared, but the three divisions remain. The first section is about the death of her mother and all women who die from domestic violence; the second travels to the past, addressing how the Civil War is remembered, life for African Americans under Jim Crow, the Native Guard, and those who survived; and the final section takes up Trethewey's relationship as a writer and a biracial person to the South in sentiments similar to Langston Hughes's ambivalent lines "the lazy, laughing South / With blood on its mouth."[15]

Structurally, Trethewey is writing in concentric circles. The innermost circle is her mother's murder and domestic violence, the next circle is her commentary on the South, and the outermost circle offers the poems on the Civil War, on national history. These circles refuse to remain discrete but connect and comment upon one another. The concerns of each bleed across the boundaries of its section, directly linking these three primary concerns. In part, the volume's movement is achieved by beginning in medias res, to borrow a fiction term, rather than chronologically with the Civil War. In a note about teaching strategies collected in her archive, Trethewey lists the advice she uses in her classes: "Do not begin at the exact beginning. Pick some point on the circle and travel all the way around to the starting point."[16] In taking her own advice, she begins with elegies for her mother, a strategy that leads her from 1985 to the 1860s, rather than the other way around. In part, this volume's structure relies on Trethewey's penchant for repetition and the circling motion it offers. She explained to Daniel Cross Turner that "those words that keep getting repeated, those motifs—cotton, ghost, cross, for example, in *Native Guard*—are also intertwined with that desire to constantly circle back."[17]

Additional motifs unify the volume: native, death, home, photographs, writing, grave, and monument. For example, the poem "Monument," placed near the volume's end, begins with the industry of ants building a hill, an image Trethewey connects to her mother's grave. In interviews, she often discusses how her mother's grave lacks a marker, which she has not placed because of indecision over which name to put on it—not her mother's married name, which would commemorate the ex-husband who killed her. Trethewey comes to the decision that she can use her mother's birth name, Gwendolyn Ann Turnbough, and that reinsertion of her mother's core identity is the truth that matters. The monument the ants are constructing and the monument for her mother connect to the Civil War and the South through the many monuments commemorating the Confederacy, which proliferated especially after 1954, indicating that their significance is less about remembering the past than about reasserting Southern segregation. For example, in the late 1970s and early 1980s, elaborate monuments were being built like the green erected at Georgia's Stone Mountain, with individual monuments to each state of the Confederacy under the looming carving of Stonewall Jackson, Robert E. Lee, and Jefferson Davis, a carving for which the Klan provided part of the funding and that was only completed in 1972. "Monument" is followed by "Elegy for the Native Guards," in which the plaque placed on Ship Island listing the names of white Confederate soldiers but not the Native Guards was erected by the Daughters of the Confederacy, while Trethewey describes herself as a "non-Daughter" in this public struggle for national memory, the personal connected to the regional and national.[18] And in part, the crosshatch writing the persona describes in the poem "Native Guard," an example of which graces the cover of the volume, physically enacts the relationship of African Americans and European Americans, lives inextricably bound up in each other and whose concepts of their very selves depend upon the other. Trethewey compares her personal history as a biracial person to the history of the United States: "This book seeks to tell a fuller story of our history as Americans. Not 'this' side, or 'that' side, because there are no sides. We are not two trains running on separate tracks in America; it is all intertwined, and here is a book that says so, such as when the black soldier is writing letters home for the illiterate white soldier, and their voices become mingled, one, as he writes for the other. The story mingles in my own blood; it is that voice that has to tell the story."[19] Thus, this volume has a center and edges, although none are discrete; it eschews a starting point or linear progression; it relies on repetition and circles back to obsessive concerns; and it writes over what has already been written to offer complicated truths.[20]

Native Guard's first section is the volume's core, the innermost circle, and its poems lament the loss of loved ones through the specific instance of the death of Trethewey's mother. This section mourns her mother's early death and all loved ones lost to violence, and this lament for the lost offers concentrated and focused poems that feel the most personal of the volume. This core of grief becomes the center around which the rest of the volume turns. The epigram that opens this section comes from "Poor Wayfaring Stranger," a gospel song about joining loved ones in heaven, and it establishes the elegiac tone, weeping for the speaker's mother who has already crossed into Jordan. These poems foreshadow her death, address her funeral, read her body for clues and evidence, futilely protest domestic violence, share the emptiness that is a child's loss, and toy with calling across the abyss between life and death. Death cannot be predicted, but the speaker reviews her family's lives for clues. "The Southern Crescent," the first poem, offers three train trips in its two sections of nine-line, unrhymed stanzas: her mother's childhood train trip, a trip the two of them take when the speaker is young, and their final trip as the Crescent ends its run. Just as trains tend to symbolize movement, these trips travel through years, marking important moments in the mother's life—her newly gained independence as a young woman, a trip in which she is the parent figure, and a final trip, as the arc of the train's existence and her own life come to a close. Accompanying her mother are absent men—her mother's father (whom she only knows by a photograph), who was supposed to meet his young daughter at the Los Angeles station and who does not show up in the space of the poem; her mother's first husband, unable to meet the train because it has derailed, much like their marriage; and her mother's final trip with her daughter in the absence of her second husband, whom she is divorcing. Throughout the trips and their accompanying losses and absences, the mother looks to the fortunate future, believing in traveling to what lies ahead rather than looking behind at what life has cost her, a poem of promise for the ever-hopeful mother and loss for the daughter, who has the hindsight of distance. The poem "Genus Narcissus" also foreshadows death from its epigraph borrowed from Robert Herrick's 1648 "To Daffodils" to its final line of what the daffodils symbolize for the mother: "*Die early.*" In Herrick's poem, daffodils symbolize the passing of human life in their short flowering period; people are likened to as short a moment as life, and the daffodils, which the daughter in Trethewey's poem gathers to please her mother, represent her mother's death at forty years old. Called "graveside flowers" by Trethewey, they treacherously whisper, predicting a death neither mother nor daughter could foretell.[21]

The physical body becomes an important image in these poems, violence written upon it becoming a text to be read. "What Is Evidence" explicitly documents the evidence of domestic violence, chronicling the damage to the mother's body: bruises covered with makeup, a black eye, a tremble in her voice, false teeth, a broken collarbone, a bullet to the temple. This unrhymed sonnet delineates the marks on the mother's body that are not enough to be entered as evidence, to keep the abuser at bay. Not even the "official document," the divorce decree, can protect her. Her ex-husband is finally convicted, but only after he kills her by shooting her twice, only then does "the landscape of her body" become enough to qualify as evidence. "Photograph: Ice Storm, 1971" enacts a similar instance, juxtaposing the mother's suffering with an early 1970s Atlanta ice storm. Those storms, which bring the city to its knees by rendering it immovable, appear eerily beautiful. Pines sparkle in the sunlight right before their limbs break, taking down power lines; the ground crunches underfoot before the walker sprawls on the ice; children get days off from school but then families run out of food and fuel. The slick and sparkly veneer, all that appears in photographs, betrays the treacherous nature of the storms, just as the photograph documenting the storm fails to reveal "what's inside—mother, stepfather's fist." The poem, which gestures toward the villanelle form with its five tercets of rhyme, lacks the villanelle's concluding quatrain, refusing to close but documenting abuse that will last for more than another decade.[22]

Alongside the poems documenting the violence enacted on her mother's body are poems about a daughter's grief. In an interview with Terry Gross, Trethewey shared her realization as a ten-year-old that her stepfather was abusing her mother, when, through the bedroom wall, she heard him hitting her and her pleas for him to stop.[23] Eric Trethewey, her father, has written about Trethewey's reluctance to talk to him about the abuse she identified, a reluctance he identified as an attempt to protect her mother, and Trethewey has described her early efforts to report the abuse to authorities at her school, authority figures who demurred at taking any action. The federal Violence Against Women Act was first passed in 1994, but in the early 1970s and the 1980s (and beyond), violence in the home was largely not prosecuted. As a child, Trethewey had few resources to turn to. Her mother, a social worker with a master's degree, was working through the legal channels to protect herself and her children, but the legal system failed her. In 1985 her mother was murdered, and her ex-husband was sentenced to multiple life sentences for murder, kidnapping, assault, burglary, and terroristic threats.[24] "What the Body Can Say" mourns in eloquent couplets, beginning with the image of a statue in the semblance of grief, an unmistakable gesture. The statue, on his knees, is also praying, asking God why his loss has been suffered. The speaker compares the statue's body to her mother's, as if her mother asked her for something wordlessly, and to her own kneeling figure, also asking God why. "Graveyard Blues," a bluesy riff on the sonnet in loose iambic pentameter, sings her mother home as she is lain to rest in the graveyard. The tidy tercets of exact rhyme (aaa, bbb, and so on) shift from the rainy churchyard to the speaker stepping forward as witness to the sun emerging as she leaves the graveyard on the road home. The closing heroic couplet describes the speaker in the graveyard, her mother's name one of the dead there, and the cold stones provide no comfort but a "stone pillow" for her head, the word "stone" connecting to the stone statue in "What the Body Can Say" and to the word "pillow," a tie to the volume's second section's reference to the Fort Pillow Massacre in the Civil War.[25]

The final four poems in this section meditate on loss. "Letter," with its focus on writing, mentions the persona's slip between "errand" and "errant," a one-letter difference, a divergent sound, marking how an outing—or a life—can change. Her loss feels the same way, unexpected, sudden, a permanent burden. "After Your Death" chronicles the chores of the living who must clean out closets, empty bowls, divest a space of the markers of a life lived. Like fruit hanging on the trees hollowed by devouring insects, the speaker feels she is "another space emptied by loss," that as she cleans, she becomes as empty as the home. "Myth," a palindrome—one of the many testaments to Trethewey's superb manipulation of poetic forms—addresses how her mother lives in her dreams, the one place where she can find her, in the space between sleeping and waking. "At Dusk" closes this section, gesturing toward nighttime, a closing of grief, the darkness of loss. The speaker can hear a neighbor calling her cat, the call almost a keening as sound becomes more important than meaning. She wonders if a similar call from her own voice might call her mother back, "certain the sounds I make / are enough to call someone home."[26]

This call to return home, to protect the home, to claim the home, resonates throughout the volume, becoming one of the motifs connecting the lament in the first section to the Civil War and to Trethewey's claim to the South as home. The physical body and the damage done to it through domestic violence and war bind the first section to the second, as do ekphrastic poems—poems about the act of writing—"stone pillows" and graves, and the writing of a history previously ignored or unknown. Domestic violence is a battle against women and connects Trethewey's mother's death in 1985 to the second section's focus on the Civil War in the 1860s. The poems in this section—the outermost, largest circle of my concentric set because it focuses on national history, the farthest echo in time and voice from the personal core of the first section—reflect on war and offer the voices of Southern women, both a nineteenth-century white woman and a twenty-first-century Black woman; a four-part poem focused on early twentieth-century Mississippi photographs; the voice of a Native Guard soldier; and an ekphrastic poem based on Winslow Homer's 1865 *The Veteran in a New Field*, marking the official end of the war.

The second section opens with an epigraph from Nina Simone's lyrics that "everybody knows about Mississippi," stopping just short of the "Goddam." This quote, which is immediately followed by the poem titled "Pilgrimage," travels into the national past through the Civil War, but it also indicates the circling of the past into the present because Simone's song was written about Medgar Evers's assassination in 1963, the Civil War violence erupting into the civil rights years when the Confederate battle flag was resurrected as a symbol for segregation. "Pilgrimage" is about the act of remembering the past and who, ultimately, owns history, to borrow Eric Foner's phrasing. To excavate how history is reified, Trethewey puns on her title pilgrimage, which describes the sacred journey she takes into the past in this section as well as the name of the two-week festival held yearly in late March to early April—Vicksburg's Spring Pilgrimage. The poem opens somberly following the Mississippi River as it carves the wide turn that brings it to Vicksburg before it turns away from the town, heading for the coast. Trethewey likens the river's turn away from the town to that of a person who "turns, forgetting, from the past." Just as the Yazoo River now fills a riverbed abandoned by the always moving Mississippi, this town, rife with history, fills its monuments with history validating the Confederacy and ignoring the contributions of African Americans. Trethewey writes that "in my dream, / the ghost of history lies down beside me, // rolls over, pins me beneath a heavy arm." These ghosts, so weighty and established over a century, fill Vicksburg and national accounts of history, and this section begins the work of lifting the "heavy arm" of history.[27]

"Pilgrimage" addresses history as told through parks and monuments, first-person accounts, festivals, museums, and historic buildings, histories Trethewey describes in her essay "On Whitman, Civil War Memory, and My South": "Monuments all around the South serve to inscribe a particular narrative onto the landscape while at the same time subjugating or erasing another."[28] Her poem describes the dead who "stand up in stone, white / marble" in Vicksburg National Military Park, established in 1899 on the site of the siege of Vicksburg.[29] Now a national park, it is dotted with monuments and statues on both Confederate and Union Avenues, roads that mark the original parallel lines occupied by the two sides in the war. The plethora of statues commemorates such figures as Jefferson Davis and John C. Pemberton, as well as states, North and South, which lost soldiers there, and Union soldiers like Ulysses S. Grant. Absent until 2004 were the African American soldiers, an absence that cultivates the false historical narrative that African Americans did not serve in the Civil War and relied on others to secure their freedom. In that year was erected the Mississippi African American Monument crafted from black African granite. This one statue only begins to correct the narrative, and Trethewey also quotes from the newspaper the *Jackson Advocate* that written materials accompanying the statue continued to downplay these soldiers' contribution to the war: "Park Superintendent Bill Nichols and Park historian Terry Winschel begrudgingly labeled the black regiments as 'supply guards' in the text on display rather than giving the men their full measure of respect as the fully recognized infantry, artillery and cavalry units that they were."[30]

From monuments, "Pilgrimage" shifts to the voice of a white Confederate woman enduring the siege of Vicksburg. Trethewey, whose notes tempt readers further into historical forays, offers her source, Mary Webster Loughborough's *My Cave Life in Vicksburg*, a first-person account from a woman who chose to remain in Vicksburg during the siege, from March to July of 1863.[31] With shells falling all around them and their homes unsafe, the residents dug—or compelled others to dig—caves to protect themselves and their households, caves Trethewey describes as catacombs, sanctuaries that sometimes became tombs. Trethewey describes this Confederate as "writing herself / into history," and Loughborough's account was published in 1864, even before the war's end. Thus, an account from the perspective of a white female enslaver could begin to shape the earliest war narratives, a privilege not extended to the African Americans in Loughborough's account, again ensuring that war accounts were created through the eyes of white Americans. The quote offered in the poem, "*what is to become / of all the living things in this place?*" comes from *Mrs. Balfour's Civil War Diary*, in an entry written in May 1863 that describes the rout of the Confederate army and the dejection of the soldiers who were hungry and defeated. Emma Balfour, like Loughborough, remained in Vicksburg during the siege. Her cry is that of the white South as they watched their homes, families, and economy destroyed, and she hopes that "there will be a fearful reckoning somewhere," not realizing their defeat is the reckoning.[32] She too, however, can write her account into history, one stored by the Mississippi Department of Archives and History. Significantly, Balfour's diary was edited and self-published by Gordon A. Cotton, the curator of Vicksburg's Old Court House Museum for thirty years, the museum "Pilgrimage" references as housing physical mementos of the war like period clothing preserved safely behind glass. Cotton, the author of more than a dozen books on local history, was awarded the Meritorious Leadership in Mississippi History, Genealogy, and Historic Preservation Award from the Order of the First Families of Mississippi in 2005—an organization that limited membership to descendants of settlers who arrived in Mississippi between 1699 and 1817 (the year Mississippi became a state).

Thus, one person produced wide-reaching accounts of the war, that of the white Mississippians, a viewpoint applauded by such a carefully circumscribed society.

The final historical narrative addressed in "Pilgrimage" is the "*living history*" supposedly to be found by staying in one of the antebellum mansions in Vicksburg.[33] These homes, many located on the bluffs by the river, have been renovated to erase their years of neglect and damage and advertise themselves as offering a window into the past, an opportunity to experience the glamour of the Old South, an advertising narrative that also contributes to a skewed portrait of nineteenth-century life. These houses, hardly as they were in their original form, pretend to offer a reconstruction of the past—one that excises the labor of enslaved people and presents a past complete with Wi-Fi, electricity, running water, and indoor plumbing.[34] They are selling not history but an experience their visitors choose to believe is reminiscent of the past, a reemergence of the Lost Cause, a story no evidence supports. This pilgrimage could be to Cedar Grove Mansion Inn and Restaurant, one of the most opulent homes, which offered Prissie's Suite as a room choice. Its website presented a glamorous version of its historical past and eliminated the desolation of war and the reality of an economy that relied upon enslaving people. In fact, the information there failed to describe the home of people who lost the war: "We welcome you to elegant and graceful Cedar Grove, a living fairytale echoing a time and a place that has long passed. Come to Cedar Grove, re-live the story, and create a memory that will last your lifetime."[35] Far from being a fairy tale, truths about the Civil War are not to be found in these narratives, but the houses themselves remain powerful in creating white Southern nostalgia for a past that did not exist. These histories, full of misinformation, are the ones Trethewey describes as pinning her down, but the poems that follow in this section begin the process of telling new truths, as does the single, opposed, and even inaccurate statue of African American soldiers in Vicksburg National Military Park.

"Scenes from a Documentary History of Mississippi" consists of four sections, each based on an image. The tone is that of a documentary film, with a narrator reading the script while the image flashes on the screen. This documentary, however, offers a new narrative about the South, a history that foregrounds African American people, as opposed to the many objectionable histories in "Pilgrimage." The first section is titled "1. King Cotton, 1907," and it uses the villanelle form, its circling, repetitive rhymes drawing intricate connections between African American labor, cotton, and the nation. This section neatly ties to "Pilgrimage" by using, as its base, a photograph taken at Vicksburg. On October 21, 1907, Theodore Roosevelt delivered an address there, and the photograph memorializes his visit as he and other European American dignitaries stand beside and walk through an arch made of bales of cotton and decorated with red, white, and blue banners.[36] The sign at the top reads "Cotton. America's King Greets America's President," and African

Americans sit on the bales and stand on the street at the photograph's edges. Trethewey's poem memorializes the president's visit, celebrated with a parade, flags, and this monument to cotton, the crop energizing the South. This image is celebratory and hopeful, marking a South with increasing wealth in its fields and a growing economy. In the third stanza, the poem steps beyond the boundaries of the image, however, with the information that only two years later in 1909 the boll weevil will arrive in the South and begin its devastation of the cotton crop, the "South's countermarch." This "plague" bears much in common with Old Testament wrath, a just punishment for an economy that excluded African Americans from its prosperity. The poem describes the African American children perched on the bales, waving flags for a president who, even in the photo, has his back to them, looking past them rather than embracing their plight. The cotton bales appear to be a barrier, even a wall, refusing progress to the people whose labor they require. The people become subject to the cotton that "surrounds them, a swell, a great mound / bearing them up, back toward us," rising up around them.[37] This economy is exposed as oppressive, even without the hindsight that its profitability will soon disappear, and the national government the president represents looks beyond the laborers hurt by the cotton economy itself.

The second section, "2. Glyph, Aberdeen 1913," is based on a photograph taken and dated by a photographer in Aberdeen, Mississippi.[38] Trethewey came across the image in her archival research, but I have been unable to locate it and suspect it resides only in the archives. This detailed ekphrastic poem replicates the image: a child's body, distorted by the heavy labor he already has to do. He is held by a man who is also gaunt—with the starvation agricultural wages of the sharecropping life—and the child's spine has been misshaped by picking cotton, giving him a humped back, the required daily labor shaping his physical body. This poem, also about cotton, does not celebrate the economic prosperity it creates, which would be disappearing by 1913 as the plague encroached; rather, here the effects of cotton on laborers' bodies are memorialized. The child's pain is the affliction of the South's poor and how the cost is foisted onto the most vulnerable: "*Look, this is the outline of suffering*: / the child shouldering it—a mound / like dirt heaped on a grave."[39] Thus, into the celebration of King Cotton is inserted an image of the physical pain caused by that very crop.

Another Southern tragedy follows in "3. Flood" about the Great Mississippi Flood of 1927, the most destructive in US history. Months of rain put the Mississippi at historic highs, submerging more than twenty thousand square miles and displacing hundreds of thousands of people. Up and down the river, the levee system began to fail, and in April Mississippi's levees began to collapse. African American laborers were particularly devastated by the disaster, and in the photograph described by the poem, they are on a barge, waiting to disembark to safety.[40] The photograph—archived in Vicksburg's Old Court House Museum, another tie to Vicksburg—pictures hundreds of people looking at the point from which the photo was taken, but what they are looking at cannot be seen. Trethewey's poem reaches beyond these boundaries of the photo to consider what has their attention—ostensibly safety and dry land—yet no one is moving. The photograph's point of view is from above, and "3. Flood" imagines that the "National Guard hunkers / on the levee; rifles tight in their fists, / they block the path to high ground."[41] Thus, instead of inserting African Americans into history, this poem clarifies the actions of European Americans in history. The National Guard, clearly present in other photographs of the flood, are not in this view, but the camera's gaze takes their place. According to the photograph's caption, the soldiers capriciously grasped this opportunity to require the refugees to perform by singing spirituals before they would be allowed to disembark, a gross misuse of their power. On the last leg of their harrowing journey fleeing the flood, the Black refugees somberly stare into the camera, caught between the river and rifles. Still, the caption also informs readers that "they refused," a powerful statement of autonomy in the face of constant national oppression. This poem captures, then, a more accurate vision of national racism and Black resistance than the many histories "Pilgrimage" addresses.

This documentary sequences close with "4. You Are Late," the final ekphrastic poem about a photograph of a child going to the library, a seeming shift from the previous three poems concerned with tragic events.[42] However, this poem continues to tell the history of Southern segregation, which permeated all aspects of life. The child has a book in her hand, ostensibly to return for another, but this library is closed, symbolically its "door / just out of reach." It bears two signs, the first faded one reading "Greenwood Public Library for Negroes," marking the segregated nature of everyday life and access to resources and literacy. The second sign reads "You Are Late," indicating that the library offers only restricted hours and probably a much less extensive collection than the library for white patrons in Greenwood, Mississippi. As Trethewey writes her into history, the girl has to enact her moment. The persona longs to reach out to her, to "say *wait*. / But this is history: she can't linger."[43] From Frederick Douglass's to Malcolm X's famous statements about the significance of literacy, the ability to read and write has been recognized as paramount in the effort for self-determination, just as the Confederate woman in "Pilgrimage" is able to write herself into history and thus control historical narratives. Denying library access to African Americans—legal after the 1896 *Plessy v. Ferguson* decision and continuing into the 1960s—is one more example of oppression. This final portrait revises the historical narrative to emphasize the everyday hardships as well as the national tragedies.

This documentary history is followed by the poem "Native Guard," a crown of unrhymed sonnets voiced by the persona of a soldier in the Native Guard beginning in November 1862, the fall during which the Native Guard was reorganized as Union soldiers. (The Native Guard, consisting primarily of Free Blacks of means, was first organized to fight for the Confederacy during spring 1861, and it was disbanded when New Orleans fell in spring 1862.) The ten sonnets travel through the three years of the Native Guard's Union existence to 1865, their lines linking as the first line of each restates the last line of the former. In an interview with Joan Wylie Hall, Trethewey underscored how few people know that almost two hundred thousand soldiers in the Civil War were African American, and she explained how she first became intrigued by the Native Guard and their assignment on Ship Island:

> I'd been going out to Ship Island—where the Louisiana Native Guards were stationed off the coast of my hometown—for years with my grandmother. It wasn't mentioned in the park ranger's tour that these black soldiers had been stationed there, that they were Union soldiers, guarding Confederate prisoners. I found out quite accidentally. I was talking to my grandmother in a restaurant, and a woman overheard our conversation. She said, "I think there's something else you need to know about Ship Island." I assumed she was a schoolteacher or a librarian, but she was more like a guardian angel because she told me this thing that sent me to the Gulfport public library. That's where I started.[44]

Trethewey did not know about the African American soldiers stationed on Ship Island because they had been left out of the public history, as she explained to Charles H. Rowell:

> When you go out there, one of the first things you notice upon entering the fort is that the Daughters of the Confederacy have placed a plaque at the fort's entry listing all the names of the Confederate soldiers who were imprisoned there, but there is no mention of the black soldiers who were stationed there. Throughout the [National Park Service's] tour you get to see the cannons and learn something about the lives of the men who were stationed on the island. But nowhere is there any kind of marker for the Native Guards. If you don't know to ask the ranger about the particular history of the island's black inhabitants, he doesn't mention it during the tour.[45]

In the face of this willed national forgetting, Trethewey marks the existence of the Native Guard, effectively creating a monument through her poetry, and her monument focuses on the importance of remembering this history of veterans whose names were not included on the plaque, in the Park Service's tours, or in the history books. The opening epigraph from Frederick Douglass sets the tone for a poem about the importance of remembering history, and the first line of the poem is "truth be told, I do not want to forget /

anything of my former life."[46] Thus begins an exquisite poetic series about remembering, about telling history, and about national memories in which the poem's persona shares his personal history, the significance of placing this history in writing, and the larger history of the Native Guard.

The persona identifies himself as a thirty-three-year-old—the age Trethewey later in the volume calls the Jesus year, an important turning point in life—formerly enslaved person born in New Orleans who was owned by Francis E. Dumas. Dumas's father was a white Creole, and his mother was biracial. He was educated in Paris and returned to New Orleans as a wealthy business and property owner. When Dumas's father passed away, he inherited the family's enslaved people, whom Louisiana law prevented him from manumitting. Denied that option, in Trethewey's poem, he taught her speaker to read and write and treated him as a servant rather than an enslaved person—and he rejected opportunities to sell the people his family had enslaved in order to protect them from worse treatment. After New Orleans fell to Union forces, he encouraged these newly freed people to join the Native Guard as he did.[47] Trethewey's persona took Dumas's advice and served until the war's end. The poems are ostensibly his journal entries, but their tone is more epistolary—informative and explanatory—rather than inwardly contemplative. They offer an account of the Native Guard, as well as a rumination on the power of writing in the creation of national monuments.

"Native Guard," like most of this volume, is a lament for the lost, lost soldiers and lost opportunities even in the moment of freedom from enslavement and the eventual Union victory. Recognizing its need for African American soldiers, the Union army recruited them, if reluctantly. The Black soldiers were treated poorly, paid less than white soldiers, provided with less food, and sometimes denied arms. Despite their numbers and preparation for battle, the persona testifies that they were "called supply units—/ not infantry—and so we dig trenches, / haul burdens for the army no less heavy / than before." The speaker is stationed at Fort Massachusetts on Ship Island and taken there, in a fortuitous historical echo, by a ship named the *Northern Star*.[48] As the Emancipation Proclamation took effect on January 1, 1863, white enslavers worried about a Black revolt and asked that the Native Guard be removed. Bowing to their concerns, on January 12, 1863, General Nathaniel P. Banks sent some of the Native Guard to Ship Island, a Gulf barrier island ten miles from the mainland, significant because "it was a strategic location for support of the Union's blockade of southern Gulf ports and was the only one of several islands framing Mississippi Sound that could sustain a large encampment of men and provide anchorage for a fleet of ships in its natural harbor."[49] The immediate duty of the Native Guard, now isolated on this desolate island, was to guard the Confederate captives held there,[50] "jailors to those who still / would have us slaves."[51]

On Ship Island, the persona lived in the sweltering Mississippi heat, walking through the sand daily. He watched the epic effects of the ocean throwing their great ships around at will, and he and his comrades learned the sea will take anything not tied down. His reflections are shared through his journal entries, written in a journal he took from an abandoned Confederate home; to record his own words, he writes across the white Southerner's entries, crosshatching each page. His accounts mingle with the language that is already there, mirroring the intricately connected lives of white and Black people in the United States, no matter the efforts at segregation: "on every page, / his story intersecting with my own." Thus, these ten sonnets, offered as journal entries, are written for posterity, for Americans who come afterward who seek the truth in history. The crosshatching in the journal ties to the scars on the back of one of the formerly enslaved people in "January 1863." This Native Guardsman takes off his shirt while they work, exposing a back that has been severely whipped, "the scars, crosshatched / like the lines in this journal, on his back."[52] The legacy of the institution of slavery and the Civil War is thus written in the persona's journal and on the bodies of survivors.

This emphasis on writing and the linking of lives pervades the sonnet sequence, tying into "February 1863," in which the Native Guard are guarding Confederate soldiers. The poem's persona writes letters home for the illiterate Confederates who both fear and need him. They worry he will write lies or distort their words, just as the history of the Native Guards has been distorted. The illiterate white men's only choice is to make their mark on the letters they have dictated to him, even while they remain unsure about what he has written down. The speaker explains that he tries to write what they want, even if they are unwilling to verbalize their thoughts: their worry of "what has become of their small plots of land" is implied when they ask, "*did you harvest enough food to put by?*,"[53] his interpretation like the many interpretations that must be made in writing history. In her notes for this volume, Trethewey wrote that "letters are important as the recording of history—in whose hands is the responsibility, the power / here a freed slave is recording history. We wouldn't know that later simply from a collection of letters. We would assume the white person was literate and wrote them himself."[54] By making her speaker the author of the letters, she upends the more usual situation of white people transcribing the words of freedpeople, and the freedperson becomes the author of history, a history missing much. These sonnets, their very form commenting on the significance of language, reflexively write this history into contemporary public history, as they comment on the significance of writing itself and the crosshatching of lives and history, the intertwining of Black and white in the United States as "truth be told."[55]

Besides emphasizing the role of African American soldiers, this poem chronicles not only the hardships of war all soldiers experience like the stench of rotting bodies, the constant hunger, and the pervasive fear of death, but it also records the particular atrocities inflicted upon the Native Guard at Pascagoula, Port Hudson, and Fort Pillow. In "April 1863" the persona writes,

> . . . Today we buried
> the last of our dead from Pascagoula,
> and those who died retreating to our ship—
> white sailors in blue firing upon us
> as if we were the enemy . . .[56]

In a skirmish in Pascagoula, Mississippi, the Native Guard had fought well—"bravely, intelligently, with several officers worthy of commendation and all deserving of praise, which [Colonel Nathan Daniels] showered on them afterward. Dumas, especially, won acclaim from the colonel for his courageous role in the fighting." When ordered to fall back to their ship, the *General Banks*, the Native Guardsmen retreated, expecting cover from white Union soldiers aboard the *Jackson*. However, the *Jackson* soldiers fired at their Black comrades rather than at the Confederate soldiers, killing four and wounding five.[57] Colonel Daniels's official report called this traitorous friendly fire merely an "unfortunate situation," phrasing ironically echoed by Trethewey, who pairs it with a line of his praise about the same battle: "The Colonel said: / *an unfortunate incident*; said: / *their names shall deck the page of history*."[58] In an address to his troops, Daniels emphasized their heroism and the martyrdom of those who died: "They have offered themselves nobly upon the shrine of their countries [*sic*] existence, and their deeds are their glory—their glory their reward.—Their names shall deck the page of history, and their process emblazon the escutcheon of our coming Republic."[59] Daniels's contradictory impulses of effectively forgiving white soldiers for killing their fellow Black soldiers and yet praising the heroism and sacrifice of the Black soldiers encapsulate much of the treatment the Native Guard received. They were necessary to the Union's victory and often commended for their bravery, but white Americans wrote them out of the historical narratives, refusing them participation in the national narratives and monuments.

"June 1863" underscores that some names will not be written into history, like the many Native Guardsmen abandoned or reported as deserters after the battle at Port Hudson, for which the exact count of Black casualties is not known, but "a loss of 50 percent would not be unusual."[60] The Native Guard fought valiantly in this major assault, and General Nathaniel P. Banks wrote his wife that "I had three regiments of Negroes—two in the fight and one at work as Engineers—They fought splendidly! SPLENDIDLY! Everybody is delighted that they did so well! Their charges upon the rebel works of which they made three, exhibited the greatest bravery."[61] Nonetheless, during a truce in which each side gathered its dead and wounded, the Native Guard soldiers were not collected, while the white soldiers were. When the Confederate Colonel W. B. Shelby asked if his soldiers could bury the dead Native Guard, since his own men were being overcome by the stench of their decomposing bodies, Banks reportedly refused, saying, as Trethewey echoes, "*I have / no dead there.*"[62] Their bodies haunt the poem's persona, the betrayed dead staring at him even while newly freed people arrive daily, ready to fight for the Union.

Just as Trethewey has argued that poets have a responsibility to tend the graves of history, her persona tends the graves on Ship Island. His duties include documenting the names of the dead and notifying relatives of their loss. He forcefully maintains that this accounting is not his alone but a national duty. The final sonnet offers a list of what must be accounted for, such as the Fort Pillow massacre. On April 12, 1864, fifteen hundred Confederate soldiers attacked Fort Pillow on the Mississippi River in Henning, Tennessee. The fort was manned by about six hundred Union troops; half were Black from the Sixth US Colored Heavy Artillery and the Second US Colored Light Artillery, and half were white from Major William E. Bradford's Tennessee Cavalry Battalion. When the Confederates gained control of the fort, they killed many of the soldiers there who were trying to surrender, including several hundred Black soldiers: "The survivors called it a massacre of men who tried to surrender; the Confederates claimed that the Federals refused to stop fighting or fleeing. Since 1973 most historians who have written about the incident have judged it a massacre."[63] In her notes, Trethewey quotes from an article in the *Mobile Advertiser and Register*, whose author wrote "an indiscriminate slaughter followed [the battle]. . . . The fort ran with blood; many jumped into the river and drowned or [were] shot." She also includes testimony from Confederate sergeant Achilles V. Clark who wrote:

> the slaughter was awful. Words cannot describe the scene. The poor deluded negroes would run up to our men fall on their knees and with uplifted hands scream for mercy but they were ordered to their feet and then shot down. The whitte [sic] men fared but little better. Their fort turned out to be a great slaughter pen. Blood, human blood stood about in pools and brains could have been gathered up in any quantity. I with several others tried to stop the butchery and at one time had partially succeeded. but [sic] Gen. Forrest ordered them shot down like dogs.[64]

His reference is to Confederate major general Nathan Bedford Forrest, who after the war became a member of the Ku Klux Klan.

In this final sonnet, the past reaches into the present with the demand that "truth be told," linking the sonnet's final line to the series' opening lines, in a constant circling motion marking the effects of the institution of slavery and the Civil War on the present United States. Its fourteen lines enumerate items that must be answered for, including the Native Guard's new 1863 moniker Corps d'Afrique, which aligns them with their African heritage rather than their origins in the United States, at which time General Banks also eliminated the Black officers;[65] the exile within the United States of "mossbacks" and freed people; all the people killed and injured during the war; the unidentified dead whose family can never be notified; the letters from soldiers that never reached their loved ones; and the dead in their graves under the ground that today's Americans walk on. The truth that Trethewey longs for is there, waiting to be unearthed, the historical truths in this monument she has created.[66]

This second section ends much as it began, noting the absence of African Americans in the many types of histories told. Following an epigraph quoting an Ohio soldier who laments the loss of so many dead in the Battle of Antietam on September 17, 1862, known as the bloodiest day in US history, with the casualties topping twenty-two thousand, their bodies arranged "like sheaves of Wheat,"[67] the ekphrastic poem "Again, the Fields" is based on Winslow Homer's *The Veteran in a New Field* from 1865, closing not only this section but also the war. Trethewey's poem captures the exhaustion of the war and its devastation in terms of blood. So much destruction then gives way to a renewal of the country, as created by Homer's painting and inscribed into Trethewey's poem. She notes the identifying Union jacket and canteen the farmer has shed onto the ground as he moves on to the task of working the land once again. The veteran is harvesting wheat, the just reward for all he fought for, the agricultural wealth of the countryside belonging to the people once again. Because it is not wheat he could have planted in the spring when the war was still ongoing; the wheat is not the reward for his own labor but instead a benediction, a blessing to the Union for a just war and deserved reward. The painting is not, then, about agricultural labor but about the Union's victory, a victory symbolically told in the terms of the land's bounty. Trethewey captures the blessed nature of wheat whose mature appearance is almost miraculous: "The wheat falls beneath his scythe—/ a language of bounty—the swaths // like scripture on the field's open page." Homer's painting imagines a harmonious future for the nation in which the South and North unify peacefully, and together they create a peaceful and successful nation. Trethewey, however, uses this picture—another way to tell history—to again point out what is missing. Her last five lines imagine the field stretching beyond the confines of the frame, and the crop being harvested shifts from wheat to cotton, the South's primary crop. This cotton is being worked by a veteran with "hands the color of dark soil," an image of an African American veteran Homer does not paint.[68] History is told through so many mediums—monuments, books, festivals, museums, buildings, photographs, archival documents, and now paintings. Through each, Trethewey inserts the voices and stories of African Americans, their history integral to a truthful rendition of the Civil War.

Native Guard's second section neatly transitions to the third—the volume's spectacular culmination—segueing smoothly from a poem based on a painting to a dream poem featuring a photograph. The transition is made by way of a Whitman quote acknowledging the endearing and the violent sides of the South, a love for the region Trethewey elsewhere describes as "complex" and "not without its stunning beauty or its stunning cruelty." Whitman's ambivalence becomes Trethewey's own ambivalence toward the South, a region she claims and confronts, loves and hates.[69] I position this section as the middle circle in my concentric circles model because it links the first section about Trethewey's mother's murder and its sense of personal loss to the second section about the Civil War and the losses incurred there. This final, powerful section synthesizes the volume's very personal core with the large national concerns, shifting to a middle ground in which Trethewey speaks to the South as a region and to her own firm claims to Southern identity and to being a Southern writer—something denied to earlier generations of African American writers.

Despite the numbers of African American writers in the South, Southern literature for too long remained a space that focused on the white Southern experience, Trethewey has pointed out. About her experience at conferences on Southern literature, she writes,

> I began to notice, after several of these panels, that someone in the audience almost always raised a question about the psyches of southern writers—*why we write the way that we do*. It seemed to me that just as often, someone on the panel would answer that question by saying something like, "We southerners write the way that we do because, after all, we lost the war." Each time I've heard this I've had to say, "My South didn't *lose* the war." On each of these occasions, the other panelists—most likely unintentionally—had responded to the question in a manner that seemed to suggest they had forgotten I was there, and that seemed to define the southern psyche and the southern experience as if they were monolithic.[70]

Instead of accepting a monolithic Southern experience as a European American Confederate experience, Trethewey asserts in an interview with Daniel Cross Turner that

> I am the quintessential Southern writer! Quintessentially American too! Geography is fate. Of all the kinds of fate swirling around my very being, this place in which I was born and this particular historical moment matter deeply. The story of America has always been a story of miscegenation, of border crossings, of integration of culture, and again, I embody this in my person. To me, I fit in as the quintessential Southerner. Perhaps even now my role is to establish what has always been Southern, though at other points in history it has been excluded from "Southernness."[71]

In her persona, then, she locates the type of crossings she writes into "Native Guard" with the crosshatched journal, the scars on a former enslaved person's back, the interlacing of Black and white lives. This final section picks up that thread, among others, and insists on Trethewey's inclusion in the canon of Southern literature. She further clarifies in an interview with David Haney that

> I have to write my way in, and it's also about asserting myself as part of one of the many traditions of poetry to which I belong. Southern poetry is indeed one of them. I have a poem called "Southern Pastoral" that I've worked on that's a dream poem. It's pretty tongue-in-cheek, but in it I'm dreaming that I'm taking a picture with the Fugitive poets and I'm right in the middle of the photograph, which would not have been the case, of course. There's the Fugitive sidestepping of race, as if we can just forget or ignore it, and it's not there. They've created a hole that I feel it is sort of my goal, my duty even, to fill.[72]

"Pastoral," the final title of the poem Trethewey refers to here as "Southern Pastoral" thus begins the grappling with the Southern canon and, to circle back to Foner's phrasing, who owns it.

In her exquisite unrhymed sonnet "Pastoral," Trethewey dreams she is being photographed with the Fugitive Poets in front of the contemporary Atlanta skyline, which has been disguised by the photographer's backdrop as a bucolic pasture filled with lowing cows. The poem is full of opposites—Trethewey paired with the Fugitives, the modern cityscape with the inauthentic nostalgic backdrop, the cows' lowing "that sounds like *no, no*" with the speaker's response of yes to the glass of bourbon offered to her, the classic Southern whiskey.[73] Robert Penn Warren is lining up the group for the photograph, even though his voice can barely be heard above the bulldozers of industrialization intent on permanently transforming the agrarian South he and the Fugitive Poets, later to become the Southern Agrarians, so valued. Trethewey imagines herself in blackface surrounded by the men who would become the New Critics, men who at least early in their careers embraced segregation in their nostalgic quest for a romanticized past, and men, like John Crow Ransom and Cleanth Brooks, whose manifestos on reading literature excised from cultural and historical contexts definitively shaped twentieth-century literary study. These critics are themselves often read outside of their context of the conservative views expressed in the 1930 collection *I'll Take My Stand*, which borrows a line from the song "Dixie" for its title. If, as Trethewey claimed, the Fugitives "sidestepped" race and she is filling the space they ignored, then she has placed herself in the midst of the men who controlled the Southern canon for much of the twentieth century, and she makes visible what they had hidden: the South modernizing in its very landscape and in the inclusion of writers beyond themselves.

Trethewey's poem captures the ambivalence of the Southern African American writer, as well as the impact white Southerners have had on a national literary tradition that until the late twentieth century was reluctant to include African American writers. The final line of Trethewey's sonnet is "*You don't hate the south? . . . You don't hate it?*," a riff on Quentin Compson's oft-quoted "I don't hate it" in response to the novel's final question "Why do you hate the South?" in Faulkner's *Absalom, Absalom!*[74] This ambiguity rings through Southern literature. The only member of the Fugitive Poets named is Warren, whose stance on racial policies moderated during his lifetime. In his 1930 essay "The Briar Patch," Warren supported segregation, aligning himself with Booker T. Washington's infamous speech now known as the Atlanta Compromise. Warren retreated from his early stance, which he himself characterized as "a cogent and humane defense of segregation" that would, by the 1960s, make him feel "uncomfortable," as he maintained in his 1965 volume *Who Speaks for the Negro*, which includes his conversations with figures from Martin Luther King Jr. and Ralph Ellison to Stokely Carmichael and Malcolm X.[75] Still, according to Paul V. Murphy in *The Rebuke of History: The Southern Agrarians and American Conservative Thought*, Warren "remained a gradualist, as wary of integration as he had ever been."[76] In Trethewey's poem, Warren directs the group in where they should stand; he organizes their presence for the photographer who encourages the group to say "race" as the photo is snapped.[77] Thus, "race" always negotiates the power dialectic between these writers, especially for a critical generation espousing elitism. The New Critics had a profound impact on literary studies. They excluded most nonwhite writers from the canon, and the New Critical legacy lived well beyond the 1960s, even through such seemingly mundane scholarly tools as the conservative early editions of Holman's *Handbook*, whose pervasive reach shaped generations of students and scholars.

However, in interviews and public talks, Trethewey speaks highly of Warren's own ambiguity and the way his personal beliefs evolved over his lifetime. *Audubon* is one of her favorite poems, and she borrows two lines from it for the opening epigrams in her volume *Thrall*.[78] Warren's words "What is love? One name for it is knowledge" are coupled with T. S. Eliot's "After such knowledge, what forgiveness?"—the word "knowledge" separating love from forgiveness in a volume of poems that investigates past deeds in the realm of racial domination and enslavement. Warren's lines come from section 6, "Love and Knowledge," in his volume about John James Audubon, the ornithologist who is remembered for his documentation of the many birds inhabiting the United States and the detailed illustrations he made of them. Audubon, whose family's fortunes were founded on enslaving people, created the illustrations he left to posterity by first killing the birds and then stuffing and painting them. Warren writes,

He slew them, at surprising distances, with his gun.
Over a body held in his hand, his head was bowed low,
But not in grief.

He put them where they are, and there we see them:
In our imagination.

What is love?

One name for it is knowledge.[79]

The conundrum becomes how can love lead to the destruction of the beloved, and is it possible for love to be so intimately tied to such destructive knowledge. This paradox may speak to the complexities in Warren's statements on race. In a 2013 interview, Trethewey said about Warren that "to see him as a man in the midst of change, someone whose position in *Segregation* was very different from his position in the '30s in *I'll Take My Stand*—I admire that about his work."[80] His 1956 *Segregation*, published in the wake of the *Brown v. Board of Education* ruling, documents the many Southern views on ending segregation, both Black and white, educated and uneducated, pro and con, militant and not. He concludes the volume with an "interview" with himself, in which he flatly states that he is for desegregation but insists that it will come gradually. He says that it will come "when enough people, in a particular place, a particular county or state, cannot live with themselves any more," and this revelation will happen "when they realize that desegregation is just one small episode in the long effort for justice."[81] Moreover, Trethewey's final lecture as poet laureate of the United States focused on Warren, and she again underscored the progress in his beliefs on race during his lifetime.[82] She claims, "Warren makes the choice to be consciously historical, and whether or not his early work bears witness to racist or unreconstructed ideas, and whether or not he reached a point of complete transformation matters less than the journey he undertakes and sets down on paper for us to see."[83]

This third section challenges not only the Southern literary canon but also the way history was taught and recorded in "Southern History." The textbook and the class itself become monuments to the Confederate South, in a class Trethewey would have taken in the 1980s. The textbook, from which the teacher reads, advanced the case of the romanticized South in which the enslaved people were content and cared for by enslavers better than they could care for themselves. The 1940 film *Gone with the Wind* was presented as a historical account of the past, and, Trethewey writes, "I watched the words blur on the page. No one / raised a hand, disagreed. Not even me."[84] Instead, her teacher condoned the lies in Southern history, the inaccuracies, the caricatures of enslaved people. Through this poem, Trethewey now challenges that account, insisting in her volume that truth be told, that the record be set straight, and she reverses her teenage complicity by putting it on paper, telling the story in couplets that make clear the lies, concluding in a heroic couplet that reverses her early silence in the most classic of forms.

"Incident" also addresses national history by focusing on another event in Trethewey's life that speaks to the South. In "Incident," an unrhymed pantoum whose title recalls Countee Cullen's poem chronicling a racist incident during his childhood visit to Baltimore, Trethewey recounts the story of the Klan burning a cross near her family's yard. Too young to remember this moment herself, the cross burning is a family memory, one that belongs to her because her family has told it so often. The warning could have been meant for her interracial family—white father, Black mother, and biracial daughter—or for the Black church nearby where a voter registration drive was being held.[85] Klansmen, "white as angels in their gowns," placed a cross "trussed like a Christmas tree" in the yard, silently lighting it and silently leaving it to burn all night, a powerful gesture of disapproval, perhaps even more powerful in its fleeting symbolism: by morning the fire had burned itself out; the charred grass would sprout again—a peculiarly Southern understatement lightly concealing an explicit threat, coding well understood by the family inside. As Trethewey writes, "When they were done, the men left quietly. No one came. / Nothing really happened. / By morning all the flames had dimmed."[86] The pantoum form with its reliance on the repetition of whole lines offers a form of containment for this horrific event. It binds the cross burning within the lines, boxing it into a controllable space, a space that can become a family memory without having to endure constant scarring. The story can be told, but it cannot escape the confines of the space the poem allows it. Cross burning became a mode of terrorism for the Klan in its second incarnation in the early twentieth century. On October 16, 1915, the Knights of Mary Phagan burned a cross on Stone Mountain, a towering granite dome near Atlanta that would be clearly visible for miles. This act was inspired by a scene from Thomas Dixon's racist novel *The Clansman*, which, in turn, inspired the infamous *Birth of a Nation*, a film that premiered on January 8 of that year and had already been screened in the White House. Beginning in 1951, states began legislating bans on cross burning, and much later in 2003 the Supreme Court ruled that states may outlaw cross burning if the intent is to intimidate. Still, in 1960, one thousand simultaneous cross burnings were held to protest school desegregation, and throughout the 1960s hundreds of crosses were burned in Mississippi every year, according to Mark Potok of the Southern Poverty Law Center.[87] The Klan, which resurged following *Brown v. Board of Education* and was revived in Mississippi in 1963, was particularly opposed to interracial marriage because of its lip service to white race purity and the chastity of white women. Intimidation is the stock and trade of these terrorists, and a cross burning, which was often followed by more violence—"arson, bombing, flogging, a midnight drive-by shooting"—was a clear threat.[88]

"Elegy for the Native Guards" also connects to national history, one more thread that connects the volume's three sections. This poem, the next to last, revisits much of the ground Trethewey covers when she explains her interest in the Native Guard. Here the speaker travels from Gulfport to Ship Island, tours the historical site, notices the plaque placed by the Daughters of the Confederacy, questions why the Native Guards are not similarly honored, and laments the losses now left to the fish and the waves. It is this trip that inspired Trethewey's interest, so it seems odd that the poem is placed so close to the volume's end. Rather than being misplaced, however, this placement allows this elegiac poem to neatly tie into the second section through the Native Guard, the first section through its focus on loss and graves, and even the volume's opening poem "Theories of Time and Space," which suggests readers travel themselves to Ship Island. The entire volume opens with the lines "you can get there from here, though / there's no going home,"[89] which reinforce that Trethewey's trip home has taken her not only there but also to unexpected places, simultaneously pulling the entire book closer to her as an individual and pushing it further away from her so that it can speak to the entirety of the nation. This trip to Ship Island offers an excursion into the past and a correction to the way that past has been written, threads that weave together the volume's concentric circles and the moments when each section escapes its confines, bleeding into the others, inserting its concerns, circling and circling.

In addition to speaking to the Southern canon and history, poems in this third section bear the weight of inserting Trethewey as a person into Southern history. "Miscegenation" presents her parents who were not allowed to marry by the state of Mississippi, Trethewey's "native" state. Mississippi passed an anti-miscegenation law against whites marrying Blacks or Hispanics in 1822, a law that was repealed during Reconstruction and then later reinstated. Like all of the sixteen remaining anti-miscegenation state laws, Mississippi's law was overturned by the *Loving v. Virginia Supreme Court* decision on June 12, 1967, but Trethewey's parents were married in 1965 in Ohio. (It is worth noting that while these laws were unenforceable, Mississippi did not officially repeal its ban on interracial marriage until 1987 or its poll tax until 1989, and it symbolically ratified the Thirteenth Amendment abolishing slavery only in 1995.) Born on April 26, 1966, Trethewey was thus legally deemed illegitimate, and on her birth certificate her mother's race is listed as "colored" and her father's as "Canadian." This classification continues to vex Trethewey, who writes, "I return / to Mississippi, state that made a crime / of me—mulatto, half-breed."[90] Evie Shockley writes that, in this poem and elsewhere, "Trethewey calls the nation to task for the politics—historical and present; raced, gendered, and classed—that ripped her parents apart and haunt her even into one of poetry's most honored offices," that of national poet laureate.[91]

Trethewey's parents shared her penchant for activism—her mother, Gwendolyn Ann Turnbough, rode with the Freedom Riders, challenging segregated interstate bus travel, and they were well aware that their marriage was both a brave and risky endeavor. Eric Trethewey, a poet himself, shared details about his early choices, and as he tells it, Natasha's parents were students at the historically Black institution Kentucky State College (now University) when her mother became pregnant. According to Kentucky State's rules, they had to get married or be expelled from college, their personal life dictated by both college rules and state law. They were prohibited from marrying in Kentucky, as in Mississippi, and so traveled to Ohio. Afterward, Natasha's mother went to Mississippi to have Natasha near her family and her home, and her father returned to Kentucky State to finish his degree that fall and join his family before his daughter's birth. Subsequently, he signed on with the navy, earning enough money for Gwendolyn to return to Kentucky State to finish her degree. Their brave marriage, barraged by so many legal and social challenges, ended in the early 1970s when Natasha was six.[92]

The very word "miscegenation" was fabricated in 1863 from the Latin *miscere* (to mix) and *genus* (race) by David Goodman Croly, managing editor of the New York anti-abolitionist newspaper *World*, and George Wakeman, a reporter on his staff. They penned a seventy-two-page pamphlet entitled *Miscegenation: The Theory of the Blending of the Races, Applied to the American White Man and Negro*, a writing meant to support the Democrats in the 1864 presidential election. The pamphlet is a nasty sort of satire ostensibly advocating racial intermarriage while clearly making a case against any such thing.[93] The term they created posited interracial marriage as "unnatural" and antithetical to the nation. The discourse spawned by anti-miscegenation laws labeled identifiably biracial or multiracial children with epithets inscribed into Trethewey's poem "Southern Gothic," such as "*peckerwood* and *nigger lover*, *half-breed* and *zebra*," "words," she writes, "that take shape outside us."[94] A persona representing her pregnant mother contemplates the "names for what grows inside her. / It is enough to worry about words like *mongrel* and the infertility of mules and *mulattoes*" in "My Mother Dreams Another Country."[95] The anti-miscegenation laws attempted to exclude adults from the social systems supporting marriage and children, as well as from their biological family and the national family. In these poems, Trethewey writes herself back into the South's history, setting on paper a history of cross-hatched identities, the interweaving of lives.

"South," the final poem, pulls together regional and personal history, and it weaves together threads initiated in the first and second sections as well, joining the personal and public history. In "South," Trethewey returns to Mississippi, "a dialectic of dark / and light" where the iconic magnolia blossoms, with their beauty and deep fragrance also symbolize Confederate white flags of surrender. She returns to a land whose topography has been changed by development, a land of cotton that killed the people who worked it; and at that moment her voice shifts from "I" to the collective "us," the cotton both clothing and killing. She returns to a land reluctant to erect markers for African American troops but busily memorializing the nostalgically rendered

Confederate South with its battle flag, roads, buildings, and monuments. She returns to a land that deemed her illegitimate, that made her parents' marriage a crime. And yet, despite miscegenation laws, Klan activity, literary prejudice, and intense discrimination from both the South and the North, Trethewey concludes her volume by stressing that she, like the Native Guard, is "native / in my native land, this place they'll bury me."[96] She returns to claim this label of native and to write her mother's murder and the Native Guard into known history.[97] In her papers at Emory, on the back of a piece of paper, Trethewey wrote the question "Who will guard the known past?," a question she answers in this volume as she becomes that guard.[98]

Chapter 4

✦

Achieving the Extraordinary

A. Van Jordan's *M-A-C-N-O-L-I-A*

In 2001, Trethewey was emceeing the 2001 Cave Canem celebration for former fellows who had published first books that year, and it was there that she first met A. Van Jordan, who was being fêted for his book *Rise*.[1] Along with such other luminaries such as Terrance Hayes, Major Jackson, Honorée Fanonne Jeffers, and Yona Harvey, Jordan was a member of the founding Cave Canem class in 1996. Two years earlier in 1994, Jordan was working as a journalist in Washington, DC, a place where a poetry reading could be found most evenings. As he began to consider the possibilities of poetry over journalism (he would complete his MFA at Warren Wilson College in 1998), he met poet E. Ethelbert Miller, whom Jordan describes as the "most patient person ever" and who spent hours marking Jordan's poems. At roughly the same time, he discovered Cornelius Eady's 1986 *Victims of the Latest Dance Craze* and "Gratitude," a poem first published in Eady's 1991 *The Gathering of My Name*. Eady's work validated in poetic form the quest of Black American poets to be poets when the educational system and established poetic world refused them. Eady resists those who oppose him, like the publishers who believe his poetry will not be profitable, the teacher who assures him he will fail, "the bullies who need / the musty air of / the clubhouse / All to themselves." Instead, "I am a brick in a house," he writes, "that is being built / around your house," a construction that combines Ezra Pound's exhortation to "make it new" with James Brown's to "make it funky."[2] By following Eady's career and his founding, with Toi Derricotte, of Cave Canem, Jordan became part of that original 1996 group of fellows. To Jordan, Cave Canem was transformative. It presented a warm, inviting place to hone his skills, a place where African American poets could cultivate their writing without bearing the burden of constantly explaining and justifying their subject matter to the uninformed. This inclusive institution, which Nikky Finney has called "the major watering hole and air pocket for black poetry,"[3] draws poets from all over the country and from educational backgrounds beyond the Ivy League, and it is from this birthplace that Jordan stepped into the poetry world. In addition to meeting Trethewey during the celebration of his first book at the Cave Canem event, Jordan met Elizabeth Alexander through Cave Canem, as well as Michael S. Harper, Frank X Walker, Camille T. Dungy, and so many more.[4]

While Alexander writes about a famous figure and Trethewey's reach stretches from the personal to the Civil War, Jordan writes about an ordinary person who did something extraordinary in *M-A-C-N-O-L-I-A*. In 1936 thirteen-year-old MacNolia Cox, who was in the eighth grade at Colonial School, won the Akron District Spelling Bee in what the *Negro Star* described as "one of the most closely contested spelling bees ever held in this state. A capacity crowd attended the finals held at the Armory and Miss Cox was given an ovation, when after eliminating her opponents she spelled correctly the winning word 'voluble.'" The capacity crowd of three thousand was "the largest crowd ever to attend a Beacon Journal spelling bee," and the audience cheered for the first African American to be crowned champion.[5] Along with a prize of twenty-five dollars, MacNolia's victory meant that she would progress to the National Spelling Bee, where she became one of the first two African Americans to make it to the finals since the bee had begun in 1925. Elizabeth Kenny, from New Jersey, placed seventh in the National Spelling Bee, and MacNolia finished in fifth place, an amazing achievement that the townspeople of Akron celebrated with a parade upon her return and a series of speeches predicting a rich future for her. However, MacNolia's victory was marred by the possibilities that she should have won the National Spelling Bee that year, that she was purposefully eliminated from the competition when she was given a word to spell that was out-of-bounds according to the contest's rules, and that the white judges in charge of the competition treated her unfairly in order to protect the illusion of white intellectual superiority, even—or perhaps especially—in a spelling contest for middle school children.

Writing historical poetry is an act of creation, not merely reclamation. For Jordan, this means theorizing into empty spaces, into the historical gaps and silences in a book that won the Anisfield-Wolf Book Award for Nonfiction in 2005, a book prize focused on addressing racism, diversity, and social justice, themes that succinctly sum up critical aspects of Jordan's achievement. The past can be recovered, but what is recovered, according to Greenblatt's theories, bears the stamp of the author's own experiences, biases, and historical moment. Like Trethewey, Jordan chose the responsibility of exhaustive research, while always knowing that more materials may exist elsewhere or appear later, just as historians accept this uncomfortable fact. He, like all of the poets covered here, chose a past that feels necessary, that represents the history needed today. Jordan is accountable not only to his hometown of Akron but to his entire audience, whom he convinces to root for MacNolia, to envision her in the spotlight of the National Spelling Bee, to hope for her, and to identify and dismantle the system of white supremacy that refused to let her perform to the best of her ability in 1936. MacNolia, for the present, is both hero and instigator, and readers respond to the emotional authenticity of Jordan's MacNolia and her extraordinary achievement.

Like MacNolia, Jordan grew up in Akron, Ohio. He discovered her in an article titled "A Way with Words" in the *Akron Beacon Journal* when visiting his family.[6] In interviews, he describes the research process that took him to additional *Akron Beacon Journal* articles written about MacNolia by Mabel Norris, the white reporter who accompanied MacNolia and her mother to Washington, DC; to the Department of Vital Statistics for information on her birth and death; to MacNolia's niece and the family documents she had (she was planning her own book and so reserved many materials for her own use); and to other locals who remembered MacNolia. Research on a hometown person brings a certain responsibility since, while most people reading Jordan's book might miss any errors, the Akron community would not,[7] and by telling MacNolia's story, Jordan tells the community's story, inserting it into national history, much as Rita Dove did for Akron. "The intersection of poetry and history has been there since the beginning of poetry. The poet has always chronicled the culture and history of a people. And so, I'm just trying to extend that tradition and work within that tradition," Jordan said in an interview.[8] Of his work in that tradition, he explained, "I spend most of my time researching. I like having search-and-rescue missions, to find erasures from our history and culture. I'm trying to connect historical events to a larger theme of the human condition. It's a way of putting the work in conversation with the world."[9]

Through Jordan's excavation of MacNolia's story, his book places her individual life in the larger history of the United States, beginning with MacNolia's obituary (from the same paper that celebrated her spelling bee victory) and her death. While the book's structure is not an exact reverse chronology of MacNolia's life, her death and adulthood come first, in the section titled "Z," and her childhood—focused primarily on the spelling bee—is covered in the second section "A," even though her life and preoccupation with language were lived A to Z.[10] Structurally, the book offers the entirety of MacNolia's life, fully lived, but it focuses on that moment on the stage when her sheer intellectual brilliance was showcased. As it exposes the systemic racism that cost MacNolia the final victory, hope is emphasized, not defeat. The past cannot be changed, but this book offers the readers the feeling that it almost could be, that we may, this time, watch MacNolia win the national competition and the world change with her. Complementing this innovative way of telling a life story are the many poetic forms Jordan uses and even creates himself, in this volume so focused on language and form that the poetry itself is an homage to a woman enamored by words from an early age.

At times, Jordan's poetry feels like Alexander's in his focus on interiority or Trethewey's with his "search-and-rescue mission." However, what he is doing with the historical poem differs from what both of them do. Jordan explained,

> I'm most attracted to poems that have high stakes around vulnerability and emotional transparency. I love speakers who struggle with what to say, those speakers who pose questions as much as they, through the transparency of the struggle, answer them. . . . That was the thing that I realized I was moved by: the emotional center of the poems—that point at which we realize the speaker has revealed something that is not easy to reveal to others. It breaks my heart every time. . . . I can get distant objectivity from the morning paper. I come to poems for the risk taking, the risk taking that most of us don't give ourselves permission to take in our daily lives.[11]

A former journalist, Jordan has written the objective newspaper stories to which he refers, and his poetry captures the emotional center he is looking for without crossing the line into sentimentality. In interviews he has also emphasized the concepts of emotional biography and emotional resonance—the terms that best describe his historical poetry. The emotional biography is MacNolia's emotive side of her story, the reality in her life that cannot be found in archives, newspaper articles, or a birth certificate and that is reliant upon Jordan and is the purview of poetry to express. Emotional resonance is the audience's reaction to MacNolia and her story; it is the elusive quality creative writers strive for, the emotional connection between MacNolia and the readers, the empathy Jordan creates. In *M-A-C-N-O-L-I-A*, Jordan successfully produces the emotional biography and resonance in a character his audience will meet only through his lyric poetry, a genre, Jordan believes, that can take readers into the interior more adeptly than fiction, which creates a more effective exterior world. Poetry does not have to maintain a narrative and offers an immediacy on an emotional level that fiction cannot match.[12] In his own poetry, he recreates the life of a brilliant yet ordinary person who achieves a victory in her youth that she will never be allowed to live up to or match a second time, a person whose potential is denied because of the Jim Crow system, which requires her to fail. By the book's end, readers know that MacNolia will not win the National Spelling Bee no matter how talented she is, yet we find ourselves rooting for her, holding our breath as she competes, willing her to win, hoping that this time the story may be different, for her and for the country.

With eloquence and precision, Jordan tells the story of African American achievement and resistance through MacNolia, whose very name he defines as "a Negro who spells and reads as well as [if not better than] any white."[13] Opposed to MacNolia's efforts is the white supremacist system, an institution that constantly rebuilt itself, responding to Black achievement with waves of oppression in regard to everything from housing and jobs to spelling bees. Jordan imagines a MacNolia who reaches beyond the scope of archival materials and who stretches into what he calls the "dead ends," the places where no information is available, the absence as enticing as presence, a space to be filled.[14] His MacNolia is placed in the larger arena of American history through poems that feature national figures like Jesse Owens, Josephine Baker, and A. Philip Randolph. While MacNolia cannot emerge the victor, the final word in this book is not that people will always be cheated by a corrupt and racist system; rather, the final word is hope. Her fifth-place finish—in the nation—challenges the edifice of white supremacy because in the contest it is made clear that without trickery, she would have won. She is the brilliant speller on the stage, and that sheer brilliance upends the central claims of white supremacy.

The poem "English" draws a portrait of a young girl on the cusp of womanhood who is beginning to sort out adult truths—her neighbor is crying because of her husband's infidelities, her skin will not lighten with bleaching cream, the lye that straightens hair also makes it fall out, boys are mysterious and enticing—and words clarify her life, offer her balance. She thinks,

> I learned the word *chiaroscuro*
> By rolling it on my tongue
>
> Like cotton candy the color
> Of day and night.

The sensuality of pronouncing the word "chiaroscuro" entices, but the word's definition—the juxtaposition of dark and light in paintings—defines her world and the forces that oppose her achievement in the spelling bee and in the rest of her life. In the poem "to," one of Jordan's many definitional prose poems—a form he is credited with creating—MacNolia's mother, Mrs. Alberta Cox, speaks, and she wishes that MacNolia would head "to" many wonderful things: to being a woman, to love, to a man who will not leave her, many of the word games this volume plays.[15]

In the midst of these changes that will propel MacNolia into adulthood, Mrs. Cox mentions that MacNolia qualified, through her love for words, for the contest addressed in "Akron Spelling Bee, April 22, 1936." This sonnet sequence—a form often focused on romantic love that here instead portrays a love for learning—offers three speakers: Maxine Schumate, John Huddleston, and MacNolia. Maxine is astonished by the fame and attention she has received; people want to take pictures with her, ask for her autograph, and put her picture in the paper, simply for spelling. She asks, "How many of you will know a love this fragile, / This immense, this short-lived and passionate?" The spotlight, however brief, that this contest offers captures Maxine, who knows that anyone could win each round—a thrill that also resonates for MacNolia, who battles through. John speaks after Maxine, admitting that while he is not much of an athlete, he makes his parents proud through his ability to spell the most difficult, impossible words: "It's a waltz through the pages of a dictionary, and I'm proud / To live this dream for those who don't have this choice." Up against MacNolia in the final round, John, who claims not to mind losing to a girl, has been told he "can't lost to a Negro; / No one ever has" in a competition that has drawn a record crowd. MacNolia's two sonnets in the final round address Maxine and John, both of whom she beats. She thinks generously of both, John, who is sweating at the end under the pressure, and Maxine, who searches for clues to spell "candelabrum," the rhythms of the word entrancing MacNolia. As the last person standing on stage, MacNolia is finally astonished: "How can I stand in so much light? / How can I stand in all this darkness?"[16]

This poem renders MacNolia's experience and astonishment at winning in unrhymed sonnets, one of many forms Jordan uses. Besides the definitional form he created and applies several times in this volume, Jordan uses syllabic poems—and had hoped to write the entire volume in syllabics but found he could not maintain the form for so long—as well as a myriad of other forms. He explained that the varied voices and experiences he was creating demanded different forms and what each could offer its content. For example, the volume begins with "Mercy, Mercy, Mercy" with MacNolia on her deathbed. In the syllabic form of alternating lines of first eight and then nine syllables—movement that, Jordan believes, creates tension in the moment where MacNolia vacillates between life and death—the quatrains draw a portrait of MacNolia's last moments in John's voice.[17] The tone is somber, MacNolia fearful, John comforting. As his father helped his mother cross over, John supports MacNolia, "sooth[ing] a dying woman's last / Days with these hands," the death, which comes to her too early, something that comes to each generation, regular as this poem's rhythm. Moreover, many of the poems bear the imprint of Jordan's interest in film, this one with stage directions—"*INTERIOR—NIGHT—Panning shot of MACNOLIA's bedroom on her deathbed*"—providing the setting.[18] "Wedding Night" sings the joy of MacNolia and John's wedding night in a series of linked tanka, alternating their voices; "Dust's" is visual, playing with spacing, lineation, and font; "Death Letter Blues Ghazal" names its form; and "Covering the Spelling Bee" is a double sestina, which breaks halfway through the second half, the form shattering as MacNolia loses on the national stage and her future shatters.

The poem "On Stage" also addresses the competition in the Akron Armory, and in it MacNolia shares her surprise that the crowd is rooting for her and her fears about the responsibility of representing the African American community in this historically white arena. MacNolia's nightmares run the gamut from worry that she will spell the wrong word and waste a year of studying to a dream featuring an announcer grown to enormous size and spitting with a forked tongue as she worries about which word she may have neglected to learn. However, instead of hostility, she finds an audience who claps in support for her. While the crowd that night was behind her, she worries they will turn on her, and her preparations run through her mind, in language reminiscent of Jamaica Kincaid's "Girl." Advice given to MacNolia from an adviser much like Kincaid's, perhaps her mother, perhaps an older relative or community member, instructs her to speak clearly, to be well groomed, to stay out of the sun, to polish her shoes, to brush her teeth, to moisturize her skin, not to look ashy, not to cry, to keep her back straight even if she loses, to wash her hair, to spell "*like there are no more words left to spell.*" The voices in MacNolia's head offer advice to help her represent the African American community in the face of white supremacy, the institution that warns John Huddleston he must not lose to her. Both young people are trained by their communities as they stand up to represent. The winning word MacNolia spells is "voluble," voluble as the voices in her head, as the worries in her heart, as the pleasure in winning the competition: "Can you spell it? A voice asks. *Can I spell it?* A voice whispers. Voluble, V-O-L-U- . . . The letters vaporize through the armory, and between each one you think of everything you must think about to get through one word." In Akron, though, she makes it through: "voluble, V-O-L-U-B-L-E."[19] She is the first African American champion of the spelling bee—an achievement she will carry with her forever.

Because she won the Akron Spelling Bee, MacNolia qualified for the National Spelling Bee, and while competing in her hometown in the northern state of Ohio was intimidating, it is in the national competition held in Washington, DC, a Southern city, where the institution of white supremacy surfaces much more clearly. The Akron bee was sponsored by the *Akron Beacon Journal*, and MacNolia was also sponsored by the Council of Negro Women, an Akron organization that inspired Mary McLeod Bethune's formation of the National Council of Negro Women. MacNolia traveled with the reporter Mabel Norris, her mother, and her teacher to the national contest. Before they left, the paper's owner, John S. Knight, shared his worries about traveling to segregated DC with Norris, saying, "It may not work to take a Negro there for competition against white children," but Norris naively assured him that she would make it work.[20] In contrast, MacNolia's mother knew what her daughter would be up against, and in the poem "Practice," Jordan shows her worries. MacNolia speaks in this poem and cannot account for her mother's hesitancy. She expects her mother to take the judges' role and follow the script: the word, the part of speech, the definition, the language of origin. Her mother's worries, however, show through as MacNolia notices that "She's still looking down / As if afraid for herself," when it is her daughter for whom she is afraid. The rules of Jim Crow, legalized or customary, were specific—as Richard Wright delineated in "The Ethics of Living Jim Crow," first published in 1937, the year after MacNolia's competition—and MacNolia's mother fears for her daughter, especially when they cross into the Southern states. Jordan's poem "National Spelling Bee Championship Montage" chronicles many of the indignities inflicted upon MacNolia and her mother: they were forced to move to a segregated car when the train crossed the state line into Maryland; they were not allowed to stay in the Willard

Hotel with other contestants and instead stayed with an influential African American doctor, Dr. T. Edward Jones; at the competition, held at the Hamilton Hotel, MacNolia has to use the back door, and she is seated alone at a small table, separate from the other contestants.[21]

White supremacy functions in waves of response to African American achievement rather than as a steady development, and it always tries to normalize itself, to be accepted as natural, and thus invisible, rather than constructed. But because it is a constructed belief system, it requires constant maintenance to survive. Segregation laws proliferated after the 1896 *Plessy v. Ferguson* Supreme Court case, and in Maryland, rail cars were separated by race in 1904; steamboats, streetcars, and hospitals followed soon after, as did schools; and miscegenation was declared a felony in 1924. The 1936 National Spelling Bee falls into an era between the wars—after the end of World War I and the Red Summer but before the economic reprieve of World War II. In these years are the Nineteenth Amendment of 1920, which gave women the right to vote but was in many ways intended to allow only white women to vote and assumed they would vote with their husbands or fathers; the 1921 Tulsa Riot, when Greenwood, known as the Black Wall Street, was burned; the Scottsboro case; and the Great Depression. In comparison, a middle school spelling bee seems like a low-stakes proposal, a moment in which the best speller should be able to win. However, historian Elizabeth Gillespie McRae documents how white supremacy permeated all aspects of American culture far beyond the segregation laws. For the ideology of white supremacy to work and remain invisible, it had to infiltrate all aspects of life, coming into the home, the church, and daily activities. Its beliefs rely on invisibility; the actions that support it need to feel ordinary and mundane in order to be readily accepted. According to an article in the highly circulated newspaper *The Afro American*, "MacNolia was regarded with much interest by the reporters and judges, and easily appeared to be one of the favorites on the rostrum because of her unflinching and unhesitating manner of spelling off the word evenly and quickly, without apparent quandary, differing from many of the other spellers."[22] White supremacy, functioning on the micro as well as macro level, however, could not allow MacNolia to win the contest because of the damage her victory would do to its struggle to remain intact.

The National Spelling Bee's rules have not excluded contestants on the basis of gender, racial identity, or ethnicity, but the national contestants come from districts that have discriminated, although it is hard to trace discriminatory practices because each district has its own, often undocumented, rules. In 1925 when the bee began, nine newspapers came together to organize the national bee, and each newspaper sponsored a finalist. Sponsorship today is similar. Newspapers serving English-speaking communities organize regional spelling bees, some as small as a county and some as large as a state or foreign country. The regional champions progress to the national bee. James Maguire documents a complaint from the Lynchburg, Virginia, branch of the NAACP in 1962 when the contest rules stipulated that no Black student would be allowed to compete. These rules were disseminated not by the national bee but by the *Lynchburg News*, the sponsor of Lynchburg's regional bee, which stipulated a whites-only contest.[23] While this case of discrimination is the only one Maguire documents, it cannot have been the only time a "whites-only" rule was enforced.

In the 1936 National Spelling Bee, the twenty thousand children who entered the regional contests that year were reduced to seventeen in the final round, and eventually only five contestants were left. The four white contestants had all come close to being eliminated, but the judges had reinstated each when the spelling they offered could be found in the dictionary as an obsolete or archaic spelling. In other words, they survived on a technicality. For example, winner Jean Trowbridge spelled "charwoman" as "charewoman" and "numbskull" as "numskull," but each time the judges found her alternative spelling in the dictionary and so allowed her to remain in the contest. MacNolia had spelled all her words correctly, looking like the strongest speller of the group, when she was given the word "nemesis."[24] The reporter for the *Afro American* wrote:

> A long and heated argument was precipitated by MacNolia's disqualification. Her teacher, Miss Cornelia Greve, white, and the correspondent from the white Akron newspaper which sponsored her, brought up the point that proper nouns were ruled out of the contest by the regulations and that "nemesis" was given in the dictionary as a proper noun, meaning the Greek goddess of retribution or revenge.
>
> The chairman of the contest, Dean George B. Woods, white, of American University, contended that the word was used just as frequently as a common noun, and that he had defined it to the girl at her request as meaning "fate."
>
> The chairman asked the judges to rule in the case. They ruled that the chairman was correct, that MacNolia had had a fair chance.
>
> Her boosters stuck it out, however, that the ruling was unfair, since, they said, they did not drill the girl in any words spelled with a capital letter in the Standard Dictionary, the authority used for the contest.[25]

According to the 1935 *New Standard Dictionary of the English Language* published by Funk and Wagnalls, *Webster's Second International Dictionary of the English Language* (1934), and the *Oxford English Dictionary* (*OED*), the definition of "nemesis" was only beginning to shift from a proper noun to a common noun in 1936. The *OED* documents many uses of Nemesis as a proper noun and only a few uses as a common noun before 1936. The *New Standard Dictionary*—the contest's authoritative text—offers the primary definition as a proper noun: "A goddess presiding over the moral and proper order of things, and visiting with retribution any violation of the natural equilibrium. She is thus a divinity of chastisement and vengeance." Only a brief secondary definition offers a use of the term as a common noun: "retributive justice," not "fate" as defined by Dean Woods. *Webster's Second International Dictionary of the English Language* (*Webster's* third edition is now the authority for the National Spelling Bee, but that change does not happen until the 1960s) confirms that the primary use of "Nemesis" was as a proper noun and its use as a common noun only a secondary definition. Furthermore, in both dictionaries, the entry "Nemesis" was capitalized, an indication to MacNolia and her teacher that she did not need to study that word since proper nouns were excluded from the context. Thus, dictionary definitions were used to offer reprieves to white contests but to deny one to the single Black contestant. Instead, Professor Woods, dean of the College of Liberal Arts at American University and a specialist in British Romantic Literature, used his exhaustive knowledge of language to choose a word with the power to eliminate MacNolia from the competition and protect the semblance of white intellectual superiority. Jordan's MacNolia says,

> Mr. Webster is
> The devil. He never taught
> Me how to spell
> *Ne-muh-sis* but now I know
> What she's all about.[26]

Jordan offers his interpretation of "nemesis": "The word in this situation stands in for injustice. There are people and forces in the world, irrespective of what you have done or prepared for or how you've comported yourself in the world, that will come with their own presuppositions about you and inflict those presuppositions upon you. [That dynamic] comes in the form of a word like nemesis. People will use that as some kind of tool to pull the rug out from under you."[27] Dean Woods became MacNolia's nemesis in an unfair battle, that of a well-educated, privileged white man who rigged the contest with a sleight of hand so well calculated that it would seem, to those who wanted to believe, that MacNolia lost fairly when she did not.

MacNolia was fêted upon her return to Akron as the champion she was: "MacNolia had a bigger parade then did our winner when we returned, though there was no luncheon at the Mayflower. Black bands came from as far away as Cleveland and MacNolia was showered with roses. The parade ended at her school with a ceremony of praise for a brave little girl."[28] Still, the experience of being denied the opportunity to perform to her potential had repercussions: MacNolia abandoned her dream to be a doctor since she could not afford college and a scholarship was not forthcoming; she dropped out of high school and went to work as a domestic. "In Service" is voiced by Dr. Wittenberg, the doctor for whom she worked, who sings her praises as a maid, one of the most damning portraits Jordan creates. Wittenberg is pleased to employ a woman who had won the Akron Spelling Bee but in a paternalistic way since, he says, he does not think she understands the meanings of the words she can spell. He expresses astonishment that she wanted to be a surgeon and suggests that perhaps her son will be able to go to college, if she can save the money. In short, Wittenberg offers MacNolia no assistance, no encouragement, no resources with which to pursue the career path he himself has chosen. He is amazed by her spelling ability but does not believe it marks intellectual potential. Instead, he brags that "she's the best damn maid in town," demonstrating his own culpability in a system of white supremacy that squanders MacNolia's potential, instead assigning her the position of facilitating the lives of white people.[29]

MacNolia's situation echoed what was happening to such national figures as Jesse Owens, Josephine Baker, and A. Philip Randolph, all of whom star in their own poems, which, according to Jordan, "place MacNolia Cox within the spectrum of African American history, and, consequently, within the spectrum of American History."[30] In the poem "Jesse Owens, 1963," MacNolia's husband John meets Owens, who, in August 1936, not even three months after MacNolia's National Spelling Bee, earned four gold medals in the summer Olympics in Berlin. Through his unparalleled success at the games, Owens defeated both his opponents and Hitler's doctrine of white supremacy. In this poem, John speaks in couplets, envisioning shaking hands with Owens as "just another baton exchange / Of the truths of life."[31] The race exhausts Owens, John, and MacNolia. As a second touchstone, Jordan offers Josephine Baker, who was by 1936 an international musical and film star, particularly popular in France but less well received in the United States. Jordan bases his poem "*Time* Reviews The Ziegfeld Follies Featuring Josephine Baker, 1936" on *Time Magazine*'s February 10 review, which calls Baker "disappointing":

> Josephine Baker is a St. Louis wash-woman's daughter who stepped out of a Negro burlesque show into a life of adulation and luxury in Paris during the booming 1920's. In sex appeal to jaded Europeans of the jazz-loving type, a Negro wench always has a head start. The particular tawny tint of all and stringy Josephine Baker's bare skin stirred French pulses. But to Manhattan theatre-goers last week she was just a slightly buck-toothed young Negro woman whose figure might be matched in any night club show, whose dancing & singing could be topped practically anywhere outside France.[32]

In a double sestina using only one envoi at the end, Jordan first presents the magazine's condescending review and then offers a response from Baker, who touts the man who loves her, the money she makes, and the accolades she receives in France, none of which will facilitate racial equality in the United States, not for an African American woman, no matter how famous. The intricately repetitive sestina form emphasizes the centuries-old repeated conflict of African American achievement with white oppression, here on Baker's part: "We could see that this show was not the *time* / For a lithe St. Louis girl of her *race* / To flaunt her flanks in front of New York *men*." A. Philip Randolph is the third figure Jordan presents, this time in a series of envelope poems. In Jordan's poem set in 1936, Randolph delivers a recruiting speech for the Brotherhood of Sleeping Car Porters, for which he had been negotiating with the Pullman Company. From that struggle a contract emerged in 1937, granting union members pay increases, shorter hours, and overtime pay. The repeating monorhymes of the envelope form's octaves perform a similar function to the sestina's repetition, which is highlighted when Jordan writes about Randolph:

> . . . Yet, he had no choice but to work
> As a porter. There's nothing wrong with the job. Nothing.
> But something's wrong—wrong with this country—when
> He has no other choice but a job his father had when
> School was not an option . . .[33]

Randolph has had opportunities his father did not but still finds himself working the same types of jobs his father did, the content and poetic form highlighting the efficacy of white supremacy and its attempt to refuse equal opportunity and progress to African Americans, one generation after another. Jordan's poems that introduce these figures and their struggles in athletics, entertainment, and politics offer a context for MacNolia—she is competing in the same circumstances as them, and her victory and subsequent loss mirror those of the most well-known African American figures in 1936.

As the first African American person to win the Akron District Spelling Bee and to place fifth in the national bee, MacNolia fundamentally changed these contests, opening the door that others easily walk through today. The National Spelling Bee is a now a national event with finalists and winners of many ethnicities and races. In 2006, a mere two years after the publication of Jordan's book, the film *Akeelah and the Bee*, a feel-good family movie, showcased an African American girl living in Los Angeles who overcomes socioeconomic obstacles to tie for first place in the National Spelling Bee with Dylan, a boy of Asian descent, a message that encourages present-day MacNolias to persevere and achieve. (As reviewers noted, the film has its issues—Dr. Larabee insists that Akeelah speak standard English only, and stereotypes about gangs, early pregnancies, woman-headed households, and model Asian minorities abound—but it emphasizes Akeelah's ability to succeed and to unify her community.) Still, the first Black person to win the National Spelling Bee was twelve-year-old Jody-Anne Maxwell, the Jamaica spelling champion, who won in 1998 by spelling "chiaroscurist" correctly, a word Jordan has MacNolia practicing in his poem "English."[34] After her victory, the E. W. Scripps Company, which runs the spelling bee, imposed a new rule stipulating that contests determining the representative for the National Spelling Bee, which is held in May, had to be held no earlier than February 1, using the logic that all champions competing would have the same amount of preparation time. Jamaica's championship, in a tradition established decades ago, is chosen in August. The Jamaican organizer was not informed about the new rule until two weeks before their bee, which could not be rescheduled that close to their competition date. Scripps did not offer Jamaica any alternatives, so the Jamaican champion was disqualified from the 1999 National Spelling Bee, an exclusion protested by Jesse Jackson and his Rainbow PUSH Coalition. Thus, even in 1999 another top Black competitor was excluded by the "rules," which naturalize white supremacy, rendering inequities seemingly logical and invisible. In Jordan's poem "My One White Friend," a blonde girl with blue eyes asks MacNolia if she thinks the judges gave her an unfair word to spell just because she is Black. The friend, a former friend from that moment on, answers her own question with "*I don't think they would have / Let you get that far just to set you up*," an opinion that forever creates a rift between them—the white girl choosing to believe the competition was fair and thus becoming complicit with the doctrine of white supremacy and the Black girl knowing that the competition, a microcosm of life, was rigged against her.[35]

Alice Walker searches for the female artists who have come before her in "In Search of Our Mothers' Gardens," and MacNolia is one of those literary mothers—a brilliant artist with words who in another time could have become an etymologist, a linguist, a philologist, a lexicographer, a poet—such is the person Jordan has created. Jordan's extensive research allows him to construct a framework, or a skeleton, upon which he can build. An archival-based framework is particularly effective in recounting the Akron District Spelling Bee and the National Spelling Bee because documents from both the Black press and the white-controlled newspapers are readily available, offering nuanced and detailed views of the events. Otherwise, MacNolia, like most people, left little archival evidence behind, so Jordan's sources concerning the remainder of her life dwindle.

Onto the framework of information that can be substantiated, Jordan writes the rest of his book, the birth of MacNolia's son, her feelings for her husband John, John's lament over MacNolia's cancer, and so much more of her life. These many poems are the product not of facts but of Jordan's theorizing MacNolia's life. As a historian constructs historical theories from the extant facts, Jordan theorizes a life, and there are many empty spaces to fill, spaces where no evidence about MacNolia's life exists. Jordan is drawn to those dead ends, which become a generative space forcing him to ask why those spaces are not chronicled. His artistic imagination, coupled with his research, responds to the gaps and silences, to the spaces lacking archival documents. A similar example exists in Jordan's *The Cineaste*, in which he inserts the African American independent filmmaker Oscar Micheaux—who has received substantial critical attention in the last few years—into film history. This volume is told in three sections; the first and third offer poems based on such classic films as *Un Chien Andalou* and *The Great Train Robbery* paired with *Blazing Saddles*, Ousmane Sembène's *Black Girl*, and the 1973 film *The Mack*. Sandwiched between this creatively unorthodox film history is an extended section on Micheaux's 1919 response to *Birth of a Nation*, the film *The Homesteader*, all copies of which have been lost, which marks it as a similar type of dead end, a space of absence that Jordan can write into being through his poetry. In the act of creating in what is otherwise a space of absence in *M-A-C-N-O-L-I-A*, Jordan writes a MacNolia who is true to the person he discovered in his research.

Beyond the printed sources, Jordan's own family offered some memories of MacNolia, community members remembered her, and MacNolia's niece Georgia Lee Gay shared a limited amount of family information. In 2008, four years after Jordan's volume was published, Gay published her own memoir about her aunt and their family titled *Whatever Happened to MacNolia Cox?* If Gay's version of the events in MacNolia's life is correct, then Jordan's recreation offers impressively few misinterpretations, although perhaps he gives John Montiere too much credit and too much blame: MacNolia did not meet John until 1969 or 1970, and they married in 1970, only six years before her death; she enjoyed a number of lovers and had an abortion in high school; she began drinking long before meeting John, partying more than her mother would have liked; and Darrell, born in May 1944, was her son with one of these lovers, not John. These differences, however, raise the question of the accuracy of Gay's rendition of her aunt's life. Accounts by family members offer clear advantages—family knowledge, memories, and documents—but are simultaneously and intrinsically biased by limited information, misremembered events, generational differences, and the desire to shape one's own (and Gay does appear in her book) and one's family's history. Gay published her story with the scandal-racked, quasi-vanity publisher Publish America (now America Star Books), which meant the book was not subject to the vetting applied to either scholarly or trade books, nor are its sources documented. When discussing his book, Jordan has been clear in interviews about how little information he was able to find about MacNolia, and in following the trail of his research, I have found his work, with what archival materials are publicly available, to be thorough and impeccable. Perhaps what is here are at least three different texts—Jordan's masterful work of poetry featuring a hero based on a real person, Gay's fond recreation of her family's life, and the historical, and still elusive, MacNolia Cox.

In his creative writing class that he titles "The Historical Hinge," Jordan advises students to tether their subjects to the present, advice he illustrates with his own youthful experience of being asked to leave, if being "asked" means being handcuffed by the police and escorted out of, a mall in Cuyahoga Falls, an Ohio city near Akron widely known as Caucasian Falls. The undeserved shame created by that incident of police harassment gave him the empathy to render fairly MacNolia's experiences with being repeatedly publicly shamed in Washington, DC. His MacNolia fully experienced the joy of achievement in her Akron District Spelling Bee victory and in placing fifth in the National Spelling Bee. She also, however, fully experienced the disillusionment of being denied the opportunity to compete fairly because of racial discrimination, and this disillusionment shapes the remainder of her life as she chooses not to strive for goals she now believes will be systematically denied to her. The portrait that emerges is of a person with great intellectual potential who pins herself into a small life so as not to face unwarranted rejection again. Jordan believes that the shame that destroyed MacNolia's intellectual curiosity widely impacted her generation, a group living before the civil rights movement, who tamped down those feelings in order to be able to cope, to live in a world where white supremacy had so much range and power.[36] His interpretation of MacNolia's life as one of stunted ambition, of immense potential derailed and deflated by racism, is one with which Gay agrees: "The trip to that spelling bee taught [MacNolia] where her place was and she knew right well how to stay there. Mac wanted no part of being kicked in the teeth again."[37] Nonetheless, MacNolia, through her life and her spirit, embodies Black resistance and perseverance, what Jordan terms African American humanity.

Chapter 5

Sampling History

Kevin Young's *To Repel Ghosts: The Remix*

Kevin Young is the Andrew W. Mellon director of the National Museum of African American History and Culture, responsible for the highly acclaimed museum that is fundamental to the representation of African Americans for the entire nation, and he serves as the poetry editor for *The New Yorker*, an influential position that allows him to shape the contemporary poetry scene. His connections to Elizabeth Alexander, Natasha Trethewey, A. Van Jordan, and the contemporary poetry world are many and began early. He met Alexander in the early 1990s at Harvard when he was an undergraduate there, and their mutual interest in visual art drew them together. She had published a review of Myron Schwartzman's book *Romare Bearden: His Life and Art* in the *New York Times* in 1991,[1] and he shared his burgeoning poems about the visual artist Jean-Michel Basquiat with her, specifically the Jack Johnson sequence. In response, she engaged his poetic project with the essay "A Black Man Says 'Sorbet,'" first published in the exhibition catalog for the traveling show *Two Cents*. In this essay, Alexander examines "the limited mainstream imaginative capacity around black men" through figures like Basquiat and Johnson who challenge that limited imagining that consistently misreads Black men.[2] Also during his undergraduate years, Young joined the Dark Room Collective, where he met Trethewey, among so many others who became the leading poets of their generation, and they worked together at Emory University for almost twelve years—her papers at Emory even contain a copy of the proofs for his book *Ardency*. Jordan and Young met on the poetry circuit soon after Jordan had published his first book *Rise*, and Young, a friend of Cave Canem, has taught in its celebrated workshops.

Young's book *To Repel Ghosts: The Remix* is about the painter Jean-Michel Basquiat, a figure famous like Sara Baartman but contemporary, living from 1960 to 1988, whom Young credits with being *the* brilliant artist of the 1980s.[3] Basquiat emerged as a New York City graffiti artist who used the tag SAMO© (the same old shit), quickly progressing to major one-person shows in New York and around the world. When he died at age twenty-seven, Basquiat had already become the highest-paid African American visual artist in history.[4] Generally characterized as neoexpressionist, Basquiat's artworks offer a complex analysis of both American history and contemporary life, a fusion of artistic influences and techniques, multiple layers of overpainting, and designs on surfaces from doors to clothes to tires to canvases. Like the other figures chosen by Alexander, Trethewey, and Jordan, Young focuses on a single figure, in his case one not forgotten or ordinary but instead, like Baartman, famous and misunderstood by many in the art world as well as by casual viewers. Basquiat often found himself the victim of racism and a figure others used for profit as his star rose. Young was drawn to Basquiat, who had only been dead three or four years when Young started writing about him, because he could relate to him. Only ten years apart in age, Young understood his references, his music, his historical moment, and Young endeavored in his poetry to capture the feeling of Basquiat's paintings and his spirit.[5] Young was writing his poems about Basquiat in the early 1990s, and before they were published in book form, they appeared in an art exhibition and accompanying catalog (with Alexander's essay) called *Two Cents: Works on Paper by Jean-Michel Basquiat and a Poetry Installation by Kevin Young*, which had showings in Florida, New York, and Los Angeles in 1995–96. Lorenzo Thomas, who celebrated this "extraordinary" exhibition, wrote that it "offered two young black men's reflections on the need to articulate their presence."[6]

A few years later, Young published two editions of *To Repel Ghosts*, the original in 2001 and the slimmer edition *To Repel Ghosts: The Remix* in 2005. In *The Remix*, "Discs" become "tracks," and all the sections are divided into smaller units and assigned titles borrowed from Basquiat's paintings—which themselves often come from text included in the painting—like "Portrait of the Artist as a Young Derelict" rather than the former "Bootlegs." The opening poem "Prehistory" is replaced with "Negative," a poem that inverts Black and white, subverting the racial binary: on television the maids are now white, the presidents are Black, music written by white people is appropriated by Black people, and the backup singers are white.[7] This racial inversion introduces Basquiat, a Black man who stepped into a role that was reserved for white men even in the 1980s, that of artistic prodigy, of a great talent that became recognizable when Basquiat was barely twenty. Although Young uses the musical term "remix," the 2005 edition's revision echoes Basquiat's technique of overpainting his pictures so that there are layers of images in palimpsest-like pieces (he also painted over Andy Warhol's art in the works they created together, startling Warhol). It also borrows Basquiat's techniques of improvisation, collages juxtaposing unlike images, gestural painting using the written word as gesture, and creating a final work with images and words scratched out, like the painting featured on the cover of the 2001 edition: on a white background is painted a blue sky, a death head, and the words "TO REPEL GHOSTS" in black and red with various versions crossed out, a technique Basquiat claimed made readers more intent on deciphering what had been painted over.[8] The title alludes to the many approaches documented in folklore that keep ghosts away, like a cross, a dream catcher, crystals, salt, garlic, or rosemary. For Basquiat, this painting may have functioned in the same way, keeping his ghosts at bay, and the ghost of the historical figure Jack Johnson appears in Young's book not as a haunting but as a Black man whose life echoes into the present. Young's book uses a musical motif, echoing Basquiat's deep investment in music in his painting, and it also imitates Basquiat's painting style in its organization and language, executing what Meta DuEwa Jones has termed "a contemporary renovative poetics."[9]

In *To Repel Ghosts: The Remix*, Young offers a heavily layered text, speaking through the lens of Basquiat and his particular interest in Jack Johnson, the first African American heavyweight boxing champion, whose choices constantly defied Jim Crows laws. Young uses the struggles of both figures to illuminate the historical parallels between talented Black men who succeeded but faced, to repeat Alexander's words, "the limited mainstream imaginative capacity." In his art, Basquiat used the technique of pentimento, a term Young also uses as a section title, which describes the palimpsestic visible trace of an earlier painting under additional layers of paint. In her 1973 novel by the same name, Lillian Hellman defined it:

> Old paint on canvas, as it ages, sometimes becomes transparent. When that happens it is possible, in some pictures, to see the original lines: a tree will show through a woman's dress, a child makes way for a dog, a large boat is no longer on an open sea. That is called pentimento because the painter "repented," changed his mind. Perhaps it would be as well to say that the old conception, replaced by a larger choice, is a way of seeing and then seeing again.[10]

Pentimento is an echo that becomes visible over time, an art term that also describes the relationship of Johnson to Basquiat. Young positions Johnson as the original, the first painting, and Basquiat as the image painted over him, a way of "seeing and then seeing again" the Black man. Even though Young's volume is ostensibly about Basquiat, Johnson's image is the underlayer that shows through, American history resurging into the present, and between them they bookend the twentieth century and illuminate the range and limits of Black men's talent and celebrity in it.

Young's *To Repel Ghosts: The Remix* begins with a visual epigram of the crown Basquiat often drew, a symbol that became his personal icon, which curator Richard Marshall calls "Basquiat's own trademark as well as a symbol of respect and admiration that he bestows on the figures that populate his work."[11] Young pairs the crown with the line from Basquiat's painting

Charles the First about Charlie Parker, the jazz great who passed away at the young age of thirty-four: "MOST YOUNG KINGS GET THEIR HEAD CUT OFF."[12] Basquiat, whose immense potential was similarly cut short by his death at twenty-seven from a heroin overdose, was drawn to figures with whom he had much in common—talent, youth, fame—solitary figures who were the "kings" of their sport or profession. In an interview, Basquiat commented on his focus on figures like Johnson: "The black person is the protagonist in most of my paintings. . . . I realized that I didn't see many paintings with black people in them."[13] Basquiat himself, as well as his range of important subjects, gave Young an opportunity to offer a concentrated, multigenerational, far-reaching poetic exploration, as he commented in an interview with Charles H. Rowell: "In my book, Basquiat becomes a lens to look at 20th-century black history and popular culture. . . . I really think of the book as a series of riffs off Basquiat's work and of historical riffs that lead into lots of other places."[14] In a 1983 interview, Basquiat was asked to define his subject matter, and his response was "royalty, heroism, and the streets," a line Young quotes in "City as School."[15] This line fuels the volume's focus on talent, fame, and racism, as well as their echoes through history.

My analysis here focuses on the extended Jack Johnson sequence, a series of eight poems that feature the volume's only historical persona. Young underscored the importance of this sequence in his preface to *Blue Laws* when he explained that it defined the volume, and in our conversation, he emphasized that it anchors *To Repel Ghosts: The Remix*. Furthermore, in an interview, he said, "The only I in the book really is 'Jack Johnson' because Jack Johnson at some level is the person of all the 'Famous Negro Athletes' whom Basquiat painted that represents a foil to Basquiat as artist, as the black male in white (high) society. So Gentleman Jack's the only person who speaks from a stance—I was trying to have his be the only authoritative 'I'—the 'I' as persona."[16] Thus, this composite yet individual persona, a foil, but I would argue also a parallel figure, speaks for himself, for African American athletes, as Basquiat's surrogate, since Basquiat was too close to Young for his voice to be taken into a speaking persona, and perhaps for Young and their generation.[17]

Throughout his career, Basquiat borrowed the boxer's stance to symbolize his own struggle in a field hostile to him. His paintings of boxers include an untitled painting known as *The Boxer* featuring the muscular upper body and head of a jubilant boxer with his gloves raised in triumph; the *The Fighter* in a much more abstract, graffiti style; *Cassius Clay* featuring the head and shoulders of the boxer in white against a red background; *Jersey Joe* wearing a crown and taking a knockout punch from a second figure; a crowned Jack Johnson raising one gloved hand in triumph;[18] a crowned head with the words "Sugar Ray Robinson"; and others, painted throughout his nine-year career. Boxers make their name in a show of strength and skill, through a physicality that may have been attractive to Basquiat since painters are not known for their physical strength, even though their art requires equal dedication and endurance; fighting his way from graffiti artist to an accepted place in the established art world would have required staying power and a pugilist mindset. Julian Schnabel, painter and filmmaker, is often quoted recounting an anecdote about how Basquiat challenged him to a match—a story told in his 1996 biopic *Basquiat*, although he shapes the anecdote to make himself the stronger contender, a shift that captures the negative spirit of the film about a painter who overshadowed Schnabel in their real competition in the art world. In her 1982 article on graffiti art, Suzi Gablik quoted Basquiat as saying, "I wouldn't be surprised if I died like a boxer, really broke, but somehow I doubt it,"[19] a sentence that simultaneously captures his fears and his overriding ambition. Boxers, like graffiti artists, often come from the streets; as street fighters, they rise from a place of adversity through the sheer power of their own bodies to become, in Johnson's case, a folk hero. The fight, for them, is literal, even if it was metaphorical for Basquiat. Moreover, in a series of photos used to advertise a joint 1985 exhibition of work by Andy Warhol and Basquiat, both men don Everlast boxing attire and gloves, the brand Basquiat also features in his painting *Per Capita*. In Michael Halsband's photographs, they are featured side by side, challenging the audience rather than each other; as winners crossing their arms on their chests and defiantly staring out of the photograph; and in a pose where Warhol is punching Basquiat when in reality the photo was scripted by Basquiat, who laid his head on Warhol's glove and grimaced as if the blow were real.[20]

Deemed the "most significant black athlete in history" by tennis great Arthur R. Ashe Jr.,[21] Jack Johnson, who lived from 1878 to 1946, was the "most famous and most notorious African American on earth," according to Ken Burns's documentary *Unforgiveable Blackness*, because he won the heavyweight boxing title in 1908, a title until then exclusively reserved for white men.[22] Not only did Johnson successfully cross that color line, holding the title until 1915 even through the famed 1910 fight against Jim Jeffries—a fight that the white sporting public expected would put a white man back in the title position but that Johnson won easily—but he also lived life on his own terms. His talent demonstrated that Black men could beat white men in the heavyweight ring, a place white men had used to define their masculinity, and his choices constantly challenged Jim Crow laws and the customary rules of white supremacy. He lived large, rich, and famous, driving fast cars, sporting expensive suits, drinking expensive liquor, and marrying, in succession, three white women after his first marriage with Mary Austin dissolved. His success disrupted the racial hierarchy at a time when *Plessy v. Ferguson* had recently been decided, and Johnson's victories offered a model of defiance to the Black community at a time when white supremacy was solidifying its hold. When Johnson defended his title against Jeffries, riots broke out in many American cities, with African Americans jubilant that he had won again and European Americans chaffing at this loss of power. In the same way that African Americans relished Johnson's successes, Basquiat celebrates Johnson, and Young finds commonalities in the success and hardships both experience.

Jack Johnson is a towering historical figure whose life is traversed by Young's eight poems. At their core, Young's poems are ekphrastic, based upon Basquiat's visual representation of Johnson, a scant figure drawn in black against a white background. Johnson's face and right hand, raised in victory, are colored in; his body is nondescript—perhaps a response to the many eroticizing photographs featuring Johnson's shirtless torso or his body in boxing attire that renders him close to naked. The iconic crown floats above his head, and his name is written below. Without the name, the figure would be unidentifiable, but the moniker, joined with the crown, constructs a context in which the few drawn lines suddenly represent the powerful body of one of the most celebrated boxers in the twentieth century. Thus, Basquiat uses the iconography of the crown and Johnson's name to elevate the sparse physical figure into a symbolic realm. Words create the man. A more classically ekphrastic poem would focus on describing Basquiat's painting, at least in part, but Young's poems instead focus on following Basquiat's lead in creating a Jack Johnson in words. His poems, in fast-moving tercets, highlight the key events that made Johnson famous, like the 1909 heavyweight championship fight against Canadian Tommy Burns in Sydney, Australia, that lasted fourteen rounds before being stopped by the police; the 1910 fight against Jim Jeffries, in which Johnson roundly beat the former champion; the day Johnson was convicted of violating the Mann Act; the fight in which he lost his title to Jess Willard in 1915; and the car crash in which Johnson died. Each of the eight poems, except the last, is paired with at least one external voice, responses to Johnson's persona that create a polyvocal, collage-like mode. These outside voices begin with the very negative and develop to the fondly positive, the portrait of Johnson, and through him Basquiat, transforming as the sequence advances.

Overall, this poetic sequence progresses from Johnson's early celebrity to his mature years when he had developed a strong sense of self and a pervasive spirit of rebellion against Jim Crow, accompanied by the support offered by important intellectuals like W. E. B. Du Bois and community figures. The first three poems chronicle Johnson's physical talents, achievement in his chosen profession, and the white community's response to him. "Black Jack" highlights his birth, only thirteen years after the Thirteenth Amendment was ratified, his success in the ring, and the audience's emphasis on his race, repeating Johnson's famous quote voiced by actor Brock Peters, "I'm black and they won't let me forget it," on Miles Davis's 1971 album *Jack Johnson*. Johnson takes pride in being Black, and he challenges boxers to come into the ring with him, sure he can beat all comers. White men, he notices, call him racist names but then bet their money on his victory. Boxing is conflated with gambling, and Johnson wittily warns his challengers that

. . . Stepping
to me, in or out

the ring, you gamble—
go ahead then dealer,
hit me again.[23]

In juxtaposition to Johnson's virtuosic display of courage and skill, Young places an excerpt from Bohun Lynch's 1923 *Knuckles and Gloves* about Johnson: "He was very strong, very quick, a hard hitter, and extraordinarily skillful in defense. He was by no means unintelligent, and, not without good reason, was regarded generally with the greatest possible dislike. With money in his pocket and physical triumph over white men in his heart, he displayed all the gross and overbearing insolence which makes what we call the buck nigger insufferable."[24] Bohun Lynch, the pen name for writer John Gilbert, portrays both men as fighting for their races, and in his telling, Tommy Burns becomes a plucky figure accepting a brutal beating while defending his race, while Johnson is rendered insufferable and "not unintelligent."

"The Upset" similarly focuses on Johnson's achievements in the ring. In this poem, Johnson fights Burns for the heavyweight championship after chasing Burns around the world goading him in order to have the opportunity to fight for the title since white fighters at the time would simply refuse to fight Black men. In Young's poem, Johnson follows Burns to Britain, France, and finally Australia, where the fight took place. Johnson's superiority in the ring was evident early in the fight; by the second round, "all bets were even / & I made him pay," Young's persona declares.[25] By the fourteenth round, when the police stopped the fight, Johnson had beaten Burns thoroughly, securing the title by a wide, and unassailable, margin. Young juxtaposes Johnson's absolute victory with Jack London's voice, who, even though he admits that "there is no use minimizing Johnson's victory," still sides with Burns: "Personally I was with Burns all the way. He is a white man, and so am I. Naturally I wanted to see the white man win."[26] While not as virulently racist as Lynch's statement, London sides with the white boxer solely on the basis of race, ignoring talent and accomplishment.

Because resentment like London's toward Johnson was widespread, white people sought a "great white hope," and Young dedicates "The Crown" to Johnson's 1910 match with Jim Jeffries, a white whale, a former champion who was pulled out of retirement for the sole purpose of beating Johnson. Like the first two poems, this poem celebrates Johnson's abilities in the ring and his success in holding onto his title two years after winning it. Young's poem likens Johnson's fists to Herman Melville's harpoons, to folk hero John Henry's hammers, to firecrackers, mighty weapons that beat Jeffries easily and quickly: "I lit Jeffries like black / powder, a fire / cracker—" declares Young's Johnson; I "beat him till he / hugged me / those last rounds." Johnson drew out the match to validate his victory and ease the disappointment of white men in the audience who had issued death threats against him. The white response was quick—mobs rioted in many American cities, beating and lynching African Americans, attempting a show of strength, even though their white representative had just been beaten in what was for a few hours the most important ring in boxing history. Into his poem, Young places headlines taken verbatim from the July 5, 1910, *New York Times*, the day following the fight:

> JOHNSON WINS
> WHITES LYNCH
> 70 ARRESTED
>
> BALTIMORE
> OMAHA NEGRO
> KILLED—

These headlines interrupt Johnson's dramatic monologue, the white violence interrupting the celebration of his win. Furthermore, the external voice speaking at the end of this poem is not a single person but lyrics taken from a contrafactum of the hymn "Amazing Grace":

> Amaze an' Grace, how sweet it sounds,
> Jack Johnson knocked Jim Jeffries down.
> Jim Jeffries jumped up an' hit Jack on the chin.
> An' then Jack knocked him down again.

This voice marks the sequence's shift from the negative external voices toward the positive. The first stanza is celebratory, although the second ends stingingly negative.[27] Despite Johnson's continued success and clear victories, he remained, for the white boxing world, a fighter who should not have achieved his victories.

Because no white boxers could be found to defeat Jack Johnson, white Americans found another way to punish Johnson for his continued success—he was charged with violating the Mann Act, an event addressed in Young's poem "The Ring." The Mann Act, also known as the White Slave Traffic Act, was a 1910 federal law meant to combat the kidnapping of (white) women who were taken across state lines and forced to participate in prostitution or any immoral purpose.[28] (The law's origins are rooted in the movement of young white women from rural to urban areas and of immigrant women into urban areas; the sexual choices of both were considered suspect.) Johnson was charged with violating the Mann Act through his relationship with two white women: Belle Schreiber, with whom he had been involved in 1909 and 1910 before the Mann Act had been enacted, and Lucille Cameron, whom he married in 1912. These trumped-up charges manipulated the law so that a Black man could be punished for his successes in the ring and in his personal life, and they prevented him from fighting. Young's Johnson describes "the bed" as "just / another ring I'd beat / them white boys in" as he "sw[ept] / the women off their feet."[29] Upon being convicted to a year and a day in prison in 1913, Johnson fled the United States, posing as a member of a Black baseball team on the way to Canada. For the next seven years, Johnson lived in Europe and Latin America, finally returning to the United States in 1920. The voices Young chooses to respond to this poem about Johnson being punished for his intimate partners belong to Booker T. Washington, who condemned Johnson for bringing shame upon the African American community, and W. E. B. DuBois, who pointed out that white American athletes were not prosecuted for personal romantic choices and that the real problem was rooted in Johnson's race, his "unforgiveable blackness." In lines Young does not include in his volume, Du Bois applauds Johnson further, as he considers why boxing has suddenly become the victim of "national disgust": "The cause is clear: Jack Johnson, successor of the Eighteenth Century John Jackson, has outsparred an Irishman. He did it with little brutality, the utmost fairness and great good nature. He did not 'knock' his opponent senseless. Apparently he did not even try. Neither he nor his race invented prize fighting or particularly like it."[30] According to Du Bois, the country has turned on a sport championed by British royalty because an African American holds the title, a defense of both Johnson and his sport.

Five years before Johnson returned to the United States, he lost his heavyweight title in a fight against Jess Willard, the subject of Young's fifth poem, "The Fix." Opinions on whether Johnson threw the fight or not are mixed, and Young's poem seems to take the side, even in its title, that Johnson did throw the fight in an effort to cut a deal to have the Mann Act charges dropped, even while pointing out that he encouraged his mother to bet on him, an indication that he may simply have been outboxed. Young writes that Johnson "did the dive," a sacrifice that cost him his title, although he was still not allowed to return to the United States until 1920.[31] The charges remained, and Johnson served his sentence in Leavenworth. Juxtaposed with these verses is an excerpt from W. E. B. Du Bois's "The Criteria of Negro Art." If Young's epigraph for the Johnson series—"Jack decided that being a painter was less of a vocation than he had supposed. He would be a boxer instead," with its clever homonym since Johnson was working in a paint store and the fine art painter Basquiat remains omnipresent[32]—showcases Johnson's choice of boxing over painting, then Du Bois's quote shifts the poem from boxing back to art. Du Bois asks his audience what they would choose if "you tonight suddenly should become full-fledged Americans; if your color faded, or the color line here in Chicago was miraculously forgotten; suppose, too, you became at the same time rich and powerful;—what is it that you would want? What would you immediately seek?" He answers his own question:

> If it were really a beautiful world; if we had the true spirit; if we had the Seeing Eye, the Cunning Hand, the Feeling Heart; if we had, to be sure, not perfect happiness, but plenty of good hard work, the inevitable suffering that always comes with life; sacrifice and waiting, all that—but, nevertheless, lived in a world where men know, where men create, where they realize themselves and where they enjoy life. It is that sort of a world we want to create for ourselves and for all America.[33]

Du Bois hopes, in 1916, for a just and equal world, rather than the world in which Johnson lived, and his hope continues, even as Johnson is unfairly incarcerated.

More than half a century later, Basquiat, the layer Young writes over Johnson, likewise enjoyed great success but was also persecuted for that success by people similar to the white men who bet their money on Johnson's victories even while trying to dethrone him. Paul Ardenne describes the art market of his time: "The 1980s were a decade of soaring prices" in which collectors began looking for younger, more affordable artists and found Basquiat, who enjoyed a substantial income in the last few years of his life. "Less than a year after his death, Jean-Michel Basquiat fetched more than $300,000 in May 1989," an extraordinary price,[34] and in May 2017, his painting *Untitled* sold for $110.5 million at Sotheby's auction, the most ever paid for a work by an American artist. To meet the demand and fill their pockets, dealers like Annina Nosei sold paintings without Basquiat's permission, paintings he at times did not feel were finished,[35] perhaps explaining why he changed dealers so often. To find space away from the demands of the art world, Basquiat disconnected his telephone to minimize the disruptions, relying on telegrams and ignoring the doorbell.[36] These telegrams become lines in Young's "Urgent Telegram to Jean-Michel Basquiat" like "HAVENT HEARD FROM YOU IN AGES STOP LOVE YOUR / LATEST SHOW STOP THIS NO PHONE STUFF IS FOR BIRDS / LIKE YOU STOP ONCE SHOUTED UP FROM STREET ONLY." In an often-repeated anecdote, as one prospective dealer left Basquiat's studio, he leaned out of the window and emptied a bowl of fruit—which she had just given him—on her head, a story featured in Young's poem about how Basquiat was exasperated by dealers hoping to profit from his work, especially this "collector showing / off her black // chauffeur."[37] Still, art dealers outnumbered the mourners at Basquiat's burial, waiting for an opportunity to profit from his art, and art dealers made, and continue to make, a stunning amount of money from his art.[38]

The virulent racism Johnson experienced in 1910 was muted by the 1980s but still recognizable in the treatment Basquiat received in the face of his own impressive victories as a rising star in the art world. White art critics too often categorized his work as primitive or considered it instinctive, dependent on pure talent or emotion, emphasizing his lack of formal training rather than categorizing him with the many self-trained white artists. They called Basquiat a cave dweller rather than an artist in residence when his studio was in the basement of Annina Nosei's gallery. They implied that his talent was entirely dependent on the drugs he used, and art dealer Bruno Bischofberger remembered Basquiat as "over-sensitive" to criticism.[39] Andy Warhol, with whom Basquiat developed a friendship and collaborated, called Basquiat's studio "a nigger's loft"—a telling phrase that Young incorporates into his poem "Campbell's Black Bean Soup"—a far cry from Warhol's own studio, The Factory.[40] Basquiat can be seen pushing back against critics in the interviews he gave in the mid-1980s as when he offered Henry Geldzahler, who patronizingly explained painting techniques that Basquiat was already using to good effect, brief circumspect comments in a refusal to engage with Geldzahler's condescension. Isabelle Graw was so off-putting in an uncomfortable 1987 interview that Basquiat at one point said, "Let's just talk and get it over with." In the interview with Graw, Basquiat shared his frustration with racism in general in the United States, using the example of catching a cab: "You can't get taxis. I go on the street, wave my hand and they just drive past me. Normally I have to wait for three or four cabs. A few taxi companies tell their drivers not to pick up blacks. . . . Black taxi drivers drive past me too."[41] In his poem "First Class (1983)," Young creates a Basquiat who flies to the United States on the elite Concorde but then has to take the subway home because no cabs will pick him up.[42] Basquiat was treated in similar ways in stores and restaurants in New York—a Black man was not expected to be where he was, doing what he was, dressed as he was, with the money that he had, successful as he was, especially in the rarefied art world—a world akin to the world of elite boxing in the early twentieth century.

The last three poems in Young's Jack Johnson sequence shift toward Johnson's proclamation of selfhood. Even though the racism does not disappear, it slides into the background, and the voices of the Black community shift to the forefront. "Last Chance" opens with his 1912 business venture Café de Champion in Chicago, the expensive art he bought for the club, and his top-drawer suits, shoes, and hats. It returns to his exile in Europe, where he lived luxuriously with his third wife, if constantly on the move from one country to the next. Young chronicles his year in Leavenworth, where he "kept cigars / & liquor & my own / private cook," and his early release for good behavior.[43] Miles Davis is the voice Young chose to respond to this poem, and Davis's commentary from his liner notes for the album *Jack Johnson* is offered. Davis describes Johnson's conviction as a "frame-up" and describes his exile in Paris as joyous, a far cry from the derision Johnson was subjected to in the United States. He also recounts the story about Johnson walking a pet leopard while drinking champagne, a representation of a daring champion living an exciting and expensive life, positive commentary that helped create the legend Johnson becomes.[44]

"Exhibitions"—a title that echoes through the art exhibitions that made Basquiat famous—likewise focuses on exploits that created the mythos of a Jack Johnson who consistently challenged Jim Crow. This poem shifts rapidly between the many spectacles featuring Johnson—the Harlem parade welcoming him home, his stunts like wrestling pythons, his demonstrations of strength like lifting three Paris showgirls at one time, his appearance in the film *Aida*, and the boxing matches he continued to fight until 1938 when he was sixty. Johnson's appearance as a captured Ethiopian general in *Aida* represents the contradictions in Johnson's life—the filmmakers sought to use his body, dressed in leopard skins, for their purposes, while Johnson responded by benefiting from and subverting the producers' goal. Johnson accepted the role but said to a reporter, "They needed a big strong fellow, and black—and that was me. I am to be the head general of Ethiopia, dressed up like Selassie with robes and all, and they take me up to Memphis—not Memphis, Tenn., but in the old country—and I am a prisoner. Boy, I mean to struggle plenty." When Johnson was asked if he would be chained as a prisoner, he responded, "They are supposed to and they'll try to, but I'll put up a good battle," a sentiment that sums up many of the events this poem scrolls through—Johnson spent much of his life subverting the white supremacy that constantly tried to subdue him. Young ends this poem quoting Johnson: "I mean to struggle plenty," a summation of Johnson's life, as well as Basquiat's.[45]

William H. Wiggins Jr., the final outside voice, responds to "Exhibitions" by recounting a story his father used to tell about Johnson receiving a ticket while speeding through Georgia. The fine was an exorbitant $50 (over $800 today), but Johnson gave the police officer twice that much and told the officer to keep the change because "I'm coming back the same way I'm going." In this 1971 article published in *The Black Scholar*, Wiggins argued that Johnson had "smashed the myth of white supremacy and given black men all over America a new vision of themselves."[46] Young's summation in his final poem "The Race (D. 10 June 1945)" is strikingly similar to Wiggins's. Both describe a man who says he spent his "life fighting /—crossing color / lines I never drew." Young, like Johnson's many biographers, emphasizes Johnson's exhortation that he be remembered as "a man, / & a good one," and Young pictures him in a race throughout his life, a constant challenger of the racial discrimination that sought to hold him down. Johnson's insistence on fast driving was his undoing, a choice that cost him his life when he hit a power pole and died:

> my Zephyr hugging
>
> like an opponent
> in the last round
> this pole
>
> of power—utility—
> my black body
> thrown free—

Still, this choice fit with the life Johnson insisted upon, a life that "broke men's jaws" and "Bigot laws," a life that was lived exuberantly and literally in the fast lane.[47] Similarly, over half a century later, Basquiat created a stupendous body of art when Black men were still not welcomed into the art world. His choice to use drugs killed him, damaging his body as surely as repeated blows damage boxers' bodies. However, both men lived with courage, forever defiant, consistently challenging the institution of white supremacy.

John Yau argues that the 1980s art critics and dealers "fail to address the fact that in his paintings Basquiat worked as an autodidact, someone who studied his subject, which was black history, both attentively and thoroughly."[48] They ignored information about how Basquiat demonstrated artistic talent at an early age, a talent nurtured by his mother, who often took him to the Brooklyn Museum, where he was a junior member, the Museum of Modern Art, and the Metropolitan Museum of Art, resources that gave him access to the world's greatest artists. A scant four years after Basquiat's death, the Whitney Museum of American Art held a retrospective on Basquiat, paying his art the serious attention it deserved. Accompanying the exhibition was Richard Marshall's book *Jean-Michel Basquiat*, which began to redirect scholarly opinion about him and his art. An essay in that volume by cultural critic Dick Hebdige affirmed Basquiat's achievements:

> Basquiat's work is as complexly coded and oblique, as passionate, as technically sophisticated, as intellectually daring as a saxophone solo by Bird or Coltrane. Like his bebop heroes, he just went to different schools. . . . The fleetness and dexterity with which Basquiat moved in and out of different voices, masks and scenes (the "street"-style magazines, the black music scene, the avant-garde "no wave" music scene, the experimental film and video networks, the East Village, the international art-star circuit) were both his strength and his undoing.[49]

Elizabeth Alexander points out, in *The Black Interior*, how the image of Basquiat as a "savage-savant" was debunked by art historian Robert Farris Thompson, cultural critic Greg Tate, and intellectual bell hooks, and she joins in that endeavor, positioning him in the pantheon of African American painters and as a person "with purpose, tutelage, family, history."[50] Young's poems, begun soon after the Whitney exhibition, direct literary attention to Basquiat and his historical subjects like Jack Johnson. Critic Rick Benjamin calls Young's historicizing one of his volume's achievements: "One comes out of the book considerably more educated about Basquiat, his artistic and cultural milieu, about the perverse and myriad ways America reifies race. As historical document, biography, as self- and other-conscious meditation on the life of the black artist in America—on all these levels, *To Repel Ghosts: The Remix* succeeds brilliantly."[51]

By borrowing the artistic technique pentimento, Young writes a historical poem about Black talent and celebrity through the lives of Johnson, the underlayer, and Basquiat, the overlayer. The layering of these two lives offers insights into how African American men were treated in the United States over the span of almost a century, and it addresses two exceptional lives of talent, achievement, and courage. By using this technique and in the trajectory of his volume, Young pursues history differently than the other authors covered here. Unlike Alexander, he is not particularly interested in the interior life of Basquiat. While he educates his readers about Basquiat, he is not reinscribing voices into history in the way that Trethewey is. Nor does Young focus on creating emotional connections to his subject in the way Jordan does. In his anthology *Giant Steps*, published in 2000, Young situates history as the primary focus of his generation, and he describes their use of history through musical terms, claiming that his generation "uses, quite comfortably, hip-hop's aesthetic and sense of history—that is, that history is ever-present, the past easily taken from ('sampled'), repeated ('looped'), collaged together, unified often only by the voice and by the rhythm of day-to-day life ('flow' and 'beat')"[52]—a claim he stands by today, a claim that describes his own work particularly well.[53] *To Repel Ghosts: The Remix* relies on the idea that history can be sampled, and Young conducts historical research with an eye for accuracy and inspiration. His poems choose a starting point, like Basquiat's painting of Jack Johnson, thus sampling the past and improvising upon it. The looping, or cycles, of history become readily apparent in the layering of Johnson and Basquiat, the same again only different but yet the same. The collaging of history so clear in Basquiat's painting becomes a technique enacted in Young's poetry, as Johnson's persona easily sits next to media headlines or Basquiat's portrait of him. This poetry carefully chooses pieces from the past for its wordplay, its puns, its sound, its rhythm, its echoes into the present because, in *To Repel Ghosts: The Remix*, the past is most relevant in how it moves forward, how it impacts the present. Young's historical poems travel beyond the limits of the elegiac, even while they lament lost people and potential, the racism inflicted on Johnson, Basquiat's shortened life, and the early lack of respect or recognition. While these poems beautifully memorialize what has been lost, they refuse to simply mourn the past. Instead, they improvise, using stories from the past to tell the stories of the present. Young's poetry demonstrates how Johnson's life foreshadows Basquiat's and how Basquiat's life was lived within the possibilities and limits placed on talented and famous Black men in the late twentieth century.

Chapter 6

✦

Reconciling the Past

Frank X Walker's *Turn Me Loose*

Frank X Walker shares a preoccupation about historical poetry with Elizabeth Alexander, Natasha Trethewey, A. Van Jordan, and Kevin Young, and he works to convince publishers and bookstores that this genre even deserves its own category and shelf.[1] Like these other poets, Walker has deep ties to Cave Canem, having been a fellow there in 2006, 2008, and 2009; he has been awarded the Lannan Foundation Poetry Fellowship, as has Jordan; and he is a Southern writer, like Trethewey. Walker's origins in Kentucky led him to coin the term "Affrilachian" to describe African American residents of Appalachia, and he was a founding member of the Affrilachian Poets and creator of the literary journal *pluck! The Journal of Affrilachian Arts and Culture*. In addition to the Affrilachian Poets, his poetry circle is anchored by institutions like Cave Canem, the decennial conference Furious Flower, and the yearly events at the Association of Writers and Writing Programs Conference. Walker describes Jordan and Camille T. Dungy as "literary cousins," confessed that he had a "poetry crush" on Natasha Trethewey, even early on writing a fan poem for her, and met Elizabeth Alexander after she delivered the inaugural poem for Obama when she was a guest artist at the University of Kentucky. Walker expansively describes his poetic influences—Rita Dove, Lucille Clifton, Marilyn Hacker, Yusef Komunyakaa—and names many more poets in his circle like Terrance Hayes, Tyehimba Jess, Nikky Finney, and Patricia Smith. His focus on innovative poetic forms engages his peers, who share his interest in form like Trethewey, and he dedicates poems in this volume to Jordan, when using the definitional form, and Jess, for a hinge poem. Walker describes his peers as a bunch of rebels who avoid the traditional canon and traditional forms, instead inventing new forms for a twenty-first-century poetic sensibility.[2]

In Walker's 2013 *Turn Me Loose: The Unghosting of Medgar Evers*, he offers the insight that "You can fill all the libraries with your version / of facts, call it history, and still not own the truth."[3] This collection uses poetry to reach closer to those elusive truths, truths necessary for this historical moment and generation, truths based on newly available historical sources, truths that present anew Evers's sacrifice and activism. This story is polyvocal, emphasizing the voices swirling around the famous figure, myriad voices that imitate how life really works, never linear but always complex and convoluted. One voice introduced here is Myrlie Evers. She is already well-known to people invested in civil rights, but this book garners her a wider audience. It is also distinctive in its inclusion of the voices of white supremacists—its attempt to create a space for a new conversation in the South—which is an unusual engagement that offers opportunities for a different type of reconciliation with the past. These voices offer a damning indictment of Southern white supremacy and illuminate how the white community supported it. These speakers are forced to reckon with their actions and, in the spirit of truth and reconciliation, to confess and change, although only one can. Moving forward requires forgiveness from the parties who have been hurt as well, forgiveness Myrlie is able to grant despite her devastating loss and without diminishing her—or the volume's—insistence on and documentation of heroic Black resistance. The technique of polyvocality, combined with accurate historical research, facilitates Walker's ability to build an emotional relationship with his audience, similar to what Jordan does. It also continues his generation's experimentation with form, and here poetic form is a space of play, the fresh innovations lightening the mood, offering a respite from the devastating subject matter. The center of the book is the assassination of Medgar Evers in 1963, one of the pivotal events in the civil rights years. In this book, however, Evers himself does not speak, and the story is told through the voices of those around him, the people whose perspective is rarely heard. *Turn Me Loose* turns attention to the unsung heroes of the civil rights movement and to the culture of white supremacy against which Evers fought.

Walker has long believed in the importance of telling stories through historical poetry, whose value as a genre is that it is "misbehaving, that it has taken on a level of activism that allows it to break new ground and is creating new poetry fans."[4] In a 2013 interview, he told Jabari Asim,

> I love history. And I think my activist instincts and my interest in reconciling what generally passes for history and what is actually true is at the core of my Historical Poetry. I've learned to appreciate how much the teller can shape and influence the story and how important it is for muted or marginalized voices to tell their own stories. I've also learned that the more participants in the story that share their often contrasting points of view, the closer we get to the truth.[5]

Turn Me Loose is Walker's fourth volume of historical poetry, all told through persona poems. Like Trethewey, he worries about the invisibility of important historical figures, and he believes that Evers is too often erased in discussions of the civil rights era that are "condensed to something as simple as 'MLK had a dream and Rosa Parks refused to give up her seat' " or focus only on the assassinations of Martin Luther King Jr., John F. and Robert Kennedy, and Malcolm X.[6] In contrast, Walker complicates those discussions by not only reinserting Evers into the discussion but also by focusing on his assassination and the aftermath. Because of the focus on the crucial moment of Evers's fatal injury and death, Evers cannot speak himself; rather, he is spoken about—by voices readers can empathize with, his wife and his brother, and by the strikingly unsympathetic voices of his assassin and the assassin's two wives. No other writer covered in this book enters into the white supremacist mindset to the depth Walker does, a disturbing journey meant to explore the roots of hatred and the Southern system of segregation Evers spent his life fighting.[7] Minrose Gwin writes that his book "takes measure of these long shadows of southern history and the bifurcated forms of memory they elicit in lingering contemporary arguments about the meaning of the Confederate flag, antebellum plantation life, and Jim Crow."[8] Dipping into Byron De La Beckwith's (hereafter, Beckwith) mind speaks to the construction of whiteness and a type of socialization that inculcates a terminal level of hatred. Walker contends that this disturbing journey, paired with Myrlie Evers's inspiring voice, helps people in the United States understand their past, an understanding necessary to reconciliation. He emphasizes his work's commitment to social justice and draws a line of influence from Langston Hughes to James Baldwin to the Black Arts Movement to historical poetry, which enacts active resistance through art.[9]

In order to create an emotional current in his poetry, Walker relies on research, imagination, and what he calls conjuring. He emphasizes the depth of his research, remarking that "it is [the persona's] roots and references to actual history that give these kind of poems legitimacy."[10] He recommends that writers conduct as much research as possible on their subject, amassing more information that they could ever put into their writing. Developing this expertise is crucial, he says, to creating accurate characters, but it is the venue of poetry that gives the historical story its "emotional strength." In the same way that *Eyes on the Prize* offers a visual narrative about the civil rights movement, to his research findings he adds, in filmmaker fashion, soundtrack, pacing, and control.[11] Walker suggests that poetry has the power to make historical figures come alive, far beyond the archive, because of its centuries-old performative nature. Good poetry is neither dry nor pedantic, and historical poetry is "more effective than traditional history because it humanizes the subjects by allowing the speakers to emote, making it easier for the reader to empathize with the subjects." Once the research is complete, "the conjuring begins."[12] In conjuring the people from the past, poets have an advantage over historians, Walker claims, because artistic license allows them to create an "emotional current," whereas a historian would be accused of bias or overly editorializing in making a similar gesture. Moreover, language mediates peoples' relationships with the past, language controlled by the person given the opportunity to tell the story. Walker offers an example from his research for *Buffalo Dance: The Journey of York*, a book about York, the enslaved man who traveled with the European American explorers Meriwether Lewis and William Clark. According to Lewis and Clark's reports, horses were stolen from their expedition by the Sioux. Walker points out that Lewis and Clark first found the horses in question on the prairie, already tamed by the Sioux, even though they were not corralled, which corresponded in the Anglo-American mind as wild rather than owned. In truth, when they took their horses back, the Sioux were merely reclaiming horses they had tamed. The word "found" is deployed to encompass the many things Lewis and Clark came across and took during their colonial exploration into lands others already occupied, underscoring the role of language in the truths of history.[13]

In addition to creating an emotional current, Walker seeks authenticity in his poems, and he argues that one way to create authenticity is to use multiple points of view, an approach he sees as "old hat in fiction" but used infrequently in poetry.[14] *Turn Me Loose* offers six voices. Myrlie Evers, Medgar's wife, is given the most poems in which to speak, and her powerful voice drives home the importance of Medgar as a pivotal political figure, the tragedy of his death, and his importance to their family and the civil rights movement. She is supported by Medgar's older brother Charles, who assumed the mantle of NAACP field secretary after Medgar was murdered. He and Medgar had "a pact . . . an agreement that one of them would stay in Mississippi and work for civil rights. If anything happened to him, they had agreed, the other would take over."[15] Also supporting Myrlie is an external voice, which Walker refers to as a Greek chorus, which explains the racist systems that existed in Mississippi and elsewhere. The other three voices in Walker's poem belong to Beckwith and his two wives, Willie (born Mary Louise Williams) and Thelma (formerly Neff), through which Walker offers a psychological exploration into the minds of white supremacists. Among the poets covered in this book so far, Alexander and Trethewey attack looming historical examples of colonial and national racism. Young demonstrates how early twentieth-century racism still echoes into the late decades of that century, and Jordan illuminates subtle and constant racism that infiltrates all aspects of life, including something as seemingly mundane as a middle school spelling bee. Alexander offers a short section from Cuvier's point of view, which is then thoroughly discredited by Baartman, and a white voice speaks in Jordan's book, but it is the largely progressive voice of journalist Mabel Norris. Walker alone creates personas of white supremacists, who speak—in this carefully balanced volume—in almost as many poems as Myrlie, Charles, and the Greek chorus combined. All of these voices swirl around Medgar, whose final words, "Turn me loose," become the volume's title.[16]

In an NPR interview, Walker emphasized that the most difficult voice for him was Beckwith's because to write in his voice Walker had to "try on the skin of someone who hates everything that I am."[17] He wanted Beckwith to be multidimensional and to accurately represent his beliefs to give readers the opportunity to measure their own biases—how far away or how disturbingly close are their beliefs to Beckwith's? Gwin argues that Walker combats "a collective unwillingness to remember the racist heart of southern and American history, a history that is ongoing."[18] In an interview with CX Dillhunt and Drew Dillhunt, Walker discussed what it was like to explore the mind of a dedicated racist:

> I really wanted to get inside his head and understand what fueled his passion, why he hated who he hated as well as why he loved what he loved. Unfortunately and fortunately there is no limit of research material on hate speech, the KKK, white supremacy, and so many images and so much material available that provided his own words. One of the devices I used to get into that space was to type in hate speech on YouTube and listen to as much of it as I could stand.[19]

Walker dedicated *Turn Me Loose* to the Mississippi Truth Project, which is concerned with truth and reconciliation. Reconciliation requires truth telling, even when it is painful, and it gathers the victims and perpetrators into the same space. This book challenges readers to consider their own socialization, beliefs, and actions through its representation of Beckwith and his two wives.

In imagining Beckwith's voice and inner life, Walker follows in the footsteps of Eudora Welty and her well-known story "Where Is the Voice Coming From?" written about Medgar Evers's assassination from the assassin's point of view, a story Walker calls "chilling."[20] Shocked by Evers's murder, which occurred on June 12, 1963, Welty wrote her story the very night she heard the news, an immediacy that she felt offered her "a kind of steely feeling about it, you know, the need for understanding a murderer, which I couldn't have done maybe if I'd thought it over for a period of time. In retrospect, I would have lost my daring, picked the story up with tongs or something."[21] Bill Maxwell and his boss William Shawn at *The New Yorker* immediately recognized the story's significance and moved swiftly to publish it. However, since Beckwith was arrested before the story went into print, changes had to be made because Welty had hit so close to the mark—a testimony itself to Welty's intimate understanding of the Southern racist psyche. In a phone call, Welty and Maxwell edited her story to remove identifying details, like the town's name and street names, that could open the publication to litigation, and it was published on July 6, 1963.[22] In a 1970 interview for the *New York Times Book Review*, Welty cavalierly commented that "the people who burn crosses on lawns don't read me in *The New Yorker*," but her flippant comment belied the truth.[23] Biographer Suzanne Marrs wrote, "All involved with the story knew that it was not only good, it was also courageous. Even before Eudora's story was in print, Diarmuid Russell [Welty's long-time agent] expressed concern about violence in Jackson and about Eudora's safety. Eudora, on the other hand, was afraid not for herself, but for her mother."[24] Exposing a system whose strength lay in its invisibility was dangerous. Much of its power came from white people's acceptance of it as natural and therefore nothing to be remarked upon or discussed, and white Southerners could face dire repercussions from disclosing and criticizing it.

What Welty did that was so courageous was to take readers into the mind of the assassin, to offer a psychological profile of a disturbing racist mindset common in the South in which she grew up. In a 1972 interview, she said, "When that murder was committed, it suddenly crossed my consciousness that I knew what was in that man's mind because I'd lived all my life where it happened. It was the strangest feeling of horror and compulsion all in one. I tried to write from the interior of my own South and that's why I dared to put it in the first person." Because she knew "the kind of mind that did this," she was in a powerful position to construct a character to embody that mind.[25] Her narrator prizes the Southern system of white supremacy, and he assassinates Roland Summers to support it, even though it had not benefited him economically. If working-class Black and white people worked together, there would be power in numbers to resist their exploitation. Racism, which splinters that group, supports capitalism through the sleight of hand that teaches working-class whites that they have more in common with wealthy white people than working-class people of other races. The privileges offered for being white and the illusionary promise of future economic prosperity convince people like Beckwith to support white supremacy, which then assumes vital significance to them because it is the only place in their lives in which they have a sense of power.

Welty's Roland Summers was a representative of change, social and economic change that so disrupted the narrator's beliefs—for what did he have besides his whiteness and illusions?—that he shot Summers, announcing to the empty sidewalk that "there was one way left, for me to be ahead of you and stay ahead of you, by Dad, and I just taken it. Now I'm alive and you ain't. We ain't never now, never going to be equals." In the narrator's mind, he must stay ahead of Summers because the racial hierarchy is absolute, and that surety dominates his thinking. Welty's text walks a fine line to reveal the narrator's thought processes while simultaneously denouncing them, which it achieves through the use of irony and the motif of heat. Thus, her narrator insists that he killed Summers for his own satisfaction but longs for approval from the governor and other powerful white people, as well as the media, which has incited the violence. He shoots Summers in the back from a great distance, a coward's shot with a sniper's skill, and in his confusion leaves his gun at the scene, but he contends that his inept actions represent expertise and make him a significant person owed gratitude. He wants "his rights," however undefined, and he sees any gains that African Americans make as his personal losses, even though he is already at the bottom of the social and economic ladder. He longs for the police to punish peaceful African American protestors: "I was already tired of seeing a hundred cops getting us white people nowhere," and he expects Blacks to be violent when he himself is the violent one. Moreover, he represents the Black community as vulnerable to white predators who knew how to get there in the dark because "it's where you all go for the thing you want when you want it the most," implying with a wink and a nod that white people are entitled to use the Black community for illicit pleasures—sex, drugs, alcohol. As the story progresses, the heat intensifies and permeates every aspect of life. The narrator waits for Summers to arrive home in the Mississippi summer heat: "It was so hot, all I did was hope and pray one or the other of us wouldn't melt before it was over." Upon his return home, the narrator feels the heat, a heat that does not break during the night that "stood without dropping, a good 92." His excuse for leaving that gun behind was that "it was scorching" and neither he nor the gun can cool off. He tells his wife that he is tired of "ever'thing in the world being just that hot to the touch! The keys to the truck, the doorknob, the bedsheet, ever'thing, it's all like a stove lid. There just ain't much going that's worth holding on to it no more . . . when it's a hundred and two in the shade by day and by night not too much difference." The next day is "hotter still," and "it looks like the town's on fire already." The heat persists at the story's end, the heat of the police pursuing him, the heat of his beliefs, the heat of guilt. The heat not only affects him but encapsulates the town, the conflagration of the South during the civil rights years, the heat of change.[26]

The one substantial error Welty made in imagining Evers's assassin was that she, as one of her friends pointed out, "thought it was a Snopes and it was Compson," a reference to the fictional world William Faulkner created in his Yoknapatawpha County.[27] Welty assigned the murderer to the social class of poor whites, Faulkner's Snopes, when really he belonged to her own class of Southern elite, if sometimes impoverished, whites, Faulkner's Compsons. In her story, the narrator's life is in stark contrast to that of Summers, who is not only a principled person but a person receiving media attention and gaining upward economic mobility. Summers drives a new white car, he lives in a nice home in a neighborhood with paved streets, his green lawn has been watered in the Mississippi summer heat, a light is left on heralding his late arrival home, and his wife is waiting up for him. In contrast, the narrator has to borrow his brother-in-law's truck, his home and neighborhood are run-down, and he cannot afford to leave lights on or water his lawn. Moreover, not only does his wife not care enough to wait up for him, but she also denigrates what he sees as his heroic assassination of Summers. Instead of offering the accolades he dreams of, his wife callously implies that the murder was not even his idea. She asks why he could not have chosen a more famous person to assassinate, criticizes him for leaving the gun behind, and taunts him that Summers will receive even more publicity in death. In this story, then, Welty created an impressively accurate depiction of the assassin, but constructing him as a Snope rather than a Compson betrays her unconscious wish to distance him from herself. While she intimately understood his mindset, she hoped it belonged to people not quite like herself, when in fact Beckwith's background and social class were uncomfortably similar to her own.[28]

When discussing the influences that taught him how to write about history, Walker mentions not only Welty's story but also Lucille Clifton's poem about Beckwith's third trial in 1994 when he is finally convicted of murdering Evers.[29] In Clifton's "the son of medgar," Medgar's son attends Beckwith's trial "to show in this courtroom / medgar's face." The son becomes the embodiment of the murdered father in a historical moment that measures how much Mississippi has changed in thirty years. Beckwith has survived to become a sick old man, once again on trial, supported by his second wife, Thelma. Myrlie attends, but Medgar was not allowed to grow old and can only be there through the visage he handed down to his son. Medgar "isn't / wasn't / won't be." This poem of tercets is a lament for Evers, but a lament that, in 1994, can feel vindicated because, as the poem's epigraph says, "*Beckwith found guilty of shooting Medgar / Evers in the back, killing him in 1963*."[30] That moment of closure changes the storyline and reduces Beckwith's impact since he has finally been defeated. Like Clifton's poem, Walker's poetry has the advantage of being written after Beckwith's conviction. This victory, although thirty years in coming, demonstrates Beckwith's weaknesses—Mississippi has changed even if he has not—and leaves space for Walker to explore his point of view. Beckwith's voice and attitude still exist in the South given the evidence that he still had supporters in the 1990s, but their time is fading away. Change and vindication have arrived by the 1990s, and, by 2013, Walker's volume exposing the unsavory reality of white supremacy was published by a Southern university press.[31]

Myrlie's voice opens *Turn Me Loose*, and she, Charles, and the Greek chorus close it down. Myrlie dominates the volume, and she reveals a life split into halves: her life before Medgar's death and her life afterward. While married to Medgar, she offers insight into their life together and Medgar's private world, as well as addressing the civil rights battle they were waging. Her poems shift in "When Death Moved In," when her life was irrevocably changed, and immediately after that she speaks to Willie and Thelma about their "sorority" of pain. After Medgar's military funeral, her voice changes again as she moves on in her life without Medgar. As she developed her own sense of identity over the course of years, she finds healing and even offers forgiveness to the Southern white community. Charles speaks in only two poems, and his poems offer the Medgar he knew as a child and his view of the atrocities they were combating. The Greek chorus illuminates the system of Southern white supremacy, offers poems debating widely diverging interpretations of Southern history, and ends the volume with an admonition that Mississippi must continue to move forward and yet never forget its troubled past.

Beckwith is the white voice of that troubled past, a voice that merges racism with misogyny, that fears race mixing, that hated being surpassed by an African American, that venerates the white working class, and that is shocked when convicted in 1994. Willie also speaks of racism, violence, and sex, and she tries to explain why she remains married to Beckwith. In Walker's telling, she may have found a modicum of truth in her twenty years with Beckwith, for in her last poem she realizes that poor whites have been duped by the wealthy. Walker himself places a lot of weight on her decision to leave the domineering Beckwith, even if it took three tries. He offers some optimism in her direction in the hope that change is possible even for entrenched white supremacists.[32] Thelma, however, sits squarely in the Far Right of the twentieth century, an adherent to the white supremacist beliefs Beckwith embraced throughout his life.

Myrlie's voice envelops the volume, offering the view of someone integrally involved in the fight for civil rights, someone whose husband had been taken, and someone who had developed into a leader herself. The unrhymed sonnet "What Kills Me" opens the volume, expressing the worry that Medgar's legacy is being lost as other civil rights figures take prominence. This poem makes clear that Evers's achievements, for which he and Myrlie paid dearly, were pivotal to the success of the movement. Similarly, Myrlie's "World War Too," with its clever wordplay, traces the civil rights movement to the World War II veterans like Evers who arrived home to find that the freedom they fought for abroad was not extended to them in the United States. Thus, they sought a "Double Victory," a slogan coined by the *Pittsburgh Courier*, against "the axis powers / of poll taxes, literacy tests, and violence." The veterans returned to fight their neighbors for rights denied to them every day. "Believing in Hymn" begins with an epigraph from the Mississippi Mass Choir, a gospel choir from Jackson, Mississippi, and Myrlie, in couplets, credits hymns for leading and consoling Evers and her. This poem securely attaches Evers's decisions to the church and its song, song that "laid down a verse over the roar / of fire hoses, attack dogs, and police batons."[33] The chorus carried them along, and Christian righteousness led their fight.

In addition to addressing the movement through Myrlie, Walker draws an endearing portrait of her private life with Medgar, one in which the few nights they had together were filled with music and the sound of their hearts beating together, a sweetness rarely included in public accounts of leaders. She personalizes Medgar, creating not only a heroic figure but one who was touchable, who loved his family and worked for their future. "Husbandry," with its title of care and cultivation, of managing resources by a woman fulfilling a traditional wifely role and of managing a husband bent on changing the world, particularly captures their relationship through Myrlie's point of view. In unrhymed couplets, the persona offers snippets about her life with Medgar: how she fell in love with a man who sought to make his home state a better place, how she left college after two years to be his wife, how she supported his dream: "wove my spine to his so he could stand / magnolia tall and blossom for all to see." This wife gave him three children to carry his name and to live for "his tomorrows." This husband heroically "spent every penny of his strength organizing / for a hate-free day." It is a poem in which both husband and wife sacrifice for civil rights, but their life together is special and apart: "we didn't waste a single night."[34]

The fight for civil rights in Mississippi was a brutal one, and the deaths did not begin or end with Evers's assassination. "After the FBI Searched the Bayou" laments those deaths, including the many bodies found during the hunt for James Chaney, Andrew Goodman, and Michael Schwerner, activists registering African Americans to vote in Mississippi. In the course of that investigation, which received national media attention and the attention of the FBI, unlike many deaths, searchers found not only the three civil rights workers but also college students Henry Hezekiah Dee and Charles Eddie Moore, fourteen-year-old Herbert Oarsby, and five other unidentified African American victims, none of whose murders the police had pursued. Myrlie's persona finds herself constantly in tears: "when they unearthed / each new corpse, / we couldn't speak for days." Walker's poems reference other highly publicized cases like the lynching of Emmett Till in 1955, a case in which Medgar had been closely involved. "Haiku for Emmett Till," a series of five linked haiku, questions what Till did, if anything, that challenged "Dixie decorum." It condemns the jury of white men who "looked at his skull / his disfigured face, smiled, and / still voted not guilty," a verdict that allowed his assassins to admit publicly to their crime in the *Look* magazine article in 1956, seven years before Medgar was killed, continuing the Southern tradition of protecting white assassins.[35]

Into this wave of atrocities are written the less celebrated cases of George Lee and Lamar Smith in "No More Fear." Walker writes in choppy, irregular lyric stanzas that stylistically mimic the chaos caused by these deaths only three months before Till visited Mississippi. Because he registered to vote, "Reverend George Lee was killed / by a shotgun blast to the face // It was ruled a traffic accident."[36] In her first autobiography, *For Us, the Living*, a title that quotes Lincoln's Gettysburg Address and echoes its admonition for the living to finish the work begun by those who died for it, Myrlie dedicates chapters to the Mississippians whose quest for equality cost them dearly. George Lee had complained to federal authorities that he and other African Americans were being prevented from voting, and he advocated voting rights in his sermons. On May 7, 1955, while driving through Belzoni in the Mississippi Delta, Lee was shot and consequently died on the way to the hospital. On behalf of the NAACP, Medgar investigated, even as the local police covered up the murder. The official story was that Lee had lost control of his car and the shotgun pellets lodged in his jaw were identified as dental fillings. No autopsy was performed. The NAACP investigation turned up witnesses who established that a tire on Lee's car had been shot out by three men following him, who then shot him in the face. However, those witnesses changed their story, refused to discuss what they saw, or disappeared. No arrests were made. "No More Fear" then addresses the case of Lamar Smith, who was registered to vote and had already exercised that right and was murdered one week before Till arrived. Smith advocated voting by absentee ballot, which allowed voters to avoid the danger involved in going to the polls. As punishment, he was shot near the courthouse of Brookhaven in a weekend crowd. Three white men were arrested for his murder, but a grand jury refused to indict them. At the end of her autobiography, Myrlie includes a damning list of fourteen people murdered for their civil rights activities, a short list of Southern atrocities.[37] African Americans who contested white supremacy by registering to vote and fighting for school integration were punished by death, as well as by rape, tax audits, loss of employment, the denial of business loans, bankruptcy, and the loss of their homes and land. Walker writes their heroic resistance into his poems.

This tragic litany continues with Evers's assassination. In the insistent couplets of "When Death Moved In," Walker presents the constant fear with which Medgar and Myrlie lived. He opens the poem with a simile likening the specter of fear to an unplanned pregnancy, ironically referring to Myrlie's unplanned fourth pregnancy—she was pregnant when Medgar was assassinated and miscarried after his death. In the poem, fear also becomes a "disfigured face," "crooked limbs and spine," and the sometimes uncomfortable space between Myrlie and Medgar in bed.[38] By the time Medgar was assassinated, progress was being made in the quest for civil rights. The tide had turned in Mississippi around 1961, a shift Myrlie traces to March 27, when nine students from Tougaloo Southern Christian College staged a sit-in at Jackson's white public library,[39] and in the wake of that turn, white violence escalated. The threat of needing new front teeth because of a beating was the reward for registering voters, boycotting segregated businesses, powerful demonstrations, television publicity, and the 1966 integration of the University of Mississippi. Medgar helped James Meredith gain admission to the university, which had denied him entrance to its law school only a few years earlier by changing its application process to systematically deny African Americans entrance. In the last three lines of Walker's poem, however, death "crawled to the front door, and spoke / its first cuss words / it sounded like a car backfired twice," the shot that killed Medgar and the second shot from a neighbor, warning others that a murderer was in their midst. In "Arlington," a poem written in tercets meant to invoke the trifolded flag memorializing Medgar's death, Myrlie watches her husband being buried in Arlington Cemetery, mourning his death but looking to the future.[40]

Mingled with Myrlie's voice is the voice of Charles, the brother who was three years older than Medgar. Like Myrlie, in the two poems in which Charles speaks, he protests the injustices of the era and looks forward, memorializing Medgar's optimism. In "The N-Word," Charles explains the connotations of the word through the reality of violence during the movement: German shepherds loosed on protestors, mobs attacking the nine students who integrated Little Rock Central High School, the four girls killed in the 16th Street Baptist Church bombing in Birmingham, the momentous losses suffered by the African American community. His raw lament makes real for readers the shattering of a window, the loss of a father, the keening of spouses. He places into the n-word all of its hateful legacy, saying, "I can't hear anything less / and absolutely nothing funny." His second poem is more hopeful, its title of "The Assurance Man" mingling Medgar's habit of giving assurance to those around him with his first job in insurance sales—going from the job of promising compensation to the activist who promises change. Charles's voice emphasizes the brother he knew before Medgar took an official position with the NAACP and the hope and optimism he had in the early days. Medgar, who refused to leave Mississippi even when threated with death, believed that Mississippi "had something beautiful to offer / her sons our freedom," and he expected it to arrive now, not in the hereafter.[41] Speaking only in couplets, Charles articulated the hope that he shared, the hope he fought for after stepping into Medgar's activist position after his assassination.

While Charles replaced Medgar in the NAACP, Myrlie moved her family to California after the second trial for Beckwith resulted in a second hung jury. In Walker's poems, Myrlie's voice progresses from the work required to refuse to hate, to the guilty verdict in Beckwith's third trial, and to the forgiveness she can finally feel, a trajectory that matches Myrlie's own assessment of the second half of her life in *Watch Me Fly*. In "On Moving to California," Myrlie deeply mourns Medgar's death, and while she had prepared for losing her husband, "climbing out from under the heaviness / of hate is the hardest thing I've ever done." That journey required that she move her family far away from Mississippi, the move away to which Medgar would not agree. In the ironically titled "White Knights"—for Bobby DeLaughter drawn as a virtuous white knight pursuing the villain Beckwith—Myrlie voices the good she sees: "For every ten Beckwiths / defending the right to wave / the Confederate flag / there's at least one Kennedy." She notes the rare but present white people who fight for civil rights: the white priest bleeding in the protest march, the "blue eyes / full of hope," the young hearts working for progress, an amazing moment of forgiveness for the loss she suffered. This poem directly follows "Last Meal Haiku," in which Beckwith enjoys a steak dripping with blood for his last meal, a poem that imagines that Beckwith has been given the death penalty.[42] In reality, he received a sentence of life imprisonment and died in prison in 2001, a final ending for his crime. The juxtaposition of these poems infers that Myrlie is able to forgive after the closure that the 1994 trial offers her, but in *For Us, the Living*, she locates that moment at Medgar's funeral. As she viewed her husband's body for the last time before the ceremony, she realized the white *Life* photographer with her had tears in his eyes: "For the first time since Medgar's death the hatred I had felt for all whites was gone. It never returned."[43]

From that moment of forgiveness, Myrlie's voice progresses to the activist she became and her hope for freedom for all. The poem "Evers Family Secret Recipe" lists the ingredients necessary to change minds—patience, smiles, generosity, kindness, hard work, commitment, and determination, as well as blood and tears. She sees the change becoming real for the next generation, a change she and Medgar helped produce, a prediction that fits the structure and argument of this volume that seeks forgiveness and reconciliation. Her admonition here is to vote, to call on the power of the ballot her generation fought and died for. Myrlie's final poem is "Gift of Time," in which she is able to come to resolutions, to find "beauty in a world / littered with scars." She finds that bullets cannot erase memories, but she has a son who resembles his father in his face, his laugh, his gait, echoing Clifton's poem. She finds that her faith is restored, and she generously—in the spirit of truth and reconciliation—forgives Beckwith. She imagines that he learned to hate for a reason, a hate that then does not have to win. At the end, she shares her conviction "that trouble don't last always."[44]

Against Myrlie's and Charles's voices of hope are juxtaposed the three Beckwith voices and the Greek chorus. Walker's poems contest the truth of the past and probe the construction of whiteness and Blackness under a separatist system. In one of the volume's most powerful poems, "A Final Accounting," Walker writes the line referenced earlier: "You can fill all the libraries with your version / of facts, call it history, and still not own the truth." In this couplet, he differentiates between the concepts of facts, history, and truth. As the introduction to this study establishes, historical representations of African American history were largely inaccurate until the 1970s, following the momentous shift when historians stopped looking *at* African Americans and began looking *as* African Americans. Walker offers two poems that present two diverging points of view on the same historical event or moment. In "Ambiguity over the Confederate Flag," a contrapuntal poem and stylistically the strongest poem in this volume, Walker offers two voices. On the left side of the page is the romanticized view of the South in which white people sat on the porch admiring their estates while Black people happily sang spirituals and willingly worked the fields. On the right side is the truthful version of the same scene in italicized font, filled with the constant, grueling labor of picking cotton, a job that destroyed people's bodies for the benefit of white property owners. The poetic lines also read straight across the page, a version telling a final truth about the work done in the United States by African Americans: "those were good ol' days *for plantation owners*." The combined voices, just as Black and white people have always lived next to each other in the South, tell a more accurate story, one that has lost its romanticized veneer. A hinge poem, "After Dinner in Money, Mississippi," juxtaposes three voices: the voice given center stage—the hinge—offers single words and phrases that read with the voices on both the left and right: on the left is a recipe for pecan pie, and on the right is a description of Emmett Till's murder. Like "Ambiguity over the Confederate Flag," the voice on the left is the romanticized view of a white South enjoying delicacies like pecan pie, a voice juxtaposed with the history of lynching in the South. For example, the center words "*pour into*" are read with "a thin crust" on the left and with "the Tallahatchie River" on the right, just as "*cover*" is read with "with pecans" on the left, and with "up the truth" on the right.[45]

The construction of racial identity is explored in several poems. "Unwritten Rules for Young Black Boys Wanting to Live in Mississippi Long Enough to Become Men" offers ten rules, beginning with "white is always right." The system of racial segregation was enforced both by law and by custom, custom being the more difficult to predict. Richard Wright illuminated this system in his 1938 essay "The Ethics of Living Jim Crow," and Walker's list is loosely based on Wright's admonitions about how to survive the South as a Black man. His rules stipulate the customary behavior required—rules that Medgar Evers constantly challenged—rules that enforced subservience and the status quo of segregation. As Wright knew, delineating the rules upon which segregation depended reduced their power because they were suddenly visible and could no longer be accepted as natural. Just as he too exposes the behavior demanded of African Americans, Walker illuminates the stakes of segregation for white people in "I'd Wish I Was in Dixie Too." This poem attacks two of the primary claims of white superiority: economic prosperity, which he points out depends on the labor of Blacks, and intellectual superiority, which depends on denying literacy to Blacks. The poem then catalogs the immense amount of work done by African Americans for European Americans, and "Dixie" becomes a moniker for a racially inequitable system, one inculcated into the way white people viewed their place in the world.[46] The white South fought to sustain its system of segregation, its sense of white privilege, and that fight resulted in Medgar's death at the hand of a white supremacist.

For Walker's volume, Beckwith is the manifestation of the white supremacist. As a murderer, he is exceptional, murder being a relatively rare crime that (usually) receives severe punishment, but positioning him, as DeLaughter did, as "the quintessence of evil" places him beyond the norm, an outlier in the white population.[47] Instead, Walker's volume presents a Beckwith as representative of the many unpunished white men who murdered African Americans in the South as a means to enforce segregation. Beckwith is allowed to murder Evers and escape punishment for thirty years because he is supported by the political establishment, like Governor Ross Barnett, who made a court appearance in support of Beckwith; by law enforcement, like the two officers who provided an alibi for Beckwith; by all-white male juries, unwilling to convict a white man for the murder of a Black man; and by a white citizenry who made threats against the white lawyers prosecuting Beckwith as well as Evers's family. As discussed with Jordan's book *M-A-C-N-O-L-I-A*, the system of white supremacy was pervasive, involving institutions from the family to the schools to the churches and to the courts. That system needed people like Beckwith—those willing to take extreme actions—and supported their efforts. Myrlie Evers documents that three lawyers defended Beckwith: "Hardy Lott, Greenwood's city attorney and a prominent member of the White Citizens Councils; Stanny Sanders, a former district attorney and Lott's law partner; and Hugh Cunningham, a partner in Governor Barnett's law firm." Not only was he defended by white men of high social and political standing, but his expenses were paid by "a newly formed White Citizens Legal Fund, with fourteen leading business and professional men on its board of directors."[48] While none of these men was a murderer, they were willing to lend their support to one and thereby sanction his actions.

In his book about the 1994 trial, Robert DeLaughter hopefully claims that "without doubt, most Mississippians, as most Americans, are decent, well-meaning people, but being 'good' is not enough. Upon the shoulders of such people falls the burden of courageously stepping in, righting wrongs, and unveiling demagoguery for what it is. All that's necessary for evil to prevail is for good men and women to do nothing," quoting the Irish political leader Edmund Burke.[49] Even though Beckwith was found guilty at this third trial, DeLaughter's claim that most Mississippians and Americans are "good" people cannot be historically supported, since the system in power rewarded white people just for being white. While perhaps not members of groups like the Ku Klux Klan, the White Citizens' Councils, or the Christian Identity Movement, as Beckwith was, these seemingly ordinary people were, in fact, not decent or well-meaning. The way they chose to live their lives supported a system that produced men like Beckwith, extremists, but extremists charged with supporting a system from which all white people benefited, the institution of white privilege.

Walker's poem "White of Way," a definitional poem using the form Jordan created for *M-A-C-N-O-L-I-A*, defines (white) power, (white) pride, and (white) privilege, all of which Beckwith embraced. White power here is "belief in the fact that all white people have the God given and constitutionally guaranteed right to exercise, encourage, promote, celebrate and defend the privilege of being born superior to other races," a doctrine that characterizes the culture that protected Beckwith. In this Southern segregationist culture, fishing, gun ownership, and country music are connected to misogyny, racism, and animal abuse, the same impulses to hunt and conquer translating from one activity to the next. Just as Beckwith takes pleasure in watching a fish die, he takes pleasure in hurting people in "Southern Sports," which opens with an epigraph from Jewish composer Abel Meeropol, who wrote Billie Holiday's hit "Strange Fruit": "Pastoral scene of the gallant south." In this South, the violence starts with name calling or a bonfire, escalating to a physical beating "for the sheer joy of causing . . . pain" or a lynching for a crowd applauding the violence. One small threat to power, and the result was a rape or a death, the enforcement of white privilege, not much of a gallant heritage. In "Humor Me," Beckwith's persona describes the rights of white men—to kick the dog, to beat a woman, to ride into the Black "side of town, looking for something funny." In his dreams—the repository of the unconscious—Beckwith is haunted by race mixing, and in "Fighting Extinction," Beckwith touts the protection of white women, the absurd sense of chivalry that stabilized his world and gave him reason for violence. Beckwith finds a mythology to support his worldview in the 1915 film *Birth of a Nation*, which galvanized a Klan resurgence, and his persona venerates the white working class, "regular, hardworking, blue collar, / proud-to-be-white folks." In "Anatomy of Hate," Beckwith admits to killing Medgar, largely for his achievements: his pressed clothes, his car, his homeownership, his education.[50] Because Beckwith cannot see beyond the system of white supremacy, the only change in the status quo he can fathom is for the binary to be reversed, with African Americans privileged and European Americans oppressed. In his "us or them" outlook, he cannot fathom the kind of world that Medgar was working toward, a world of equal opportunity that could exist beyond the binary of black and white. Whiteness is the only accomplishment Beckwith has, and even he recognizes its constructed and fleeting existence and so fights all the harder to hang onto that one bit of power, an obsession that allows him to kill to maintain it.

Speaking alongside Beckwith are his wives, Willie, to whom he was married for twenty years despite their two intervening divorces late in the relationship, and Thelma, whom he married in 1983. In her two poems, Thelma, a steadfast white supremacist, brazenly lectures Myrlie that Beckwith was generous to shoot Medgar in the back instead of the face and claims victory well into the twenty-first century since it took forty-five years for the United States to elect an African American president after Beckwith murdered Evers. Her voice reminds readers that the Far Right perseveres in the United States, despite progress. Willie's persona is given six poems, and she represents the white people who supported Beckwith, as well as the white women who choose to be intimately involved with murderers. In "Fire Proof," Willie connects sexual passion with racism, explaining that Beckwith's Klan meetings spurred their sex life. As long as she ignored the concrete signs of his activities—the smell of gunpowder or the need to burn his clothes—she could stay with him without feeling she had to judge his choices. In making that argument, however, she makes her own choice: staying with a violent white supremacist is a sign that she tacitly agreed with his views. Beckwith's violent nature emerged in the brutality in their relationship, from physical to psychological violence, exposed in her dreams of being lynched or chained. Still, she stayed, a choice she underscores in "Stand by Your Man," quoting Tammy Wynette's song, which flouted the emerging feminist principles. This song, number one on the US country charts for three weeks in 1968, encourages women to forgive their man, although he's hard to understand, a sentiment that inanely describes their troubled twenty-year marriage.[51]

Still, as mentioned earlier, Willie's adherence to the segregationist system falters as the volume progresses. A poem in which Beckwith decries race mixing follows directly after Willie describes the many unpunished and unchallenged white men who raped Black women, and men as well, a crime rarely pursued until the later twentieth century.[52] She says, "thus began / our great tradition / of not knowing and not wanting to know," the choice on the part of white women who looked away from the crimes their men committed but took no action to stop them. As well as acknowledging that some white men were sexual predators, Willie acknowledges that the segregationist system is failing economically. In "Harriet Tubman as Villain: A Ghost Story," she verbalizes the Southern fears associated with the Great Migration, that the Black laborers would entirely leave the South, leading to the decimation of the Southern economy. In her poem, the white farmer and his wife freeze to death in the field trying to pick the cotton upon which their finances depend, an admission that white people are reliant on Black labor but one that stops far short of advocating better conditions for workers. Then, in "Epiphany," she confesses that even while she feels no kinship with Blacks, she realizes that poor whites have been used by the white elite: "we were too dumb to know / we were just their rugs." In her life, Willie was an alcoholic and physically abused by Beckwith (as established by Reed Massengill), and when she finally divorced him for the third time, she lost their son to Beckwith's supremacist community. Her progress, if indeed it is that, is meandering, but she does begin to recognize the institution of white supremacy that Walker is intent on exposing. This final poem in which Willie speaks is an unrhymed sonnet, the most complicated poetic form Walker offers to any of the Beckwiths.[53] The consistency of their voices in repetitive couplets and tercets indicates a lack of imagination and an inability to move beyond the ingrained patterns of thought that offer them a modicum of power.

By the volume's end, Walker offers a step toward truth and reconciliation. Over the years since Medgar's assassination, Myrlie finds peace and progress in racial relations in her life. Beckwith, on the other hand, is shocked by the verdict in his 1994 trial, by a South that had progressed from producing lynching postcards to the "Judases / that helped find me guilty / the third time" in "What They Call Irony." Still, he refuses to budge, insisting on the sanctity of the racist right. He imagines that he is now the victim instead of a justly convicted murderer, that he is now the one being lynched by the unrecognizable South in which he finds himself. Willie inches toward realizing truths about the South, understanding at last that racism isolates groups of the working class, denying them the power of numbers in dealing with the wealthy who exploit all of them, but Thelma remains just as entrenched in her white supremacist beliefs as Beckwith. The Greek chorus has the final poem in the volume, and it entreats Mississippi to remember the past, to remember "the entire weight of history / and southern guilt" and to "move, in any direction, as long as it is forward." This poem, titled "Heavy Wait," offers both a lament for the past and optimism for the future, a future dependent on a clear-eyed historical understanding of the world in which a person like Medgar Evers lived and died.[54]

Walker's *Turn Me Loose* focuses on the web of voices that surround Evers, the people and historical forces that create the United States in which he lived. It not only brings Medgar into the contemporary discussions of the civil rights movement but also introduces Myrlie as a significant voice for the movement. Walker's carefully structured volume balances hope for the future with the underlying concern about resurgent white supremacy, and it painstakingly exposes the system that makes a Beckwith not just possible but probable. The volume ends with a timeline, much of which is a litany of the dead from Emmett Till, Denise McNair, Cynthia Wesley, Carole Robertson, Addie Mae Collins, John F. Kennedy, James Chaney, Andrew Goodman, Michael Schwerner, Malcolm X, Martin Luther King Jr., Robert F. Kennedy, and Fred Hampton to James Byrd Jr., James Anderson, and Trayvon Martin. Myrlie is able to offer forgiveness as her faith is restored, but forgiveness is only offered to those who ask for it.[55] And asking for forgiveness requires repentance, as Walker's volume asks its readers to come forth, face their country's truth, and move into a better future.

Chapter 7

✦

Excavating Captive Lives

Camille T. Dungy's *Suck on the Marrow*

"When I am writing, it is always about history. What else could I be writing about? History is the synthesis of our lives," declares Camille T. Dungy.[1] As a writer in the historical poem genre, Dungy's development as a poet is deeply interwoven with the other writers covered in this study. She has described Elizabeth Alexander's *The Black Interior* (2004), as well as Terrance Hayes's *Muscular Music* (1999), as formative books in her development as a poet, and she recalled Natasha Trethewey's pleasure at signing her well-worn copy of *Domestic Work*, a book that spoke directly to her and allowed her to envision her future poetic project clearly.[2] A fellow at Cave Canem in 2001, 2002, and 2004; a finalist for the Cave Canem poetry prize in 2000, 2001, and 2002; and an editor on the anthology celebrating Cave Canem's first decade, *Gathering Ground*, Dungy's entrance into the poetry world mirrors that of the other poets covered here. Her work as an editor means she is simultaneously participating in the poetry circles and creating them. As one of the two cofounders, Dungy supported emerging poets through From the Fishouse, a website that features largely new poets through audio recordings, capturing the oral tradition of poetry, as well as in its anthology by the same name, and she edited *Black Nature: Four Centuries of African American Nature Poetry*, which includes poems by ninety-three poets from across the centuries, including Alexander, Trethewey, and Walker. From Alexander's *The Venus Hottentot* in 1990 to Dungy's 2006 first book of poetry *What to Eat, What to Drink, What to Leave for Poison* is a mere sixteen years for two poets only ten years apart in age, what will eventually be viewed as less than half the span of a literary generation.

Like the other poets addressed in this study, Dungy is deeply invested in history, and she describes her poetic goals as exploring who we are now, how we got here, and who we are becoming,[3] links that draw the past into direct conversation with the present and the future. In a 2005 interview with Rita Dove, one of her poetic influences, Dungy described Dove's work in terms that can be applied to her own. She said, "I see in your work several different approaches to history. There's history from an official sense—this is the story that happened, let me reinvestigate the story. There's the personal history. . . . And there's the speculative history. . . . You reimagine what might have been the story of that story, or the story behind the story."[4] In Dungy's 2010 book of historical poetry *Suck on the Marrow*, these three goals govern the story: to tell the official history told by historians and archives, to incorporate her personal exploration of the historical materials and sites, and to create a speculative history, what she makes of these materials to tell a story that re-creates the past and echoes into the future.

Unlike many historians writing before the 1970s, about whose biases John W. Blassingame notes that "although [they] examin[ed] practically all kinds of accounts written by white eyewitnesses, they have largely rejected those written by former slaves,"[5] Dungy, born in 1972 into the emerging wealth of primary materials written by African Americans, plumbs those materials to create both convincing personas who resist the institution of slavery and a verisimilitude of antebellum life from the point of view of enslaved people. The volume's emphasis is on the Black community, both enslaved and free, and it is their voices that control the poems, confiding their fears, but also living beyond the concerns of the enslavers in an intact and even joyful community. The poems address issues of particular relevance to the two decades covered—the kidnapping of free Blacks, the Free Black community, sexual oppression, and the journey to freedom—all the while emphasizing African American agency in the antebellum years.

Dungy incorporates, first, official history, history as written by the historians. However, she deftly avoids the trap of accepting the traditional narratives by focusing on comparatively unknown history and positioning the poems in *Suck on the Marrow* in the years between 1831 and 1850, after the end of the international slave trade in 1808 and before the passing of the Fugitive Slave Law, the event that anchors many explorations of the institution of slavery, like Toni Morrison's *Beloved*. Dungy, instead, focuses on the two decades preceding that law, years in which states, hungry for enslaved labor, had to rely on the birthrates of enslaved people already in the United States, illegal importation of captive Africans, or enslaving free Blacks. To prepare to tell stories about that era, Dungy completed four to five years of research in North Carolina, Georgia, Virginia, and Pennsylvania, visiting archives and historic sites.[6] In a conversation with poet Adrian Matejka, she testified to the expansiveness of her research and its accuracy: "I visited plantations; I crawled through Underground Railroad hideouts; I held abolitionist newspapers in my own hands; and I took a book's worth of notes (a much thicker book than the book I ended up writing)." Dungy stresses that her book is "deeply accountable to facts," which extend to the physical place of Philadelphia and the visual representation of Virginia. She explains, "I found a map of Philadelphia from the time when Joseph Freeman was kidnapped. I also found a Green Book, which was a sort of White Pages/

register of black people in a community, and which listed people's names and occupations and addresses. So I found the street on which my fictional character would have lived, and I walked on that street with my real nonfictional feet, and I had it in my mind as I drafted my poems." The photograph that graces her book's cover comes from central Virginia, similar to the plantation her character Joseph could have lived on after being enslaved, and it visually resonates both back to his world and forward to the contemporary Virginia that Dungy knows.[7]

The second historical category is a personal exploration of historical materials and sites, and Dungy has published many essays connecting her own life to that of her ancestors by, in one instance, visiting the historic sites in Ghana like Cape Coast Castle, where Africans were held during the slave trade. In "A Brief History of Near and Actual Losses," she connects the loss of people during the slave trade, especially the mothers who lost children, to her own experience of almost losing her two-year-old daughter to a wave on Ghana's unpredictable coast. She weaves together the history of the Underground Railroad and the Civil War in Maine with the discomfort of her visiting Maine, where many white people had never met a Black person and so behaved with invasive curiosity in "A Shade North of Ordinary." For Dungy, the past constantly echoes into her present, into her relationship with her neighbors and her country, and, in a third example, into the church she decided to stop attending when the minister prayed for "those who are on the outside of our society looking in," displaying a blindness that people in "those" categories, like Dungy, were already in the congregation, already an integral part of the nation, their past part of the national past.[8] Additionally, Dungy has deep ties to Virginia: her mother was born in Lynchburg and lived there for the first ten years of her life; her grandfather was professionally born there, a pastor at Court Street Baptist Church in Lynchburg and a professor at a local seminary; and Dungy herself lived in Virginia for seven years.[9] If, as Dungy writes, "history is the synthesis of our lives," then history is immensely personal, the past creating our present. Her poems take place in the Virginia she knew and Philadelphia, just across the Mason-Dixon line and, for her while writing *Suck on the Marrow*, an affordable drive. She is always aware of what has transpired before she arrives in a place, and her essays trace the lines of influence from the past to now. Thus, the past is within grasp of the present, not lost to time, but offering echoes that can be located and reimagined.

The third category is "speculative history," by which Dungy meant speculative in the sense established by Octavia Butler's *Kindred* or Margaret Atwood's *The Handmaid's Tale*.[10] Atwood defines speculative fiction:

> If you're writing about the future and you aren't doing forecast journalism, you'll probably be writing something people will call either science fiction or speculative fiction. I like to make a distinction

> between science fiction proper and speculative fiction. For me, the science fiction label belongs on books with things in them that we can't yet do, such as going through a wormhole in space to another universe; and speculative fiction means a work that employs the means already to hand, such as DNA identification and credit cards, and that takes place on Planet Earth. But the terms are fluid. Some use speculative fiction as an umbrella covering science fiction and all its hyphenated forms—science fiction, fantasy, and so forth—and others choose the reverse.[11]

While Atwood's dystopia looks to an alternative future where the democracy of the United States has been replaced by the totalitarian Republic of Gilead, an eerily familiar government particularly intent on controlling women and their bodies, Butler's time-traveling neo-slave narrative dwells in the real past of the United States from 1815 to 1831, corresponding to the time frame chosen by Dungy. Butler's *Kindred*, with its title referencing familial relationships that stretch from past generations to the present, addresses the institution of slavery during the time when immense profits were made by focusing on women who could bear children often, the sale of those children, and enslaving free Blacks. The novel opens in 1976, tellingly the year of the United States' bicentennial, when Dana, a Black woman, is pulled into the past to ensure the survival of her white ancestor and thereby her family's line. Besides addressing issues facing enslaved people—beatings, rapes, brutal working conditions, and murder—Butler considers how white people became, on the one hand, conductors on the Underground Railroad, like Dana's white husband Kevin, who accidentally accompanies her into the past, or, on the other hand, brutal enslavers like her ancestor Rufus. Through Dana and Rufus, Butler explores how "slavery of any kind fostered strange relationships,"[12] just as she considers power and intimacy in much of her writing. Like Butler, Dungy writes stories about things that happened somewhere, viable truths that can be historically verified, and like Atwood, her writing "employs the means already to hand"—national history—and "takes place on Planet Earth." In *Suck on the Marrow*, Dungy speculates on lives that could have been lived, and she creates individual personas who speak for the people who lived very similar lives, much like the personas created by Trethewey. As she said to Dove, Dungy reimagines "what might have been the story of that story, or the story behind the story,"[13] the story enslaved people and their early descendants were unable to tell, art transforming emotion into something permanent, shareable, transformative, and manageable.

Dungy describes *Suck on the Marrow* as a novel in verse, a story that ended up being more suited to poetic form than an extended narrative.[14] Her volume focuses on locations in Virginia and Pennsylvania, places important because of their proximity to the border between freedom and enslavement, particularly before 1850. Free Blacks in Philadelphia were vulnerable to the kidnappers looking to drag African Americans south into enslavement, and Virginia, while a substantial distance from the free North, was not the Deep South. Personas narrate much of the volume, which is organized around the stories of individual characters: Joseph Freeman, a free Black man living in Philadelphia who is kidnapped and enslaved; Molly, an enslaved woman who lives on the Jackson Farm in Virginia where Joseph now lives; Rebecca and Dinah, enslaved people who run to quite different forms of freedom; and Melinda, Joseph's wife in Philadelphia who mourns his absence and eventually remarries. The volume ends with a found poem incorporating a wide range of voices and an abecedary cleverly offering information generally found in a notes section. Throughout, time refuses a chronological march forward, instead existing independently within each speaker's section. Thus, Joseph's first section begins in 1831 as he is kidnapped and ends seventeen years later, after Melinda has reluctantly remarried; Molly's voice speaks for only two years; Rebecca and Dinah run in 1842, one ending up as a sex worker in the South and the other in Philadelphia where she meets Melinda; and Melinda's section begins with the loss of her husband, wanders through her grief, and concludes with a new marriage and thoughts of Joseph on his thirty-second birthday. These disparate sections overlap, intersect, and engage each other, and the reader is given the impression that the lives are being lived simultaneously, as, in fact, they are. They offer a complex reconstruction of two decades told through personas, who bear well Dungy's caveat that "any resemblance to real people or events is not the least bit coincidental."[15]

The settings of the poems, Virginia and Philadelphia, physically mark a liminal space, which figuratively becomes representative of the constantly shifting tension between freedom and enslavement in the United States. In *The Philadelphia Negro*, W. E. B. Du Bois wrote: "Philadelphia was the natural gateway between the North and South, and for a long time there passed through it a stream of free Negroes and fugitive slaves toward the North, and of recaptured Negroes and kidnapped colored persons toward the South."[16] Similarly, Virginia, while not bordering Pennsylvania—which did border three states where enslaving people was legal—was part of what was known as the Upper South, closer to the line demarcating the ostensible transition from slavery to freedom, a far cry from the Deep South. Both places are on distinct sides of the Mason-Dixon line, but since they are so close to that demarcation that decides one's life, they highlight the constructed sense of freedom—how can a person be free by stepping over an often invisible boundary or enslaved by being dragged back across it? As a binary, then, freedom and enslavement are opposites that exist uncomfortably close and define each other. This line, even before the 1850 Fugitive Slave Act, was constantly crossed by figures like Dungy's "Trapper," who looks for free Blacks who assume their freedom is a constant, something that is real and solid; this surety, in his eyes, makes them vulnerable.[17] The kidnapping of people clearly demonstrates the permeability of this line, since Joseph, a man who has not had an enslaved person in his family since 1773, finds himself suddenly enslaved on a Virginia plantation. He is betrayed by a false certainty of freedom in a country in which the issue of who can be enslaved shifts constantly, especially throughout the nineteenth century, as tensions rise and laws tighten. Freedom and enslavement are, then, separated by a permeable border, often crossed, in a country in which the federal and state governments kept relegislating the space in which a person shifts from free to enslaved and sometimes back again. This indeterminacy over what freedom means is a constant tension in the early to mid-nineteenth-century United States.

Dungy's tale begins in Philadelphia since Joseph lives there until he is kidnapped in 1831. According to historian Julie Winch, the Free Black population in Pennsylvania was 30,202 in 1820,[18] and the large free population combined with the proximity to slave states meant that most of the nation's kidnappings took place in Pennsylvania, Maryland, and Delaware.[19] Eric Foner also comments on the prevalence of kidnapping: "Philadelphia, less than two dozen miles from the border with slavery, witnessed frequent abductions. An investigation in 1826 revealed the existence of an interracial gang based in Delaware that had lured nearly fifty black men, women, and children onto ships in Philadelphia and transported them to be sold in the South. As late as 1844, the abolitionist weekly *Pennsylvania Freeman*, in an article entitled 'Kidnappers,' complained, 'Our state is infested with them.' " African Americans who were kidnapped had few ways to establish their identities as free people. White kidnappers could match them to an ad for an escaped enslaved person of similar appearance, they could "obtain certificates of removal from unscrupulous public officials," or they could simply take their victims with few fears of being questioned.[20] Joseph is matched to a description of a man named William, which becomes Joseph's new name, when he is transported from Wilmington, Delaware, less than forty miles from Philadelphia, to Richmond, Virginia, and then further inland. In 1806, to offer one of the most famous examples, the prominent Philadelphian leader Richard Allen, who established the African Methodist Episcopal Church, was kidnapped by a white man intent on taking him south under the guise of capturing a self-emancipated person. Because Allen was so very well-known, he prevailed in establishing his identity as a free man, but the attempt to kidnap even a person of his stature underscores the vulnerability of less-renowned free people. Kidnapping, in Pennsylvania, was illegal, but it was a crime difficult to prosecute because most of these crimes involved crossing state lines, no national anti-kidnapping statute existed, and African Americans were not allowed to testify against European Americans in court in many states. Groups like the Pennsylvania Abolition Society, which helped Allen, worked to free kidnapped people, but their resources were limited and the profits for kidnapping substantial. Historian Carol Wilson points out that "the toleration of kidnapping was a way for whites to enslave free blacks without admitting that they were doing so."[21] Moreover, the constant threat of kidnapping kept free Blacks, and their possessions, vulnerable. One's identity as a free person, then, was always in question and hard to prove; it was itself a liminal and precarious space.

Joseph's rich life as a free person is established in the poem "You are not the one Melinda sings her underbreath song to please," a sequence of three sonnets. His life revolved around his family, his wife, his church, and his status as a free person, underscored by his surname "Freeman." His bass singing voice would ring out during the service's hymns, and he sat in church surrounded by a brother, parents, an uncle, old friends, and the community. The pew itself shaped its wood, in a seat he had used for years, to hold him securely in that space. At home, Joseph and Melinda lived in two generous rooms, and they talked to each other of desire, love, and hope for the future.[22] Dungy describes "fudging the form" in the volume and calls these poems "rogue sonnets."[23] Unrhymed and more syllabic than metrical, these are sonnets of improvisational form, a choice that fits the life they describe, one that fits a prescribed, and taken-for-granted, form only so far and then loses its strict form when Joseph is kidnapped and forced into an unexpected life as an enslaved person. The lineation and spacing in each sonnet draw attention to the volta, and each sonnet's concluding sestet reinforces what Joseph has lost: he is not the one who can now hear Melinda's new song, he can still desire but no longer touch Melinda, and instead of singing, now he stays silent to avoid pain.[24] Still, while decrying his personal tragedy, Joseph's Philadelphia community emerges as strong and intact, a community of tight bonds and rising song, one of familial love and devout lives.

In comparison with his life as a free person are the horrors of Joseph's new life as an enslaved person, told in the epistolary sequence "From the Unwritten Letters of Joseph Freeman," thoughts Joseph would like to confide to his wife but cannot in an existence that turns his mind from hopes of communication and escape to simply survival. These lyric letters date from 1841 to 1848 and draw a picture of life on the plantation: brutal whippings over minor infractions, a lack of food, stealing to survive, crowded living quarters, and the use of women's bodies to produce more enslaved people and to nurse white babies. A group of enslaved people more recently arrived than Joseph runs away, a few of them successfully escaping, one girl wounded and recaptured, and a boy, Ben, who dies in the escape. Doctor Jackson, the enslaver, displays Ben's body as a warning to the other enslaved people, and eventually the doctor gruesomely reassembles Ben's bones in his study, a testament to his medical knowledge and the irony of a supposed healer being so brutal. He punishes any encroachment on his possessions decisively, and Joseph concludes that "A man / whose livelihood depends on stealing / the toil of other people's bodies / must keep a keen eye on his own / most dear and precious things." Throughout these horrors, however, Joseph thinks of his wife and his son Jacob, whom he imagines growing into the man he himself was. Joseph worries about whether Melinda can pay their rent and what her life is like now. He confesses in an uncharacteristically simple clause that "I am frightened," but part of his mind remains Joseph Freeman, a free man who lives in Philadelphia with his beloved family, signing these letters with variations on "ever your beloved husband."[25] The poem "Survival" implies that Joseph dies in bondage, never to return to his family, like Solomon Northup, the famous author of the 1853 slave narrative *Twelve Years a Slave* and subject of the 2013 Hollywood film of the same name, did. Dungy explains that she wrote "From the Unwritten Letters of Joseph Freeman" before becoming aware of Northup. Serendipitously, she penned this poem at the artists retreat Yaddo in Saratoga Springs, New York, the town where Northup and his family lived: "I've always marveled about that synchronicity, or the haunting, or the visitation or whatever you will call it that allowed me to write my poem in the same town where a famous and similar incident happened, even when I didn't yet know about the incident."[26]

Like the liminal places of Philadelphia and Virginia, the concept of a free Black was a contested identity throughout the antebellum United States, despite the long existence of free communities of color. Free Blacks fit neither of the dominant communities, enslaved or white, and so they made white Americans uncomfortable and threatened the system of racial hierarchy being constantly reinforced, as when states began passing a variety of laws restricting the rights of free Blacks. To offer only a few examples, in 1836 Texas forbid free Blacks from entering the territory, in 1837 free Blacks lost the right to vote in Pennsylvania, Georgia (1842) and North Carolina (1844) denied citizenship to free Blacks, and in 1844 Oregon Country passed the notorious "Peter Burnett Lash Law," which required that all African Americans, free and enslaved, leave the territory. Still, the free Black community in Philadelphia wielded power in influence and sheer numbers. In 1820, Philadelphia boasted the largest free Black population, only surpassed in 1850 by Baltimore, with New York following in third place.[27] Historian Erica Armstrong Dunbar explains that in Pennsylvania "slavery began to draw to a close in 1780 with the enactment of the Gradual Abolition Act, which initiated the process of formal emancipation in Pennsylvania." Over the next half century, slavery slowly ended in Pennsylvania leaving, in 1830, only eleven enslaved people in Philadelphia. By the 1840s, slavery and indentured servitude were eliminated, and instead in Philadelphia lived "a free black community supported by autonomous religious and mutual aid organizations that were sustained by a mature leadership."[28] Gary B. Nash also emphasizes the many achievements realized in Philadelphia: the first organized protest against returning Blacks to Africa, the first independent Black religious denomination (African Methodist Episcopal Church), and the first meeting of the National Negro Convention Movement, as well as the many Black Philadelphians who became prominent in politics, education, literature, history, and journalism.[29]

Through Melinda, and her grief over losing Joseph, *Suck on the Marrow* offers a window into Philadelphia's Free Black community. Economically, the community was diverse. Well-off people had houses on the main thoroughfares, but they lived side-by-side with the working class and the poor. Melinda and Joseph lived on an alley in a home of two rooms, a common housing arrangement. As a bricklayer, Joseph's skills would have been in demand as Philadelphia grew quickly, but he would also be competing for jobs with whites who sought to bar African Americans from many professions and trades. When Joseph was kidnapped, their son was only a toddler, and Melinda supports Jacob for the next thirteen years as a single parent. She works as a servant for the Cartwright family, who do not own people but participate in the institution of slavery because Mr. Cartwright makes his money in textiles, an industry reliant upon the labor of enslaved people. In the poem "Complicit," Melinda describes her uncomfortable position: she needs the income, but her employers implicitly support the institution that stole her husband. Not only do the Cartwrights benefit from textiles, but they also consume other goods produced by enslaved people's labor in simple acts like serving cakes to their friends. Melinda, who now refuses to use goods produced by the labor of enslaved people, namely, sugar, cotton, rice, coffee, and tea, notes that "the production of sugar for a family of five requires several months' *labor* / from one slave." During the summer, Melinda insisted on wearing wool rather than cotton even in the stifling heat until a free labor store selling cotton opened in Philadelphia. In this golden shovel poem—a form that merges the fight against slavery into each line describing Melinda's working days—the italicized words running down the right margin form an advertisement when read alone, indicating that "the free goods and labor store" has opened and offers "cotton cultivated by well remunerated labor," rather than the labor of enslaved people.[30] Dungy comments on the intertextuality of her poems:

> I used actual documents (advertisements, newspaper articles, marginalia written by living human beings), and enfolded them into my fabricated world. That was part of the process of crafting this book. I thought a lot about what I called hidden texts—those coded messages that some people know how to read and which are invisible to other people. Some of my borrowed text was planted in a way that was completely independent from the rest of the poem, and some of the text was inextricable from the language of the rest of the poem. I believe this is the way society works. Sometimes you can take the black body/text out of the white world and the white world will keep going; sometimes, without the black body/text, the white world would collapse.[31]

In "Complicit," if the words of the ad for a free store were removed, the poem's meaning would be lost, lines would be oddly incomplete, textually marking the interdependence of the Black and white worlds, as well as the complicit nature of lives lived in the United States. Melinda protests the institution of slavery by reducing her diet to vegetables, legumes, and fruit, none produced by enslaved laborers, but she needs the wages paid by the Cartwrights. The Cartwrights, on the other hand, are fully complicit in that institution as well as oppressing free Blacks.

The Cartwrights' friends recommend sending free Blacks back to Africa, the scheme of the American Colonization Society (ACS). The ACS paternalistically argued that a return to Africa was best for free Blacks, whose lives were so circumscribed in the United States, and "white colonists wanted blacks to be removed from the country, voluntarily or against their will. Racism was central to white colonization ideology; it was hostile at best."[32] Mrs. Cartwright "looks to Rev. Finney to learn which acts will prove her faith," a reference to Robert Finley, a Presbyterian minister who helped establish the ACS, even while she is loath to lose her household help like Melinda.[33] By trying to have it both ways, appear faithful to Finley and her friends as well as keep her household servants and her family's income, Mrs. Cartwright inadvertently highlights the importance of African Americans to Philadelphia and the nation. While many white people sought to eliminate the presence of free Blacks, they were simultaneously heavily reliant on Black labor, enslaved and free. The ACS's goal was to help free Blacks emigrate to West Africa, primarily Liberia, and some people did indeed go, like John Jenkins Roberts, a businessperson who became Liberia's first president.[34] However, most free Blacks opposed the scheme and understood that the ACS presented a very real threat. In 1817, nearly three thousand African Americans rejected this proposal, joining together in protest at Mother Bethel Church, a significant moment in Black resistance.[35]

Although Melinda has to spend her days working for the Cartwrights, her nights are spent with her family and organizations like the Vigilant Committee of Philadelphia—opportunities for love and rebellion. Jacob is growing up, and while she laments that Joseph is missing these changes, she notices that Jacob's "thighs are growing the same tensed muscles / that flexed his father's." She waits for Joseph but eventually recognizes she cannot expect him to return and, after thirteen years alone, marries Richard, a good man, a man of "flesh that answers questions, / each limb real as furniture," who provides them with a home and teaches Jacob a trade. Melinda attends meetings with the Vigilant Committee, a secret committee in existence from 1837 to 1852. It raised money and resources to help runaways and kidnapped victims, endeavors both expensive and illegal. Melinda comments that "The Committee calculates / it has aided nearly two hundred men through Philadelphia / and on to Canada this year," even though the need is much greater.[36] For her part, she and Richard participate in the Underground Railroad, housing freedom seekers in their home, risks the Free Black community regularly took.[37] Choosing to harbor freedom seekers and attend meetings planning illegal actions presents a tangible threat to her family; breaking laws was an excuse used to enslave free Blacks, but she does it for Joseph: “Lord bless his body / if he lives.”[38]

In the midst of risk and hardship, Melinda still has time for joy. In “Observation on the Return of Migratory Birds,” Melinda records when each species returns after the winter: the blue jay on March 1, pigeons and robins before her birthday, chickadees at the end of April, information Dungy found in handwritten notes in an almanac from the 1830s.[39] In this poem alternating tercets with one-line stanzas, Melinda celebrates the natural world, whose rhythms are part of her own world. She takes time to notice the birds that fly down her alley and sing from nearby rooftops, creatures who have so much freedom and yet are tied to the seasons. In the following poem, “Unravel and Weave,” Melinda ponders who she is now since she is no longer her young self and no longer Joseph’s wife because of his long absence. While she considers taking Richard’s last name, she longs to be herself, “just Melinda,” who is, at that moment, literally waiting to cross the road, a symbol for the moment of her life, a crossroads at which she will finally give up on Joseph and move forward with Richard. Just as she waits every year for the birds’ return, she has waited for Joseph, hoping against hope that he will return from his forced southern migration, but he does not return with the birds. Still, Melinda makes choices and finds joy in the world around her: “When these flitters return / to my block of the black ward one morning and stay / on into the evening, always, I notice, I smile.”[40] With all the injustices in her life, Melinda has a son she loves, and she celebrates the natural world.

Juxtaposed to Melinda’s life are the enslaved lives of Dinah and Rebecca, who, along with many men, are subjected to sexual oppression. Molly tells the beginning of Dinah’s story when she comments on Dinah’s mother, Lena, in the contrapuntal poem “Code.” Molly’s words, on the left, join the text of an ad italicized on the right that offers enslaved people for sale, people who are likely herself and her husband, Shad. While Molly believes she thoroughly understands the farm she works on and criticizes Lena for not understanding her position and the power of Miss Amy Jackson, she herself does not realize that the Jacksons are planning to sell her, “*the female . . . not to be surpassed as a cook, . . . washer, . . . and ironer too*,” and Shad. She comments that Doctor Jackson “roll ’round the ’taters with a *servant* / girl name of Lena.” Lena’s story is then picked up in Dinah’s section in “Conditions of the Sale,” which offers the information that Lena produced three boys, who were sold, as well as Dinah, who is allowed to stay with her, but during her fifth pregnancy, she lost the baby and became infertile, now “useless / to Jackson but all the more subject to Miss Amy.”[41] For some unexplained and mysterious transgression, Doctor Jackson ordered her death in a particularly gruesome way, as Dungy described in an interview: “At one point there is a story (borrowed from a placard I read at a museum) of a woman who was killed when she was rolled down a hill while shoved in a whiskey barrel with ‘nails jutting through the cord,’ ” an incident she called the “documentation of the most vile parts of our history."[42] Following her death, Jackson is haunted by Lena's ghost, a ghost who becomes corporeal in her daughter Dinah, "her skin looking delicious / as morning cream, or while she was bent to sweep the floor in Jackson's rooms."[43] His wife sells Dinah away before Jackson can replace Lena with her—his own daughter—and Dinah finds herself sold to a lawyer named Jennings who repeatedly rapes her, just as Jackson had done to her mother.

Another form of sexual slavery addressed in Dungy's poems is bringing in a man chosen for his virility and strength to sleep with many of the women enslaved on the plantation in an attempt to produce physically superior children. In "Born on This Place," Molly comments that "my father was the stud who worked this farm one week, / a wedding gift from the Missus' father to his newest son. / Twelve children born on this place in March of '33."[44] Once the international slave trade ended in 1808, enslavers were dependent upon US birthrates to produce the labor force they wanted to use, so to increase their wealth, they became focused on women's reproductive possibilities, which they tried to control and exploit. According to historian Marie Jenkins Schwartz, some demanded to approve marriages with an eye to the children the marriage would produce, while others would bring to their plantation men with the physical characteristics they hoped would be passed on and require that enslaved women have sex with them. Because the gynecological profession was in its infancy as white male medical doctors took the place of midwives and so little was understood about the reproductive cycle, these pairings did not always produce pregnancies, and enslavers took the step of contracting with local doctors to attempt to increase the number of children born on their plantations. These doctors were serving the enslavers' interests rather than the lives of the enslaved people and often caused harm through their ignorance and greed.[45] In *The American Slave Coast*, Ned and Constance Sublette emphasize that the primary supplier of enslaved people after 1808 was Virginia, where the Jackson farm was located.[46] Because so much of the South's wealth was located in people's physical bodies, increasing those bodies took precedence during this period. Moreover, the financial gain was dependent upon selling people, which resulted in the dissolution of more families.

"Lesson" is a winged poem about yet another form of sexual slavery, the tradition of using enslaved women as wet nurses for white people's babies. On the left side of the page is the column beginning "the child of the breast gets," a line opposed to, on the right side, "*the child of the womb*," setting up the conflict between the white child who nurses from the enslaved woman and the Black woman's own child who nurses only afterward. The two columns or "wings" of the poem are uneven, the spacing in lines is awkward, not all of the lines match up horizontally—all of which combines to create a discordant tone. The woman's own child "*eats . . . scraps*," while the white child gets "the best milk and claims the labor . . . of working hours."[47] The act of forcing a woman to be a wet nurse is naturalized by the very term "wet nurse," for how can being a nurse, a person whose profession is helping other people, be a negative? Better phrasing would consider the act to be theft, the stealing of milk as described by *Beloved*'s Sethe, who is "nursed" by schoolteacher's two nephews, a type of rape that takes the only tangible thing she can offer her children, milk and through that life and a future. Thus, the white child is stealing the stuff of life from the biological child. Dungy points out that the uneven construction of the poem is meant to underscore the uneven positions of the two children,[48] the poem's very shape and language imitating the discord between the enslaved and free people. And it is in this poem where the volume's title is located: hope is reserved for the white child who "*sucks . . . the marrow*," a phrase echoing Henry David Thoreau's statement in *Walden* that he wanted "to live deep and suck out all the marrow of life,"[49] a claim written just a few years after the two decades covered by Dungy's book, by a man who championed the abolitionist movement, participated in the Underground Railroad, attacked the Fugitive Slave Law, and supported John Brown. Still, it is the white child in Dungy's poem who has the opportunity "to live deep," an injustice the poem protests.

While for many people like Joseph or Molly escape was impossible, Dungy's volume offers stories of enslaved people who successfully escape through Rebecca and Dinah. The poem "*and thou shalt be called a new name, / which the mouth of the Lord shall name*" interweaves lines from Isaiah 62, an Old Testament book about the salvation of Israel, with lines describing Rebecca's plan to escape enslavement, to reach her own salvation. Finding a dying buck, Rebecca uses the decomposing body to scent the clothes she will run away in, the stench masking her own smell from the tracking dogs. As she chooses a new life, she chooses the name Rebecca, this name replacing the name given to her by enslavers.[50] The poem loosely cites verses 1–4 of Isaiah 62 but leaves out the second half of verse 4, which mentions the name Hephzibah, the name Jennings uses for the continuous string of enslaved women who work in his kitchen, introducing the possibility that Rebecca, like Dinah, is running from Jennings and sexual slavery. Rebecca's journey, however, takes her to a safer place in the South rather than ending in the North. Significantly, Rebecca is unaided by white abolitionists but is taken in by Madame Jane—probably Jane Hawkins—an African American brothel owner in the Buzzard's Roost neighborhood of Lynchburg, Virginia. In their study *Free Blacks of Lynchburg, Virginia 1805–1865*, Ted Delaney and Phillip Wayne Rhodes offer information about this community of free Blacks living in a slave state. They establish that "although free blacks comprised only a small portion of Lynchburg's population, they were among the wealthiest and most highly skilled residents of the city. Free people of color provided essential services that supported and benefited the entire community." The self-emancipated could blend into this community easily because of its dense housing and the busy traffic on the river it faced.[51]

Rebecca's choice to run into the heart of Lynchburg rather than heading further north feels antithetical, but sex work offered a form of freedom. Dungy explains that brothel owners "had a level of power and access in the city that was unrivaled by others—because of the clients they served and the manner in which they served them. I found it fascinating that these women would wield that much power and wealth, in a public way, given their occupations."[52] Delaney and Rhodes explain that the 1860 census documents that sex workers made up 7 percent of the free Black population, and four of the twelve wealthiest free Blacks were in the trade. They write that "free women of color appear in the earliest records of local 'houses of ill fame.' . . . Prostitution was the single most lucrative occupation per capita for free blacks (male or female) in antebellum Lynchburg. The wealthiest black woman in Lynchburg in 1860, and the second wealthiest free person of color, was Jane Hawkins, a thirty-three year old woman of 'ill fame' residing in Buzzard Roost."[53] Dungy's Rebecca can escape the institution of slavery by entering into sex work since her former owner cannot afford to let it be known that he frequents the brothels. As sex work has always been visible and yet invisible, Rebecca cloaks herself with it.

"At Madame Jane's" is a three-part poem in which the persona of Jane explains the realities of life in her brothel. Like the real Jane Hawkins, Madame Jane wields power in her community: her house is expensive, and she decides who is allowed inside the doors, controlling the physical space of the house, which manages to sit outside the usual confines of enslaved and free communities. The women who work for her are given much better living conditions than enslaved people: they get a room, have a bed, are allowed plenty of food, and have access to a doctor's care. To obtain even this form of freedom though, Rebecca has to jettison her dream of claiming her own name because Jane cannot afford to harbor a person marked by her previous identity in any way. Instead, Rebecca has to shape herself to fit the fantasies of the brothel's clients who will pay a week's wages to have their wishes fulfilled. Jane points out that the fulfillment of sexual desire is what Rebecca has been doing as an enslaved person and could be forced to do again:

> There's an auction outside the Congress Hotel this evening
> remember
> you been naked all your life
> good for little more than breeding dirty dreams
>
> I say it's time you see that profit
> And that power

The women who work in her house fulfill scatological fetishes, fetishes of necrophilia and incest, sadomasochistic fantasies, anatomical explorations, the many desires for the forbidden. The clients, Jane says, "pay for promise in my house." Working there, Rebecca is "nobody and everybody," but, as Jane points out, this job offers an element of power and choice. Jane tells her, "Work for me a year you'll have money for a trunk of dresses / and a steamer ticket out of here / if you believe there's anywhere to go." This life may simply be the first stop in Rebecca's journey out of the South, but Jane suggests that there may not be more power and profit to be had elsewhere.[54]

While the stories of enslaved people running north are most well-known, enslaved people escaped through a myriad of means. Dinah, like Rebecca, contemplates "how she might rid herself" of Jennings, determined to escape sexual bondage and enslavement in total. She chooses to mail herself to the North, her feat echoing the well-known case of Henry "Box" Brown. From Jennings's drunken ramblings, Dinah located a man willing to help her escape, and she accumulated the funds to pay for the box and the shipping cost. Shipped north, "Dinah spent twenty hours with her face by the breathing hole, her body curled / like a nursing child's, wondering what order of thanks she would offer the man / who opened her crate."[55] Escapes of this type were not always successful: the white people necessary to mail and receive the box could betray the person reliant upon their help, white people along the shipping route could discover the escaping person, and the conditions of being packed into a box for a somewhat undetermined amount of time were punitive. Brown decided to run after his wife and children were sold to a Methodist minister heading to North Carolina. Deprived of his family, he had no reason to remain enslaved in Richmond, Virginia, and developed a plan to ship himself north. Brown's hardships were probably shared by Dinah. He was packed tightly into as small a box as possible; he spent hours upside down, effectively standing on his head; the heat was stifling; he could not drink or eat; his box was thrown off a wagon in one instance; and he spent more than twenty-four hours in the box. Famous images memorialize the moment when the box was opened and Brown stepped out of it and into the living room of a northern abolitionist.[56] Brown became a speaker for the abolitionist cause and his story was made public. In an interview, Dungy clarifies that Brown was one of many enslaved people who escaped this way:

> "Dinah in the Box" was triggered by reading several accounts of women who freed themselves by packing themselves into boxes and having those boxes shipped to border states. We know the story of Henry Box Brown because that became a famous narrative, but the abolitionist newspapers had lots of accounts of women doing the same thing. In fact, I read more about women then about men. I wondered what would drive a woman to do this. I also wondered about why we don't hear these women's stories more often.[57]

In this poetry, then, Dungy ensures that women's stories are reinscribed into public memory through Dinah's daring escape.

The poem "*Runaway* Ran Away" commemorates Dinah's escape, its title reminiscent of Robert Hayden's "Runagate Runagate," which incorporates voices like the language of advertisements for freedom seekers, the voices of people running for freedom, and the wanted posters for Harriet Tubman. Dungy's poem likewise integrates the language of the archives through an ad for a "*Runaway*," italicizing this word to mark it as a direct quote. Dungy explained that she "used advertisements I found in proslavery newspapers. . . . These advertisements I enfolded into the poems written from the perspective of my black characters. In this way, I was able to give voice to the white slave-owning segment of the population, using their own words rather than my own."[58] According to the ad, Dinah is nineteen, illiterate, 5'3" with a birthmark on her face and a gap between her front teeth. This external language, that of an enslaver looking at his captive, is interwoven into the poem that illuminates much that he did not know about her. In the owner's view, he owned another person, which gave him the right to "store" her in his apartment for his use. In his view, the outside of her body, what he can see, is what is relevant, as is her illiteracy, which he regards as a lack of intelligence or the inability to negotiate the world beyond his property. Dinah never speaks in this poem, but the poem makes clear that her real self is not what her enslaver knew: "thought he knew her *well* / *when* she was in there with him." Instead, Dinah successfully escapes in an impressively complicated plan, leaving him and his ability to rape her far behind. In the volume's fourth section, Melinda meets Dinah, who is now living in Philadelphia.[59] Dinah's life as a free person is precarious because the risk of kidnapping looms, but at the volume's end she is still free and may head for Canada.

Throughout its four sections, *Suck on the Marrow* speculates on what might have been, writing the story behind the story, told in voices that could not speak during their time. They tell of terrible hardships through kidnapping, sexual oppression, and enslavement, but they also reveal a strong Free Black community, journeys to freedom, and joy. The United States in which they live from 1831 to 1850 is one in which freedom and slavery constantly shift, in meaning, in physical spaces, in the law. Nonetheless, they look toward the twenty-first century, a time when their stories can be told and their history can be part of the present, retold and reimagined. Dungy's poetry plumbs years of hardship and years of agency, emphasizing resistance and an intact community that endures to the present. Her past is constantly in conversation with the present, the two inextricably linked and reaching toward the future.

Conclusion

✦

The Historical Impulse, the Zeitgeist of a Generation

Looking forward, we see that the wave of historical poetry continues to surge. The contemporary Black historical poem is successfully writing African American history into public memory, in and beyond the academy. And writers keep joining, the earthquakes of contemporary events raising a tidal wave of historical poetry. Robin Coste Lewis's *Voyage of the Sable Venus and Other Poems* (2015) is ripe for exploration, with its verses of found poetry borrowing language from art about Black female figures from 18,000 BCE to the present; Tyehimba Jess recreates the life of blues musician Huddie William Ledbetter in *leadbelly* (2005) with exquisite attention to form; Amaud Jamaul Johnson writes about the violence of 1919 in *Red Summer* (2006), a subject Eve L. Ewing's *1919* (2019) addresses as well; Adrian Matejka's *The Big Smoke* (2014) also takes up the life of boxer Jack Johnson; Vievee Francis addresses the Mexican-American War in *Blue-Tail Fly* (2006); and such accomplished poets as Yona Harvey, Honorée Fanonne Jeffers, Douglas Kearney, Fred Moten, giovanni singleton, Lyrae Van Clief-Stefanon, and so many more are writing about history, revising the past and changing the present.

While many authors, like the six addressed in this study, dedicate extended sequences or entire volumes to a historical event or person, authors take a range of approaches. Major Jackson, for example, calls the use of history the zeitgeist of his generation, and he talks about himself as a poet who constantly uses history in his work but as appetizers rather than entrées.[1] "The Augustan Suite" of the section titled "XXV. Italy" in *Roll Deep* references the *Romanus Pontifex*, the 1454 papal bull that gave King Afonso V of Portugal the right to enslave Africans, and describes the role of Africans in the European artistic imagination, that of "the slave boy delivering clothes to a nude Pollux" on an amphora created by the artist Exekias in the black-figure technique, as well as the many paintings of an infant Christ who seemingly "craves the adoration of a / black Magus."[2] Similarly, "Stand Your Ground (a double golden shovel)," based on Robert Hayden's "American Journal" on the left margin and Gwendolyn Brooks's "Beverly Hills, Chicago" on the right, references Noah's ark, Klan activity and eugenicists' tirades, and the historically African American fraternity Iota Phi Theta and sorority Delta Sigma Theta, among other references like allusions to Langston Hughes and Allen Ginsberg. History in these poems is ever present but evading the poem's primary focus, appetizer rather than entrée.

While history permeates Jackson's work in this plethora of allusions, Mendi + Keith Obadike create installation art through images, music, and words, and they emphasize scrutinizing the naturalized, seemingly seamless historical narratives. *Big House/Disclosure* is about the institution of slavery. It asks performers to follow three discourses: graphic scores for music, text scores for instructions, and lyrics to be spoken, sung, or simply thought and felt. The Big House has rooms, as opposed to the typical housing for enslaved people, and this house has ten locations that are used in the performance. The violence in the house is hidden. Houses typically feel safe, but a Big House during antebellum years was not. This house is connected to house music, to interviews, and to the Chicago Slavery Disclosure Ordinance that required corporations in business with the city to research and then disclose any gains they made from the institution of slavery. The "For the Record" section states, "Nations are built on narratives. Every narrative has a backstory,"[3] and this artistic work brings forth narratives connecting the enslavement of people and economic gains.

Other poets use specific historical references more sparingly in single poems that revise history. In *a gathering of matter a matter of gathering*, Dawn Lundy Martin offers a poem about the African American soldiers who fought in the Revolutionary War in "Bearers of Arms: 1775–1783." Her five sections begin with the Middle Passage, with the European settlers and the enslaved Africans they brought with them, with "boot prints" on a "new" land that cartographers will now draw in light of colonization.[4] As the Native Americans are forced off their land, the invaders claim it for their own and construct Native Americans and Africans as savages, ripe for domination. She references the people Thomas Jefferson enslaved and the many enslaved people who ran north for freedom, people who hoped to be part of the new nation and so fought on the side of what would become the United States. They found inspiration in institutions and in the cry of European settlers for liberty. Martin uses quotes from the white settlers protesting British taxation in the lines "liberty, liberty," which when echoed by enslaved people also seeking liberty were dismissed by Henry Laurens, a merchant and delegate to the Second Continental Congress, who had made his fortune as a partner in Charleston's House of Austin & Laurens, the largest firm in North America selling enslaved people. Martin quotes Laurens, who described the Black protestors as acting in "thoughtless imitation" in their own calls for liberty, men who went on to fight for that liberty in the Revolutionary War.[5] At the poem's end, the people who fought, who wore military uniforms, find that while a few are freed, most are still enslaved, so fighting for the cause of US liberty gained them only a "tentative freedom."[6]

Quraysh Ali Lansana's volume *They Shall Run: Harriet Tubman Poems* takes yet another approach by layering historical poetry onto the paintings of the consummate storyteller Jacob Lawrence, an intersection that produces a rich retelling of national history. Lansana's volume chronicles Tubman's work in helping enslaved people escape in persona poems featuring Tubman, her husband John Tubman (they were married from 1844 until she escaped north five years later), a freedom seeker named Isaiah, a hunter of freedom seekers, and a chorus offering dreams, incantations, a parable, and a song. These personas echo through history, like Jacob Jackson, a free Black to whom Tubman sent a coded letter in December 1854 asking that he ready her brothers for the coming journey north, language that Lansana echoes in his poem. The persona in "John Ross" speaks of meeting at the cabin of Tubman's father, Ben Ross, so that Tubman can take a group of enslaved people north. Moreover, a revolver speaks in a poem, as does a dog chasing freedom seekers, a freedom seeker named Joe, and even Joe's back, through fresh wounds inflicted by the enslaver. Also included is the artifact of an advertisement offering a $2000 reward for the "ranaway" Joe.[7] Lansana employs a layering technique, Tubman at its base with mythic, historical, and visual representations of others informing his poetry and Tubman as Moses on one of her famous journeys juxtaposed with language and incidents from historical documents.

The cover of Lansana's volume features an image from Jacob Lawrence's second Harriet Tubman series, paintings completed in 1967 (as opposed to his first Tubman series, 1939–40). Seventeen of these were included in the 1968 *Harriet and the Promised Land*, a children's volume published by Windmill Books, an imprint of Simon and Shuster. Before the book's publication, the paintings were exhibited in December 1967 at New York's Terry Dintenfass Inc. (Dintenfass represented Lawrence for twenty-five years.) In these paintings Lawrence tells a story of Tubman that becomes a layer in the story told by Lansana. For example, the poem "Reason," in which the revolver speaks, responds to Windmill Books' rejection of Lawrence's painting *Forward* because in it Tubman carries a gun with which she forces a reluctant freedom seeker to continue the journey north.[8] Similarly, the original version of *Canada Bound* featured blood in the footprints of fleeing freedom seekers, blood that was removed before the book was finalized.[9] Early in his career Lawrence established himself as a visual storyteller of African American history with his extended series on pivotal figures like Tubman, Frederick Douglass, and Toussaint L'Ouverture. Patricia Hills declares Lawrence "a pictorial griot—telling stories of his own African American community."[10] His stories become bound up in Lansana's Tubman story, one of its many inflections, all of which commingle to create a multilayered twenty-first-century telling.

Poet Evie Shockley engages history in two venues: her influential scholarly writings and her poetry. In her 2011 article "Going Overboard: African American Poetic Innovation and the Middle Passage," she notes the "trend in American poetry toward the historical poem" in both African American poetry and poetry being written by white women and explores the work of poets writing about the institution of slavery. In her poem "dependencies" from *the new black*, published in the same year, she takes on the contentious national history of Thomas Jefferson and his relationship to that institution. Through four discourses, "dependencies" illuminates the contradictions lived by Jefferson, embodied in his estate Monticello, and written into the founding documents of the United States. On the left side of the page are stanzas varying from six to nine lines long that introduce the conflict between the persona and Jefferson. On the right side of the page, in bold, are quotes from the Declaration of Independence, the juxtaposition clarifying the irony inherent in this document. Also on the right side are interspersed words, sometimes italicized, that augment the critique of Jefferson's declaration of freedom for all, while he himself enslaved people. A center column of speech is quoted from the "Guide for Visitors—Monticello," which Shockley notes that she obtained during a visit in 2009; these italicized words are direct quotes.[11] These discourses demonstrate the simultaneous existence of various versions of history—from contemporary and informed voices to the Thomas Jefferson Foundation's interpretation of the monument of Monticello and the Declaration of Independence.

The persona opens the poem with the lines "visiting Monticello was / an education" and proceeds to share with her readers "the myth"—constructed as carefully as the plantation itself—of Jefferson taught by the monument of Monticello. History, and how it is transmitted, exists not only in books, paintings, and photographs but also in places like the home of the third president of the United States. The house is the focal point of Monticello, and Shockley pairs information about the aesthetic and scientific principles undergirding Jefferson's estate design with the information that efficiency and aesthetics meant placing the living and working spaces for enslaved people "beneath and behind" the house, physically locating the "dependencies" partially underground, in a space where they would be unnoticeable in the functioning of the house and in the principles of the nation. Placing the people almost underground figuratively positions their place in the new nation as invisible and literally buries their place in history. While the space of his "dependencies" was buried in the house's design, Jefferson's wine cellar was a focal point in the house, and the persona points out that the wine traveled from that cellar to the dining room via a dumbwaiter manned by another unseen enslaved person whose labor made dinner possible but whose visage also remained hidden. Thus, the presence Monticello presented to the world was that of efficiency and scientific progress, but its presentation was dependent upon the labor of enslaved people to whom Jefferson's words "we hold these truths to be self-evident, that all men are created equal" were not applied. Shockley's poem ends by merging the three discourses, offering a line that could read in many ways based on the spacing, lineation, and lack of punctuation: "I prefer your words, depending on them to be better than you."[12]

Finally, Tracy K. Smith's magnificent sequence "I Will Tell You the Truth about This, I Will Tell You All about It" was written for a Smithsonian exhibit and the resultant National Portrait Gallery's *Lines in Long Array: A Civil War Commemoration*, a volume of contemporary poetry, photographic images, and poetry written during the Civil War created for the 150th anniversary of the war—a national space sponsored by government institutions where public history is being revised.[13] Her sequence of ten sections is a found poem whose language is taken from two books about the war that preserve primary texts written by African Americans during and after the war. Ira Berlin and Leslie S. Rowland's *Families and Freedom* provides the sources for the first nine sections, and the tenth relies upon Elizabeth A. Regosin and Donald R. Shaffer's *Voices of Emancipation* for its voices as well as the poem's title. Smith describes herself as a "curator" who presents African Americans' experiences in their own words: "It became clear to me rather quickly that the best way of breaking my own silence would simply be to move over and give these men and women the opportunity to 'speak' through my poem—or, rather, to allow myself and my potential readers to take those actual, factual voices in unison, without the filter or intrusion of my own voice." She calls the result "a kind of composite of various pleas and arguments and assertions about the nature of justice, freedom and nationhood."[14] Her poem retains the original documents' language and cadence by reproducing most of the nonstandard spellings, capitalizations, punctuation, and spacing and steps into the documents' lines sometimes at the beginning and sometimes in medias res; phrases or sections are excised without the use of ellipses, and the order of the sentences or phrases is occasionally altered—all creative choices that transform the original discourse into compelling poetry.

Smith's creative method and the poem's thematic concerns are clear even in the title. Its first phrase "I will tell you the truth about this" comes from a deposition made on November 21, 1906, by Ellen Wade. In Wade's application to receive benefits for her husband's Civil War service, she has much to explain—names that changed after the institution of slavery ended, relationships and children she and her husband had with other people, the date of their marriage, and the circumstances of her claim. With no paper trail, her claim would be decided on the basis of the information she shared, the oral history of her community, and corroboration by others. Throughout her winding explanation, which condenses years of her life into a brief narrative, Wade maintains that she is telling the truth, one that can be verified even though it was not supported by written documents. The second phrase in the title, "I will tell you all about it," is excerpted from Mary Jane Taylor's May 13, 1919, deposition. Also claiming a Civil War widow's pension, Taylor similarly explains her marriage, which followed the tradition of marriages between enslaved people rather than the legally recognized marriages that followed the abolition of slavery. She assures the government questioner she will tell him "all about it," and she patiently explains how her community did not know they were free until a full year after the war ended, the circumstances of her first marriage, which she did not consider legal, and her subsequent legal marriage to Samuel Taylor. The circumstances that both Wade and Taylor describe are clearly foreign to their questioner, who repeatedly asks for more information when their accounts do not fit his expectations, expectations established by legal traditions nonexistent for enslaved people. Nonetheless, the two women offer truths even if the government found them difficult to accept since they did not fit the legal norms regulating the lives of white Americans. By using the voices of Wade, Taylor, and others, Smith offers their histories, not accounts of battles or combat or officers or Lincoln's assassination or even daily duties, but the truths of ordinary people who emphasize family ties, the love they bear their family, and their struggle to free their entire family, as well as the poor treatment they receive from the military and the government.

These voices explain important issues in the African American community of the time and make their case eloquently and persuasively. Smith's editorial process layers and splices these voices, a process not unlike Kevin Young's admonition to treat history like music, which can be sampled and collaged together.[15] As they are transformed into lyric, free verse poetry, the voices become larger than their single tone; they claim the biblical "I" of authority and speak for the many people in their situation. In an interview with Clair Schwartz, Smith commented on this war poem and history:

> I also want to find ways of enacting some of my anxieties and feelings that have to do with the history of the now. A couple of years ago, I was invited to contribute a poem about the Civil War for an exhibit at the Smithsonian. I wouldn't have otherwise written a Civil War poem, but I feel like it's so relevant to these problems that we're finally speaking about in terms of race and the justice system. I want to marry all that together somehow.[16]

Thus, this poem's personae offer insights into their own difficult situations, but Smith's poem "marries" those with today's issues of social justice—equal treatment from the government and government support for families, two of the many ways in which the past continues to speak to the present. History is, at its core, just as much about the present as the past, as this book returns to James Baldwin's declaration that "the great force of history comes from the fact that we carry it within us, are unconsciously controlled by it in many ways, and history is literally *present* in all that we do."[17]

In a 2013 interview given while she was the national poet laureate, Natasha Trethewey was discussing which stories make it into the history books and which are excluded when she quoted George Orwell: "Who controls the past controls the future; who controls the present controls the past."[18] If, from appetizers to single poems to extended sequences to entire volumes, post-1960 poets are writing historical poetry, then they are challenging that control. Into a genre uniquely positioned to capture the ambiguity of history, poets write lyric history necessary to the present, poetry with the power to correct the past, realign the present, and create a hopeful future.

By challenging control and dissemination of the traditional historical narrative, the poets covered in this study lead in the struggle for social justice. They are able to make deep inroads into righting the narrative of American history because of the poets who came before them, most significantly Robert Hayden, Michael S. Harper, and Rita Dove. From "Middle Passage" through *Debridement* to *Thomas and Beulah*, these three influential writers created a space where historical poetry could flourish. Their generation—just before and in the mainstream of the civil rights years—was also instrumental in the evolution of how African Americans were portrayed in history, that shift in 1970 mirroring the changes happening in literature.

Postmodernism destabilized both fields. It shifted focus away from a single dominant historical narrative to new ways of not only validating what was historical evidence but also how history could be told. Historians, confronting Hayden White's claim that the form through which history is told integrally shapes history itself, began to train in creative nonfiction. In turn, writers grappled with similar contradictions and uncertainties, which led to the rich opportunities now available in how history can be told through creative writing since history—capital *H* and lowercase *h*, as Rita Dove formulates it—is no longer expected to be a singular monolith. As a result, what Catherine Gallagher and Stephen Greenblatt called counterhistories—the spaces, absences, and gaps in history—are no longer counter to a dominant version of history; instead they have moved squarely to center stage. No longer are stories of Sara Baartman, the Native Guard, MacNolia Cox, Jack Johnson and Jean-Michel Basquiat, Medgar Evers, and free and enslaved Blacks from the early nineteenth century marginalized. The writers addressed here place them into the core narratives of American history. As poets joined historians in writing a new public history of the United States that redefines what it means to be American, Natasha Trethewey made the stunning pronouncement that "poetry can be a genre of history."[19]

What we inhabit is the present, but the ghosts of the past linger, critically impacting how we understand the world. If James Baldwin was correct that "it is to history that we owe our frames of reference, our identities and our aspirations,"[20] then the way into a progressive future is to right the past, as much as we're able in our particular moment in time with the tools we currently have. The poets covered here accept that responsibility and through their myriad of approaches, write a past that is necessary, one that frees readers to change the present and envision a just future.

NOTES

Preface

1. Edwards, Lee, and Esposito, "Risk of Being Killed."
2. Foner, *Who Owns History?*, xiii.
3. Chang, "Public Life of Poetry."
4. Gabbin and Alleyne, *Furious Flower*, xxv.

Introduction

1. Hughes, *Poems from Black Africa*, 11.
2. Young, introduction, 5.
3. Alexander, *The Black Interior*, 91–92.
4. T'Shaka, "African Studies Department History," 13; Rooks, "Beginnings."
5. Holt, "African-American History," 212.
6. Young, introduction, 6.
7. Alexander, "Negro Digs Up Her Past," 465.
8. Dungy, "In Others' Voices," 17.
9. Jackson, "Historical Poem," 6.
10. Evie Shockley in discussion with the author, October 29, 2016.
11. Quoted in Dungy, "In Others' Voices," 17.
12. Quoted in Dungy, "In Others' Voices," 16.
13. Trethewey, "Why I Write."
14. Chang, "Public Life."
15. Jackson, "Historical Poem," 5.
16. Jackson, "Historical Poem," 6.
17. Rowell designates these writers as second and third wave, post-1960s in *Angles of Ascent.*
18. Taleb-Khyar, "Gifts to Be Earned," 79.
19. Trethewey, "Why I Write."
20. Ramsey, "Terrance Hayes and Natasha Trethewey," 125, 126. Ramsey also uses the 1960 border, which he calls "a generational 'tipping point,' " contending that "this generation was *formatively* shaped in a changing landscape." Besides sharing this border designation, Ramsey and I part ways in our interpretations: for example, his habit of misreading such basics as hair care when he argues that "shampoo has no racial essence—it chemically cleans any kind of hair" and similarly missing historical significance in the readings of Natasha Trethewey's and Terrance Hayes's poetry.
21. Baldwin, "White Man's Guilt," 410.
22. Grossman, "History and Literature," 5, 6.
23. White, *Practical Past*, 10.

24. White, "Historical Text as Literary Artifact," 91.

25. Holt, "African-American History," 211–12.

26. Ellison, "An American Dilemma," 315–16. In *Ralph Ellison: Emergence of Genius*, Lawrence Ellison offers this account:

> Ellison's most consequential analytical work for 1944, however, was not published, probably because he had to ship out to sea in the wake of the opening of a second theater of warfare off the coast of France in June. While biding his time and waiting for the last possible minute to go, he had developed ties with *Antioch Review*, a young intellectual and academic journal published in Yellow Springs, Ohio, since the beginning of the 1940s. Through the pages of *Antioch* he had first gotten to know Stanley Hyman and see the work published of his *New Masses* colleague Edwin Berry Burgun, along with such critics as Granville Hicks. The editorial staff arranged for Ellison to review *An American Dilemma*, the book that had piqued the American public's conscience, still blistering after the 1943 riots.
>
> Ellison found the study by the Swedish social scientist Gunnar Myrdal (aided by Ralph Bunche and Sterling Brown) dangerously flawed. Instead of devoting volumes to prove that Negro society suffered at the hands of white racism, what was called for, Ellison said, in his famous paraphrase of Joyce, was Negro cultural self-determination: "What is needed are Negroes to take it [Negro culture] and create of it 'the uncreated consciousness of their race.' " More interesting than the tragedy of Negro life in America, he said, should have been an analysis of the cultural forms and rituals that Negroes had actively chosen in the face of the "higher values" of white America. And he had not given up his interest in the class dynamic of the wielding of power, which he said Myrdal misunderstood. "All of this, of course, avoids the question of power *and* the question of who manipulates that power." He was reminded of his college days and the white philanthropist who came to Tuskegee to be entertained and to dictate the future of the black race. Ellison saw condescension in the Carnegie Commission's decision to hire a Swede, instead of any number of qualified black researchers, to study the important question of racism. His review was a little too hot for *Antioch*, which begged off publication. Ralph Ellison would grow accustomed to confirming the acid of his views to literature. (302–3)

27. Holt, "African American History," 212.

28. For a thorough discussion of the complexity of the *Brown v. Board of Education* decision, its implementation, and its effects, see Klarman, *Brown v. Board of Education.*

29. Hall, "Long Civil Rights Movement," 1235. Terms, parameters, and periodization are often hotly contested, and these are no different. A full accounting of the many studies of historiography is well beyond the scope of this study, but for another valuable view, see Cha-Jua and Lang, " 'Long Movement' as Vampire."

30. See Debo, "Reflecting Violence in the Warpland."

31. Harding, "Beyond Chaos," 278–79.

32. Harding, "Beyond Chaos," 279.

33. Painter, "Remembering Herbert Gutman," 336.
34. Painter, "Remembering Herbert Gutman," 336–37.
35. Harris, Jr., "Coming of Age," 108.
36. Zinn, *Politics of History*, 36.
37. Quarles, *Black Mosaic*, 182.
38. Yetman, "Ex-Slave Interviews," 193.
39. For historiographies of the studies of the institution of slavery, see Yetman, "Ex-Slave Interviews"; and Charles B. Dew, "Slavery Experience."
40. White tells this story in "My History in History," 97. This new classification based on *Ar'n't I a Woman* was first noticed by Schwalm, who recorded it in "Ar'n't I a Woman?" In note 5, Schwalm documents that Sheridan Henry, reference librarian at the Library of Congress, explained that the heading was proposed on February 13, 1985, specifically because of White's book, and approved on March 5, 1985. Additionally, in "My History in History," White chronicles the difficulties in choosing this dissertation topic, the roadblocks in completing her research, and the many press rejections before it was published.
41. Cade, *Black Woman*, 10–11.
42. Novick, *That Noble Dream*, 16.
43. Novick, *That Noble Dream*, 17.
44. Gallagher and Greenblatt, *Practicing New Historicism*, 6.
45. Gallagher and Greenblatt, *Practicing New Historicism*, 16–17.
46. Montrose, "Professing the Renaissance," 20.
47. White, "Historical Text," 82.
48. White, "Historical Text," 82.
49. White, *Practical Past*, x.
50. White, *Practical Past*, 65.
51. White, *Practical Past*, 23.
52. Morrison, "Site of Memory," 113.
53. White, *Practical Past*, 23.
54. Baldwin, "Black English," 154.
55. Gutkind and Fletcher, *Keep It Real*, 76–78.
56. Goodman, editorial in *Rethinking History*, 1.
57. Major Jackson in discussion with the author, April 4, 2016.
58. Alexander, "One Who Went Before," 125.
59. Davis, *Southscapes*, 38.
60. McHaney, "Interview with Natasha Trethewey," 55.
61. Plante, "Interview with A. Van Jordan."
62. Medina, "Persona Non Grata," 361.
63. Elizabeth Alexander in discussion with the author, April 11, 2017.
64. McHaney, "Interview with Natasha Trethewey," 46.
65. Notes in box 7, folder 4. Natasha Trethewey Papers, Stuart A. Rose Manuscript, Archives, and Rare Book Library, Emory University. Atlanta, GA.
66. Rambsy II, "Catching Holy Ghosts," 549.
67. Mendi Obadike in discussion with the author, October 29, 2016.
68. Browning, "Making a Necessity of Memory."
69. Sara Kaplan, "Interview: Natasha Trethewey," 39.
70. Alexander, "Negro Digs Up Her Past," 465.
71. Foner, *Who Owns History?*, xi.

Chapter One

1. Alexander, "One Who Went Before," 125.

2. Young, introduction, 4.

3. Shockley, "Black Arts Movement," 188. See also Shockley's *Renegade Poetics*.

4. Alexander, *The Black Interior*, 63.

5. In *Robert Hayden*, Pontheolla T. Williams documents that while in the WPA, Hayden's work included writing on the abolitionist movement in Detroit and Illinois, as well as supervising research in local history and folklore (16).

6. Hayden, *Collected Prose*, 80.

7. Hayden, *Collected Prose*, 123, 80.

8. Williams, Jr., "Covenant of Timelessness," 74–75.

9. Potter, "Remembrance," 51.

10. Mirsch, "Mean to Be Free," 685.

11. Davis, "Robert Hayden's Use of History," 96.

12. Fetrow, "Portraits and Personae," 43.

13. Benét, *John Brown's Body*, 308.

14. Hayden, *Collected Prose*, 162.

15. For a more complete account of *The Black Spear*'s metamorphosis, see Friedlander, "Robert Hayden's Epic of Community." Per Andrea Beauchamp, assistant director, Hopwood Awards Program at the University of Michigan, Hayden actually won a Hopwood Major Poetry Award. In those days, the awards were classified as major and minor, based on the old English public school system where if two brothers attended, the older was called Smith Major and the younger Smith Minor. For the Hopwoods, undergraduates entered the Minor Contest and graduate students the Major Contest Seniors were allowed to decide which competition they would like to enter. Email with the author, November 14, 2016.

16. Hayden, *Collected Prose*, 169–70.

17. Hayden, *Collected Prose*, 170.

18. Hayden, *Collected Prose*, 170.

19. Nielsen, *Writing between the Lines*, 122–23.

20. Hayden, *Collected Poems*, 54; Hayden, *Collected Prose*, 170. For significant readings of "Middle Passage," see also Fetrow, "Middle Passage"; Howard, "Resistance, Sacrifice, and Historicity"; Kutzinski, "Changing Permanences"; Raphaël Lambert, "The Slave Trade"; and Eben Wood, "Private Lives of System."

21. Jackson, "Historical Poem," 5.

22. Hayden, *Collected Prose*, 178.

23. Hayden, *Collected Prose*, 162.

24. Hall, "Larger Stage," 21.

25. Hayden, *Collected Prose*, 168–69.

26. Alexander, "Negro Digs Up Her Past," 465.

27. Alexander, *Crave Radiance*, 240.

28. Hayden, *Collected Prose*, 180.

29. Hayden, *Collected Prose*, 11.

30. Harper, "Every Shut-Eye Ain't Asleep," 9.

31. Hayden and Harper, "Robert Hayden and Michael Harper," 984.

32. Stepto, "Michael Harper's Extended Tree," 423.

33. Hayden and Harper, "Robert Hayden and Michael Harper," 985.

34. Harper, "Remembering Robert Hayden," 183.
35. Randall and Harper, "Interview with Michael S. Harper," 17.
36. Antonucci, "Map and the Territory," 501–2. In Treseler's "Office Hours," Harper shared, "When I published Robert Hayden's *American Journal* in 1978, in limited edition by Effendi Press, I had to *buy* a press to get it published" (109).
37. Alexander, *Black Interior*, 63.
38. Major Jackson in discussion with the author, April 4, 2016.
39. Brouwer, Review, 208.
40. Harper and Nielsen, "Conversation" 82.
41. Harper, *Dear John, Dear Coltrane*, 62.
42. For a full and insightful reading, see Antonucci, "Spirits of '76."
43. Harper, *Images of Kin*, 20, 27; see Dodd, "The Great Rainbowed Swamp."
44. Harper, *Healing Song for the Inner Ear*, 60.
45. Harper, *History Is Your Own Heartbeat*, 6, 22.
46. Harper, *Debridement*.
47. Rowell, "Down Don't Worry Me," 792. Young's *Brown: Poems* contemplates the significance of "Brown" in a myriad of manifestations, including a radical John Brown who irrevocably alters the nation in poems about Kansas.
48. Loewen, *Lies My Teacher Told Me*, 177.
49. Harper, *Debridement*, 8; Du Bois, *John Brown*, 158.
50. Harper, *Debridement*, 40; Du Bois, *John Brown*, 123.
51. Du Bois himself meant to write a biography of Frederick Douglass and signed a contract to that effect with the Philadelphia publishers George Jacobs and Company, but the opportunity to write about Douglass eventually was reassigned to Booker T. Washington, leaving Du Bois still with a book contract, as his literary executor Herbert Aptheker recounts in *Nat Turner's Slave Rebellion*. When asked for a new biographical subject, he offered to write about Nat Turner, and the publishers requested he write about the white abolitionist John Brown instead, with the resulting volume published on the fiftieth anniversary of Brown's death, a recovery itself recovered in 1970 (i–ii). For letters about the biography's subject, see Herbert Aptheker, *Correspondence of W. E. B. Du Bois, vol. 1*, 60–65, and for an analysis of Du Bois's *John Brown*, see Keith E. Byerman, *Seizing the Word*.
52. Du Bois, *John Brown*, 162; Harper, *Debridement*, 3.
53. Du Bois, *John Brown*, 55; Harper, *Debridement*, 4.
54. Du Bois, *John Brown*, 128, 150.
55. Du Bois, *John Brown*, 29.
56. Harper, *Debridement*, 21.
57. Bennett, Jr., *Negro Mood*, 101–2.
58. Reynolds, *John Brown, Abolitionist*, 498.
59. For other scholarship on Harper, history, and *Debridement*, see Saul's excellent article "Triple-Conscious Brothers in the Vein"; Ronda's thorough study *Reading the Old Man*; Clark, "Michael S. Harper," which praises his use of history and recovery of a John Brown and his Black compatriots but also points out that critics often call this volume poorly structured; and Lehman's negative review, which characterizes Harper's book as an attempt "of a more historical nature to illuminate the black experience in America" that is too pat, "simply not daring, not sharp, not surprising enough" in "Politics," 175.

60. In *Every Shut Eye Ain't Asleep,* Harper and Walton included work by poets born between 1913 and 1962 who had published at least one volume with a commercial press and whose poetry met their artistic quality standards. Hayden and Dove are also well represented in Harper and Walton's other anthology, *The Vintage Book of African American Poetry.*

61. Rowell, "Interview with Rita Dove: Part 2," 722.

62. Dove, *Grace Notes*, 64.

63. Taleb-Rhyar, "Gifts to Be Earned," 86.

64. Dove, "Poet's Choice."

65. Ratiner, "Chorus of Voices," 103.

66. Bellin, "Tricking the Muse," 126.

67. Alexander in discussion with the author, April 11, 2017.

68. Righelato, "Rita Dove and the Art of History," 765, 762.

69. Throughout Dove's body of work, history is at the forefront, as in *Museum.* Besides the poetry covered here, history takes center stage in many single poems throughout Dove's work but most consistently in *On the Bus with Rosa Parks* (1999), particularly in its titular fifth section, and in *Sonata Mulattica* (2009) about the biracial musical virtuoso George Augustus Polgreen Bridgetower who lived from 1778 to 1860. However, neither of those volumes had the fortuitous timing of *Thomas and Beulah*, so while they are significant and influential, neither had its impact.

70. Frank X Walker in discussion with the author, February 1, 2017.

71. Bingham, "Interview with Natasha Trethewey," 63.

72. Rowell, "Interview with Kevin Young," 43–44.

73. Dungy, "Interview with Rita Dove," 1029, 1025.

74. Rowell, "Poem Is Smarter," 915.

75. Rowell, "Interview with Rita Dove," 723.

76. Cavalieri, "Brushed," 139.

77. Ingersoll, "Not the Shouted Slogan," 185.

78. Vendler, "In the Zoo," 50.

79. Moyer, "Poet Laureate Rita Dove."

80. McClain, *Contributions of Blacks*, 134.

81. Schneider, "Writing for Those Moments," 112.

82. Love and Giffels, *Wheels of Fortune*, 113.

83. *WPA Guide to Ohio*, 345.

84. Love and Giffels, *Wheels of Fortune*, 48–49.

85. Dove, *Thomas and Beulah*, 26, 60.

86. Dove, *Thomas and Beulah*, 22.

87. Walsh, "World Has to Fall Away."

88. Love and Giffels, *Wheels of Fortune*, 113–17.

89. Dove, foreword, viii.

90. Many critics have offered readings of *Thomas and Beulah.* For critics focused on history, see Steffen's outstanding chapter in *Crossing Color*; Steinman, who argues that the poems are "history allowed to speak for itself" in "Dialogues between History and Dream," 433; Wallace, who claims that "Dove is preoccupied with . . . American history and history more generally" in "Divided Loyalties," 12; and Boone, who argues that "the political consciousness Dove

forges in her poetry is based on a complex understanding of history and the dialectic between history and the individual" in "Resignation to History," 74.

91. Vendler, "In the Zoo," 50.

92. Schneider, "Coming Home," 117.

93. See Keller's chapter on Rita Dove and Brenda Marie Osbey on the long poem in *Forms of Expansion*; see Lindner who claims that part of the *Thomas and Beulah* success is that it offers valuable examples of "enacting the tension between the lyric and the narrative" in "Eloquent Silences," 105.

Chapter Two

1. Alexander in discussion with the author, April 11, 2017.
2. Alexander in discussion with the author.
3. Eady, introduction, 3, 4.
4. Derricotte, introduction, 5–6.
5. Mullen, introduction, 8–9.
6. Hoppenthaler, "Interview with Michael S. Harper."
7. Alexander, introduction, 6.
8. Dungy, "In Others' Voices," 17.
9. Jackson, "Historical Poem," 5.
10. Gould, *The Mismeasure of Man.*
11. Gould, "Hottentot Venus," 20.
12. Alexander in discussion with the author.
13. The best two full-length biographies about Baartman are Crais and Scully's *Sara Baartman and the Hottentot Venus* and Rachel Holmes's *African Queen.* The bare outline of Baartman's life I have offered here is summarized from Crais and Scully's biography, and I have relied on their spelling of her name. Although Holmes conducted original research and her more lively writing style offers a good read, Crais and Scully's extensive documentation of their primary and secondary sources indicates that their biography offers more accuracy and less speculation.
14. Chase-Riboud, *Hottentot Venus.*
15. Alexander in discussion with the author.
16. Alexander, *Venus Hottentot*, 6.
17. Alexander in discussion with the author.
18. Alexander, *Venus Hottentot*, 5.
19. Alexander in discussion with the author; Morrison and Stepto, "Intimate Things in Place," 478.
20. Alexander in discussion with the author.
21. Alexander, *Venus Hottentot*, 6.
22. Alexander, *Venus Hottentot*, 9.
23. Crais and Scully, *Sara Baartman*, 135.
24. Alexander, *Venus Hottentot*, 10.
25. Phillip, "Interview with Elizabeth Alexander," 502.
26. Pereira, *Into a Light*, 220.
27. Morrison, "Site of Memory," 113.
28. Young, *Grey Album*, 23.
29. Alexander, *Venus Hottentot*, 52.
30. Sellar, "Making History," 50.

31. hooks, *Black Looks*, 62–63.

32. See Nisco, "Dark Histories, Bright Revisions," for an overview of even more creative works inspired by Baartman's story. For additional scholarly analyses of Alexander's poem, see Werbanowska, "Reclaiming the Commodified Body"; Pinto, *Difficult Diasporas*; Willis, introduction to *Black Venus 2010*. See Hobson, *Venus in the Dark*, for an analysis of Baartman's role in the larger discussion of the black female body; Baartman's case has received a vast amount of scholarly and cultural attention since the 1980s.

33. It is worth noting that not all recent creative or scholarly projects addressing Baartman revise the original colonial narrative. For example, reviewers credit the 2010 film *Vénus Noire (Black Venus)*, directed by Abdellatif Kechiche, for condemning Baartman's oppressors as well as all exploitative entertainment, but they also notice that it refuses her a voice, as its action circles around her largely mute form. Brett Bailey's Exhibit B, a recreation of the nineteenth-century "human zoo" put on by European colonizers, is considered by some viewers as a critique of those zoos and by others as merely reenacting and thus reinforcing them. Furthermore, scholar Natasha Gordon-Chipembere in "Claiming Sarah Baartman" objects to Chase-Riboud's novel and Parks's play, which, she argues, "collude with the master narrative" and "[condemn] Baartman to a self-destructive, sexually excessive, drunken stereotype which echoes Cuvier et al." (303).

34. Trethewey, "Far, Deep Things."

35. *Miss Crandall's School for Young Ladies and Little Misses of Color* has received little scholarly attention. It is a noteworthy comparison to *The Venus Hottentot* because it focuses on a relatively unknown school for young African American women in Connecticut, a subject quite unlike Baartman, but one of equal importance since it focuses on the quest for education. This volume demonstrates the depth of Alexander's historical knowledge on the school headed by Prudence Crandall, a white woman. Alexander and Nelson offer a historical introduction, each contribute twelve sonnets for a total of twenty-four sonnets that tell the school's story, and the concluding authors' notes explain their personal pilgrimage to the Prudence Crandall Museum, their rationale for writing such a book in the sonnet form, and their collaborative process.

36. Alexander in discussion with the author.

Chapter Three

1. Pereira, *Into a Light*, 220.

2. Schwartz, "Natasha Trethewey."

3. This chapter on *Native Guard* builds on my new historicist analysis of Trethewey's *Bellocq's Ophelia*; see Debo, "Ophelia Speaks."

4. Eady, introduction, 2–3.

5. Strange, "Dark Room Collective."

6. Bingham, "Interview with Natasha Trethewey," 64.

7. Turner, "Southern Crossings: An Interview."

8. In 2020 Trethewey published *Memorial Drive: A Daughter's Memoir*, a heartbreakingly gorgeous memoir. The memoir form, and perhaps the years that have passed, facilitates Trethewey's revealing journey into her past, her relationship with her mother, and the damage done by her stepfather.

9. Teresi, "Interview with Natasha Trethewey," 121.

10. Hall, "Larger Stage," 20, 21.
11. Haney, "Conversation with Natasha Trethewey," 28.
12. Trethewey, *Native Guard*, 1.
13. For additional scholarship on *Native Guard*, see Atkinson, "Natasha Trethewey's Joe Christmas," for an analysis of the meaning of native ties in Trethewey and Faulkner; Birdsong, "Memories that are(n't) mine," for a reading of Trethewey's volume through trauma theory with an emphasis on matrilineal lineage; De Cenzo, "Natasha Trethewey," for a general gloss of the volume and its focus on history; Davis, "Enfoldments," for an analysis of Trethewey's use of photographs and visual art, as well as her insightful reading of Trethewey's claiming of the South in *Southscapes*; Goad, "Throwaway Bodies," which analyzes the photography; Henninger, "What Remains," for a reading of Trethewey's autobiographical personae through the position of an adult child; Jee Eun Kim, who explores miscegenation in "His Story Intersecting"; LeMahieu's excellent article "Robert Lowell, Perpetual War," in which he briefly considers Trethewey; McHaney's superb "Natasha Trethewey's Triptych" on physical and historical bodies; Pereira, "Re-reading Trethewey," for an analysis of Trethewey's biracial identity; Nagueyalti Warren, "History, Memory, and Nostalgia," for close readings of Trethewey's poetry and nonfiction through a loosely synthesized lens of history, memory, and nostalgia; and Queen, "Natasha Trethewey's Palimpsestic Poetics," for an analysis of history's role in Trethewey's palimpsests.
14. McKee, "Conversation with Natasha Trethewey," 141.
15. Hughes, *Collected Poems*, 26.
16. Box 8, folder 1, spiral notebook, Trethewey Papers.
17. Turner, "Southern Crossings: An Interview."
18. Haney, "Conversation with Natasha Trethewey," 29.
19. DeVries, "Because of Blood," 107.
20. Reviewer Ange Mlinko describes *Native Guard*'s structure as "a dialectic, in three parts: the autobiographical as thesis, the historical as antithesis, and the intertwining of the personal and the historical as synthesis" (59). In "History, Memory, and Nostalgia," Warren suggests that "another way to think about the structure is memory (of her mother); history (of the Native Guard); and nostalgia, a desire for what is lost" (84). McHaney in "Natasha Trethewey's Triptych" also notes the repetition and circling in *Native Guard*, a volume she reads as one wing of a triptych with *Bellocq's Ophelia* and *Thrall*.
21. Trethewey, *Native Guard*, 7.
22. Trethewey, *Native Guard*, 11, 10.
23. Gross, "Poet Natasha Trethewey."
24. Solomon, Native Daughter, 15.
25. Trethewey, *Native Guard*, 9, 8.
26. Trethewey, *Native Guard*, 12–15.
27. Trethewey, *Native Guard*, 19, 20.
28. Trethewey, "On Whitman," 53–54.
29. Trethewey, *Native Guard*, 19.
30. Qtd. in Trethewey, "On Whitman," 54.
31. For a replica of Loughborough's romanticized cover, see Aiken and Bolton, *Mississippi*, 69.
32. Balfour, *Mrs. Balfour's Civil War Diary*, 12.

33. Trethewey, *Native Guard*, 20.

34. See Church, Moore, and Shockley, "Incident in the Lives," which describes a time when these writers found themselves unexpectedly hosted in a former enslaver's home. They describe their fraught experience in a house that "reeked of the rot of slavery; we could smell and hear and feel its wounding history in every inch of the structure. Unquiet, peaceless spirits wandered the halls and brooded in corners" (282). Essays like this combat the narrative put forth by the likes of the Cedar Grove Mansion.

35. The Cedar Grove Mansion Inn and Restaurant was sold in 2020, so the information presented here (and used in Trethewey's poetry) can no longer be found on its website.

36. For a replica of this photograph see Akin and Bolton, *Mississippi*, 98.

37. Trethewey, *Native Guard*, 21.

38. McHaney, "Interview," 104.

39. Trethewey, *Native Guard*, 22.

40. This photograph and its caption can be found in the section of images following p. 126 in Barry, *Rising Tide*.

41. Trethewey, *Native Guard*, 23.

42. A replica of this photograph can be found in Akin and Bolton, *Mississippi*, 93.

43. Trethewey, *Native Guard*, 24.

44. Hall, "Larger Stage," 21–22.

45. Rowell, "Inscriptive Restorations," 1032.

46. Trethewey, *Native Guard*, 25.

47. Hollandsworth, *Louisiana Native Guards*, 26.

48. Trethewey, *Native Guard*, 25, 26.

49. Weaver, *Thank God My Regiment*, 1.

50. Hollandsworth, *Louisiana Native Guards*, 39.

51. Trethewey, *Native Guard*, 27.

52. Trethewey, *Native Guard*, 26.

53. Trethewey, *Native Guard*, 27.

54. Box 14, folder 7, Trethewey Papers.

55. Trethewey, *Native Guard*, 30.

56. Trethewey, *Native Guard*, 28.

57. Weaver, *Thank God My Regiment*, 41, 42. Hollandsworth offers another point of view, interpreting the *Jackson*'s action as an accident: "Unfortunately, a shell from a six-inch rifled cannon fell short and exploded, killing four and wounding five of the native Guards as they scrambled aboard the *General Banks*" (46).

58. Weaver, *Thank God My Regiment*, 42; Trethewey, *Native Guard*, 28.

59. Quoted in Weaver, *Thank God My Regiment*, 87.

60. Hewitt, "An Ironic Route to Glory," 95.

61. Quoted in Weaver, *Thank God My Regiment*, 113.

62. See Hollandsworth, *The Louisiana Native Guards*, 59–60; and Hewitt, "Ironic Route to Glory," 96. Hewitt oddly refuses to identify Banks's claim as racist, instead writing "inexplicably, the Federals left untouched the area where the Native Guards had charged—in stark contrast to their actions elsewhere on the battlefield." Trethewey, *Native Guard*, 28.

63. Cimprich, "Fort Pillow Massacre, 150; Regosin and Shaffer, *Voices of Emancipation*, 69.

64. Quoted in Cimprich, "Fort Pillow Massacre," 157, 158.

65. Hollandsworth, *Louisiana Native Guards*, 71.

66. In an interesting aside, Trethewey considered identifying her persona as a woman but worried that would be interpreted as a sleight of hand. Box 14, folder 15, Trethewey Papers.

67. Wiley and Milhollen, *They Who Fought Here*, 264.

68. Trethewey, *Native Guard*, 31.

69. Trethewey, "On Whitman," 51, 57.

70. Trethewey, "On Whitman," 51–52.

71. Turner, "Southern Crossings: An Interview."

72. Haney, "Conversation with Natasha Trethewey," 29.

73. Trethewey, *Native Guard*, 35.

74. Faulkner, *Absalom, Absalom!*, 395.

75. Warren, *Who Speaks for the Negro?*, 11.

76. Murphy, *Rebuke of History*, 208.

77. Trethewey, *Native Guard*, 35.

78. Natasha Trethewey in discussion with the author, September 20, 2016.

79. Warren, *Audubon*, 30.

80. Hall, "Larger Stage," 25.

81. Robert Penn Warren, *Segregation*, 64.

82. Trethewey's final lecture can be found on the Library of Congress's website (https://www.loc.gov/item/2021689419/), and her essay adapted from this lecture, "The Quarrel with Ourselves: Robert Penn Warren's 'World of Action and Liability,' " was published in *AWP*.

83. Trethewey, "Quarrel."

84. Trethewey, *Native Guard*, 38.

85. Gross, "Poet Laureate"; Trethewey, "The Quarrel with Ourselves"; Trethewey, *Memorial Drive*, 34–36.

86. Trethewey, *Native Guard*, 41.

87. Mark Potok in discussion with the author, May 21, 2010.

88. Newton, *Ku Klux Klan*, 13, 265.

89. Trethewey, *Native Guard*, 1.

90. Trethewey, *Native Guard*, 46.

91. Shockley, "Black Arts Movement," 192.

92. Eric Trethewey wrote two essays about his family: "Walking Home" about his college and early family life and "Connections and Correspondences" about the death of Trethewey's mother. This second essay, published in the wake of Trethewey's Pulitzer Prize and increasing fame, feels uncomfortably invasive, delving into the life of a woman he divorced years before and the life of his daughter, whose poetic accomplishments by 2008 had well outstripped his own. This tension contributes to the theme of colonization in Trethewey's *Thrall*.

93. Kaplan, "The Miscegenation Issue," 277.

94. Trethewey, *Native Guard*, 40. In *Memorial Drive*, Trethewey again emphasizes that her mother "knew, too, that language would be used to name and thereby attempt to constrain me—*mongrel, mulatto, half-breed, nigger*—and

that, as on the back of the mule, I would be both bound to and propelled by it. My mother wanted only that I not be destroyed by it" (42).

95. Trethewey, *Native Guard*, 37.

96. Trethewey, *Native Guard*, 45, 46.

97. Kevin Young comments, "But the culture black folks made promised a kind of belonging in the idea of nativeness, even in the midst of exile. For black culture, 'going native' was less a dangerous excursion than a reclaiming of the home they found themselves in. *Native Son, Notes of a Native Son*, Natasha Trethewey's *Native Guard*, the native Tongues hip-hop collective: African American conceptions of nativeness mean belonging, a nativity holy and human. It is exactly this nativity that some would seek to deny our first black president." *Grey Album*, 148.

98. Box 14, folder 7, Trethewey Papers.

Chapter Four

1. Trethewey in discussion with the author.
2. Eady, introduction, 143.
3. Quoted in Schwartz, "An Interview with Toi Derricotte," 158.
4. A. Van Jordan in discussion with the author, April 10, 2017.
5. "Champion," 1.
6. Price, "A Way with Words."
7. "Interview with A. Van Jordan."
8. Romain, "Tragedy of MacNolia Cox."
9. Silverstein, "Writing a Poem," 30.
10. Jordan explained that his poetry volume began as a young adult book, something akin to Thanhha Lai's *Inside Out and Back Again*, but he found the subject matter worked better as a volume of poetry aimed at adults. Moreover, he first wrote the volume in chronological order but had a hard time finding a publisher. Then, in a workshop, when he advised a student to use the tried-and-true technique of reading their manuscript backward, he realized the same approach might work with his own volume. After reordering his manuscript into a form that emphasized transcendence, he sent it back out to publishers, who eagerly vied to publish it. Jordan in discussion with the author.
11. Plante, "Interview with A. Van Jordan."
12. Jordan in discussion with the author.
13. Jordan, *M-A-C-N-O-L-I-A*, cover (brackets in the original).
14. Jordan in discussion with the author.
15. Jordan, *M-A-C-N-O-L-I-A*, 75, 80–91.
16. Jordan, *M-A-C-N-O-L-I-A*, 97–99
17. Jordan in discussion with the author. John Montiere was MacNolia's husband.
18. Jordan, *M-A-C-N-O-L-I-A*, 17, 15.
19. Jordan, *M-A-C-N-O-L-I-A*, 103, 102, 103.
20. Chesley, "Spelling Bee," 3B.
21. Jordan, *M-A-C-N-O-L-I-A*, 95, 112–17.
22. Collins, "Best Speller Stumbles."
23. Maguire, *American Bee*, 80.

24. All accounts of the spelling bees assert that a list, rather than the entire dictionary, was used, but I have been unable to locate a list for the 1936 competition. Scripps purchased the National Spelling Bee in 1941, and their spokesperson maintains that they have no files prior to that date. MacNolia's niece, Georgia Lee Gay, claims to have MacNolia's diary and to have borrowed the following from it: "The word I missed was *Nemesis*. It was supposed to be spelled with a capital letter and was not part of the official list, so the judges ruled me out of the contest." *Whatever Happened to MacNolia Cox?*, 39.

25. Collins, "Best Speller Stumbles."

26. Jordan, *M-A-C-N-O-L-I-A*, 116.

27. Romain, "Tragedy of MacNolia Cox."

28. Chesley, "Spelling Bee," 3B.

29. Jordan, *M-A-C-N-O-L-I-A*, 36.

30. Ahl, "Interview with A. Van Jordan."

31. Jordan, *M-A-C-N-O-L-I-A*, 39.

32. "New Plays in Manhattan," 47.

33. Jordan, *M-A-C-N-O-L-I-A*, 83, 90.

34. "Spelling Her Way," 144.

35. Jordan, *M-A-C-N-O-L-I-A*, 129.

36. Jordan in discussion with the author.

37. Gay, *Whatever Happened to MacNolia Cox?*, 59.

Chapter Five

1. Alexander, "Magic of the Commonplace," A36.

2. Alexander, *Black Interior*, 139.

3. Rowell, "Interview with Kevin Young," 49.

4. Tate, "Nobody Loves a Genius Child," 233.

5. Kevin Young in discussion with the author, September 21, 2016.

6. Thomas, *Extraordinary Measures*, 227.

7. Young, *To Repel Ghosts: The Remix*, 3.

8. Young writes that Basquiat "said he crossed out words in his paintings so you saw them more. Life in all these words, black life I suppose, is necessarily analog, a mixtape of sorts that seeks to approximate life itself—practicing the exacting art of inexactness." *Grey Album*, 13.

9. Jones, "Renovating New Rhythms," 214.

10. Hellman, *Pentimento*, 3.

11. Marshall, *Jean-Michel Basquiat*, 16.

12. The most complete *catalogue raisonné* of Basquiat's work is the Galerie Enrico Navarra's three-volume edition titled *Jean-Michel Basquiat*.

13. McGuigan, "New Art, New Money."

14. Rowell, "Interview with Kevin Young," 49.

15. Geldzahler, "Interview with Jean-Michel Basquiat," 202; Young, *To Repel Ghosts: The Remix*, 17.

16. Rowell, "Interview with Kevin Young," 44.

17. Young discussion with the author; Lorenzo Thomas compellingly calls Young's Jack Johnson persona "ventriloquial." *Extraordinary Measures*, 227.

18. Young pointed out that an early version of the Johnson painting has Basquiat's name on it, and Basquiat kept that painting for himself. Discussion with the author.

19. Gablik, "Report from New York," 36.

20. Rosenthal, "Exclusive Story."

21. Ashe, *Hard Road to Glory*, 42.

22. Robert Hayden, whom Young credits as an influence, placed Jack Johnson in his poem "Summertime and the Living . . . ," a title that echoes the song "Summertime" written by George Gershwin for the 1935 opera *Porgy and Bess.* Hayden shortens the title of Gershwin's song, which imitates African American spirituals, eliding the words "is easy," and instead writes a poem about how the summer is "the poor folks' time / of year." Johnson appears at the poem's end in his luxurious limousine, which "set the ghetto burgeoning / with fantasies / of Ethiopia spreading her gorgeous wings," a figure that offered a promise of change. *Collected Poems*, 39.

23. Young, *To Repel Ghosts: The Remix*, 44.

24. Lynch, *Knuckles and Gloves*, 149.

25. Young, *To Repel Ghosts: The Remix*, 46.

26. London, *Jack London Reports*, 258.

27. Young, *To Repel Ghosts: The Remix*, 50–51.

28. Rape against Black women was seldom prosecuted at this time. See Danielle L. McGuire, *At the Dark End*, for a history of the fight against the rape of Black women.

29. Young, *To Repel Ghosts: The Remix*, 52.

30. Du Bois, "Prize Fighter," 181.

31. Young, *To Repel Ghosts: The Remix*, 57.

32. Batchelor, *Jack Johnson*, 16.

33. Du Bois, "Criteria of Negro Art," 292–93.

34. Ardenne, "Art Market," 108.

35. Graw, "Interview," 67.

36. Geldzahler, "Interview with Jean-Michel Basquiat," 205.

37. Young, *To Repel Ghosts: The Remix*, 291, 126.

38. Hoban, *Basquiat*, 3.

39. Birschofberger, "Reflections on and Experiences," 65.

40. Warhol, *Andy Warhol Diaries*, 519. Pat Hackett, who worked for Warhol, compiled this text, which muddies its accuracy. According to Hackett's introduction, she and Warhol would talk every weekday morning. She would take notes, and immediately after the conversation, she would type them up. Furthermore, the published account of 807 pages was created from an original twenty thousand pages; it offers what Hackett felt was "the best material and the most representative of Andy" (introduction, 17–18).

41. Graw, "Interview," 67.

42. Young, *To Repel Ghosts: The Remix*, 113–15.

43. Young, *To Repel Ghosts: The Remix*, 62.

44. Davis, *Jack Johnson*, liner notes.

45. Finis Farr, "Jack and the Game"; Young, *To Repel Ghosts: The Remix*, 67.

46. Wiggins, "Jack Johnson as Bad Nigger," 46.

47. Young, *To Repel Ghosts: The Remix*, 69–72.

48. Yau, "Street Song," 88.
49. Hebdige, "Welcome to the Terrordome," 65.
50. Alexander, *Black Interior*, 136, 135.
51. Benjamin, "Mixed-Up Medium," 195. Keith Gilyard's review offers valuable insights, particularly his argument that "in general, though *To Repel Ghosts* is a tribute, Young's lines are stronger the more he writes *around* the work of Basquiat rather than more directly *to* it" (512).
52. Young, *Giant Steps*, 6.
53. Young in discussion with the author.

Chapter Six

1. LoVerde-Dropp, "Interview with Frank X Walker."
2. Frank X Walker in discussion with the author, February 1, 2017.
3. Walker, *Turn Me Loose*, 58.
4. LoVerde-Dropp, "Interview with Frank X Walker."
5. Asim, "Interview with Frank X Walker," 32–33.
6. LoVerde-Dropp, "Interview with Frank X Walker"; Dick and Yerman, "Still Chasing These Words," 412.
7. One other poet who adopts the voice of the conservative Far Right in order to critique it is Patricia Smith in "Skinhead."
8. Gwin, *Remembering Medgar Evers*, 21.
9. Walker in discussion with the author.
10. Dillhunt and Dillhunt, "Frank X Walker."
11. Walker in discussion with the author.
12. Dillhunt and Dillhunt, "Frank X Walker."
13. Dick and Yerman, "Still Chasing These Words," 415, 416.
14. Dillhunt and Dillhunt, "Frank X Walker."
15. Evers, *For Us, the Living*, 332.
16. I have struggled with how to refer to the speakers in Walker's book. In her autobiography *For Us, the Living*, Myrlie Evers makes clear her preference to be addressed as Mrs. Medgar Evers because in Mississippi, while white women would always be addressed with a title, Black women were addressed by their first names—one of the ways in which white supremacy was enforced through custom. When faced with testifying in court about her husband's murder, Mrs. Evers declared that "I am called 'Myrlie' only by my friends. Others are treated with courtesy in court, and I expect the same treatment" (353). However, by the time Mrs. Evers wrote her second autobiography and was by then Mrs. Evers-Williams, *Watch Me Fly*, she firmly claimed her identity as an individual, and she uses her first name to differentiate herself from the role of Medgar Evers's wife and the mother of his children. Thus, I will follow her lead in referring to her as Myrlie, as well as using Medgar's and Charles's first names for clarity. I find I resist using Beckwith's first name, not out of respect but in an effort to distance myself from him, but I have used his wives' first names for clarity as well.
17. "Civil Rights Turmoil in Verse."
18. Gwin, *Remembering Medgar Evers*, 161.
19. Dillhunt and Dillhunt, "Frank X Walker."
20. Dick and Yerman, "Still Chasing These Words," 412.
21. Royals and Little, "Conversation with Eudora Welty," 265.

22. Freeman, "Interview with Eudora Welty," 183.

23. Clemons, "Meeting Miss Welty," 31.

24. Marrs, *Eudora Welty*, 308.

25. Kuehl, "Art of Fiction XLVII," 83, 100.

26. Welty, *The Collected Stories*, 603–7. For thorough readings of Welty's story, see Marrs, *Eudora Welty*, 181–85; Gwin, *Remembering Medgar Evers*, 31–61; and Harrison, "It's Still a Free Country." Harrison particularly analyzes the assassin's white supremacist mindset.

27. Buckley, "Southern Imagination," 101.

28. Gwendolyn Brooks offers a poetic model for exploring not only the white supremacist mindset but also the point of view of the white wife of a man who commits a heinous hate crime in "A Bronzeville Mother Loiters in Mississippi. Meanwhile, a Mississippi Mother Burns Bacon" (*Blacks*, 333–39). This poem about Emmett Till's murder speaks through the voice of the wife of a murderer, ostensibly Carolyn Bryant, whose husband, Roy Bryant, along with his half-brother, John William Milam, murdered Emmett Till. As Molly Littlewood McKibbin argues, "Brooks is insisting that white women shoulder some responsibility for the violence carried out in their names." "Southern Patriarchy," 667. Using a ballad form, Brooks's persona attempts to force what has happened into a typical romance paradigm with herself as the maiden, her husband as the hero, and Till as the villain, but what has happened cannot be refashioned as a heroic plot, nor will it remain within the rhyming quatrains of a conventional ballad. A former high school beauty queen and mother of two, Carolyn was twenty-one years old in 1955 when Till was killed at age fourteen. Brooks's persona combs her hair and applies lipstick before breakfast since her beauty is part of the character she is playing, a beautiful white woman who needs to be protected by white men, the touted Southern chivalry used as an excuse for decades of violence against African Americans. After throwing away the burnt bacon and cooking more—from the beginning the story fails to progress smoothly—she calls her two sons and husband to the table, as orderly as her thoughts are disordered by what has happened. The reality that the villain was a "child / Of fourteen, with eyes still too young to be dirty, / And a mouth too young to have lost every reminder / Of its infant softness," only a decade or so older than her two sons, belies the myth and forces her to question what he had done "or if anything had been done" (335). She sees that "the breaks were everywhere" in the "pattern" that had organized her life in Mississippi, and Brooks explores the system of white supremacy through the interiority of a white woman who is simultaneously oppressed and privileged by that system. Brooks's generous portrayal of her draws a person awakening to a system of social relations that now disgusts her, as do her husband and his acquittal: "a hatred for him burst into glorious flower, / And its perfume enclasped them—big, / Bigger than all magnolias" (339). Her dismal realizations segue into "The Last Quatrain of the Ballad of Emmett Till," in which Till's mother sits with his body, her son the victim of white supremacy. Historically speaking, Brooks's portrayal of Mamie Till has proven to be more accurate than that of Carolyn Bryant, who testified on her husband's behalf at his trial and spoke little on the record after that. However, in his book *The Blood of Emmett Till*, historian Timothy B. Tyson shares the interview Bryant, now Carolyn Bryant Donham, granted him in 2008 in which she admitted to fabricating

the story of assault she told in court. Tyson is also in possession of Bryant's attorney's notes, and his conclusion is:

> In this earliest recorded version of events, she charged only that Till had "insulted" her, not grabbed her, and certainly not attempted to rape her. The documents prove that there was a time when she did seem to know what had happened, and a time soon afterward when she became the mouthpiece of a monstrous lie.
>
> Now, half a century later, Carolyn offered up another truth, an unyielding truth about which her tragic counterpart, Mamie, was also adamant: "Nothing that boy did could ever justify what happened to him." (7)

Brooks's poem remains hopeful that white women in Bryant's position can gain insight and change, and Bryant has finally gone on record recanting her testimony—although far too late to save Till or punish the men who murdered him. During the summer of 2022, investigators located an unserved arrest warrant dated August 29, 1955, for Carolyn Bryant, but a grand jury in Mississippi declined to indict her, claiming there was insufficient evidence for charges of kidnapping and manslaughter.

Many critics have written about "A Bronzeville Mother Loiters in Mississippi. Meanwhile, a Mississippi Mother Burns Bacon." See McKibbin, "Southern Patriarchy," for a thorough analysis of Brooks's poem, as well as an account of its critical reception.

29. Dick and Yerman, "Still Chasing These Words," 412.

30. Clifton, *Collected Poems*, 507. In addition to Clifton, Marilyn Nelson, whom Walker met through a workshop at Cave Canem, influenced Walker's historical poetry. Walker said that Nelson, and specifically her book *Carver: A Life in Poems* about George Washington Carver, offered a model in "what it did and how it did it." Walker in discussion with the author.

31. The third trial encouraged other creative and biographical ventures. Oh the scholarly side, Minrose Gwin's 2013 *Remembering Medgar Evers* is hands down the most comprehensive and important work on Evers; Adam Nossiter wrote his 1994 biography *Of Long Memory* with a particular focus on an outsider's view of the South; Reed Massengill, the nephew of Beckwith's first wife, published an unauthorized biography of Beckwith in 1994; and Michael Vinson Williams published his 2013 biography *Medgar Evers: Mississippi Martyr*, which carefully contextualizes Evers's life and illuminates the many dangers facing African Americans when they challenged white supremacy. Most well-known is the Hollywood film *Ghosts of Mississippi* (1996), directed by Rob Reiner, that focused on the 1994 trial, a moment that offered an outcome to celebrate and an opportunity to decry Beckwith's beliefs. Ostensibly about Medgar, Myrlie's determination, and the legal system in Mississippi, the film actually focuses on Assistant District Attorney Robert (Bobby) DeLaughter and his efforts to bring this case to trial once again. DeLaughter takes center stage, and his heroic figure tries to right the wrongs done in the past. The film recreates a Southern system in which his late father-in-law, a fervent segregationist and judge, has the gun that killed Medgar in his collection; his wife Dixie leaves him, in large part because he pursues this third trial and so could embarrass her in front of the entire state; and his and his family's safety are threatened. Against a white supremacist system still willing

to punish those seeking to diminish it, DeLaughter steps up, and because of his efforts the case against Beckwith goes to court. Much to Beckwith's astonishment, he is found guilty, a satisfying ending for a late twentieth-century audience. However, the film, not unlike *The Help* (2011), is about white redemption rather than Medgar or Myrlie, who are pushed into the background, while DeLaughter, as the principled white man, is given center stage, a problem Myrlie Evers-Williams addresses in her second autobiography, *Watch Me Fly: What I Learned on the Way to Becoming the Woman I Was Meant to Be*. After reading the script, she wrote Reiner about her disappointment:

> The film they were making wasn't really about Medgar, but rather about Bobby DeLaughter. Certainly, I had no desire to minimize DeLaughter's contribution; he was a good friend and an important ally, and without him I would never have seen justice done. But there would have been no trial in the first place if Medgar hadn't worked toward change in Mississippi.

Myrlie accepted Reiner's reply as sincere when he said, "I'm White, Myrlie, and I can't make a movie about Medgar. . . . But maybe someone like Spike Lee will." She also believed that "the executives at Castle Rock Entertainment subscribed to the Hollywood presumption that to make a *big* movie, a White man, in this case Bobby DeLaughter, had to be the central hero" (217). The successful third trial also produced a book by DeLaughter himself, *Never Too Late: A Prosecutor's Story of Justice in the Medgar Evers Case*. DeLaughter's book focuses on the trial and the process of building a final case against Beckwith, a focus that allows a useful exploration of the white supremacist system that supported Beckwith in the 1960s and that, while it has diminished but not disappeared, resulted in death threats to DeLaughter and his defeat when he ran for a judgeship a few years later.

32. Walker, in discussion with the author.
33. Walker, *Turn Me Loose*, 30, 31.
34. Walker, *Turn Me Loose*, 22.
35. Walker, *Turn Me Loose*, 36, 37.
36. Walker, *Turn Me Loose*, 38.
37. Evers, *For Us, the Living*, 155–58, 169–70, 377–78.
38. Walker, *Turn Me Loose*, 39.
39. Evers, *For Us, the Living*, 235.
40. Walker, *Turn Me Loose*, 39, 48.
41. Walker, *Turn Me Loose*, 8–9, 64.
42. Walker, *Turn Me Loose*, 53, 62, 61.
43. Evers, *For Us, the Living*, 315.
44. Walker, *Turn Me Loose*, 63, 65.
45. Walker, *Turn Me Loose*, 58, 4, 29.
46. Walker, *Turn Me Loose*, 23, 12.
47. DeLaughter, *Never Too Late*.
48. Evers, *For Us, the Living*, 355.
49. DeLaughter, *Never Too Late*.
50. Walker, *Turn Me Loose*, 18, 10, 7, 33, 17, 19, 51.
51. Walker, *Turn Me Loose*, 50, 59, 20, 21.
52. See McGuire, *At the Dark End*.

53. Walker, *Turn Me Loose*, 32, 34, 60.
54. Walker, *Turn Me Loose*, 52, 60.
55. Walker, *Turn Me Loose*, 65, 66.

Chapter Seven

1. Dungy, *Guidebook*, 45.
2. Camille T. Dungy in discussion with the author, March 2, 2017.
3. Dungy in discussion with the author.
4. Dungy, "Interview with Rita Dove," 1029.
5. Blassingame, *Slave Community*, xvii.
6. Dungy in discussion with the author.
7. Dungy and Matejka, "Full of Many Stars," 20, 32–33.
8. Dungy, "Unwelcome in My Church."
9. Dungy in discussion with the author.
10. Dungy in discussion with the author.
11. Atwood, "Aliens Have Taken the Place."
12. Butler, *Kindred*, 230.
13. Dungy, "Interview with Rita Dove," 1029.
14. Dungy in discussion with the author.
15. Dungy, *Suck on the Marrow*, 81.
16. Du Bois, *Philadelphia Negro*, 15.
17. Dungy, *Suck on the Marrow*, 17.
18. Winch, *Between Slavery and Freedom*, 62.
19. Wilson, *Freedom at Risk*, 10–11.
20. Foner, *Gateway to Freedom*, 50, 51.
21. Wilson, *Freedom at Risk*, 120.
22. Dungy, *Suck on the Marrow*, 18, 19.
23. Dungy in discussion with the author.
24. Dungy, *Suck on the Marrow*, 20.
25. Dungy, *Suck on the Marrow*, 27, 21, 22.
26. Dungy and Matejka, "Full of Many Stars," 30.
27. Winch, *Between Slavery and Freedom*, 85.
28. Dunbar, *Fragile Freedom*, 3, 71.
29. Nash, *Forging Freedom*, 7.
30. Dungy, *Suck on the Marrow*, 70.
31. Dungy and Matejka, "Full of Many Stars," 33–34.
32. Dunbar, *Fragile Freedom*, 49.
33. Dungy, *Suck on the Marrow*, 70.
34. Winch, *Between Slavery and Freedom*, 71.
35. See Diemer, *Politics of Black Citizenship*, for a full analysis of colonization and the Free Black community.
36. Dungy, *Suck on the Marrow*, 66, 73, 66.
37. For information on the Underground Railroad and African Americans in Philadelphia, also see Switala, *Underground Railroad in Pennsylvania.*
38. Dungy, *Suck on the Marrow*, 73.
39. Dungy and Matejka, "Full of Many Stars," 25.
40. Dungy, *Suck on the Marrow*, 72, 71.
41. Dungy, *Suck on the Marrow*, 42, 57.

42. Dungy and Matejka, "Full of Many Stars," 44.
43. Dungy, *Suck on the Marrow*, 57.
44. Dungy, *Suck on the Marrow*, 31.
45. Marie Jenkins Schwartz, *Birthing a Slave*, 22–25, 34.
46. Sublette, *American Slave Coast*, 3.
47. Dungy, *Suck on the Marrow*, 43.
48. Dungy in discussion with the author.
49. Thoreau, *Walden*, 88.
50. Dungy, *Suck on the Marrow*, 47–48.
51. Delaney and Rhodes, *Free Black of Lynchburg*, 37, 32.
52. Dungy and Matejka, "Full of Many Stars," 27.
53. Delaney and Rhodes, *Free Black of Lynchburg*, 40.
54. Dungy, *Suck on the Marrow*, 50–55.
55. Dungy, *Suck on the Marrow*, 61–62.
56. See Ruggles, *The Unboxing*.
57. Dungy and Matejka, "Full of Many Stars," 25–26.
58. Dungy and Matejka, "Full of Many Stars," 37.
59. Dungy, *Suck on the Marrow*, 60, 68.

Conclusion

1. Major Jackson in discussion with the author, April 4, 2016.
2. Jackson, *Roll Deep*, 42.
3. Mendi + Keith Obadike, *Big House/Disclosure, 82*.
4. Martin, *a gathering of matter*, 39.
5. Berlin, *Many Thousands Gone*, 160.
6. Martin, *a gathering of matter*, 41.
7. Lansana, *They Shall Run*, 31.
8. Hills, *Painting Harlem Modern*, 93; Nesbett and DuBois, *Jacob Lawrence*, 163.
9. Wheat, *Jacob Lawrence American Painter*, 116.
10. Hills, *Painting Harlem Modern*, 75.
11. Shockley, *new black*, 101.
12. Shockley, *new black*, 23–26.
13. This sequence has now been published in Smith's *Wade in the Water* in the second section, which offers other historical poems. Her notes in this volume offer a comprehensive guide to the sources she used in writing this found poetry.
14. Smith, "Back to Earth."
15. Young, *Giant Steps*, 6.
16. Schwartz, "Moving Toward," 191–92.
17. Baldwin, "White Man's Guilt," 410.
18. Chang, "The Public Life."
19. Browning, "Making a Necessity."
20. Baldwin, "White Man's Guilt," 410.

BIBLIOGRAPHY

Ahl, Lindsay. "Interview with A. Van Jordan." *Shadowgraph Magazine*. Summer 2013. https://www.shadowgraf.com/interviews/interviews-with-writers/a-van-jordan/.

Akin, Edward N., and Charles C. Bolton. *Mississippi: An Illustrated History*. Staunton, VA: American Historical Press, 2002.

Alexander, Elizabeth. *The Black Interior*. Minneapolis: Graywolf Press, 2004.

———. *Crave Radiance: New and Selected Poems 1990–2010*. Minneapolis: Graywolf Press, 2010.

———. Introduction to *Gathering Ground: Celebrating Cave Canem's First Decade*, edited by Toi Derricotte, Cornelius Eady, and Camille T. Dungy, 6–7. Ann Arbor: University of Michigan Press, 2006.

———. "The Magic of the Commonplace." Review of *Romare Bearden: His Life and Art* by Myron Schwartzman. *New York Times*, March 24, 1991, A36.

———. "The Negro Digs Up Her Past: 'Amistad.'" *South Atlantic Quarterly* 104, no. 3 (Summer 2005): 463–80.

———. "The One Who Went Before." *American Scholar* 75, no. 1 (Winter 2006): 122–25.

———. *The Venus Hottentot*. Charlottesville: University Press of Virginia, 1990.

Alexander, Elizabeth, and Marilyn Nelson. *Miss Crandall's School for Young Ladies and Little Misses of Color*. Honesdale, PA: Wordsong, 2007.

Antonucci, Michael. "Spirits of '76: Michael S. Harper's 'Bristol: Bicentenary Remembrances of Trade.'" *Worcester Review* 35, no. 12 (2014): 165–79.

———. "The Map and the Territory: An Interview with Michael S. Harper." *African American Review* 34, no. 3 (2000): 501–9.

Aptheker, Herbert, ed. *The Correspondence of W. E. B. Du Bois*. Amherst: University of Massachusetts Press, 1973.

———. *Nat Turner's Slave Rebellion*. New York: American Institute for Marxist Studies, 1966.

Ardenne, Paul. "The Art Market in the 1980s." Translated by Michel Vale. *International Journal of Political Economy* 25, no. 2 (Summer 1995): 100–128.

Ashe, Arthur R., Jr. *A Hard Road to Glory: A History of the African-American Athlete 1619–1918*. New York: Warner, 1988.

Asim, Jabari. "An Interview with Frank X Walker." *Crisis* 120, no. 3 (Summer 2013): 32–33.

Atkinson, Ted. "Natasha Trethewey's Joe Christmas and the Reconstruction of Mississippi Nativity." In *Faulkner and the Black Literature of the Americas*., edited by Jay Watson and James G. Thomas Jr., 245–55. Jackson: University Press of Mississippi, 2016.

Atwood, Margaret. "Aliens Have Taken the Place of Angels." *The Guardian*, June 16, 2005. https://www.theguardian.com/film/2005/jun/17/sciencefiction fantasyandhorror.margaretatwood.

———. *The Handmaid's Tale*. New York: Ballantine, 1985.

Baldwin, James. "Black English: A Dishonest Argument." In *The Cross of Redemption: Uncollected Writings*, edited by Randall Kenan, 154–60. New York: Vintage, 2010.

———. "White Man's Guilt." In *Price of the Ticket: Collected Nonfiction 1948–1985*, 409–14. New York: St. Martin's Press, 1985.

Balfour, Emma Harrison. *Mrs. Balfour's Civil War Diary: A Personal Account of the Siege of Vicksburg*, edited by Gordon A. Cotton. Vicksburg, MS: G. A. Cotton, 2006.

Barry, John M. *Rising Tide: The Great Mississippi Flood of 1927 and How It Changed America*. New York Simon and Schuster, 1997.

Batchelor, Denzil. *Jack Johnson and His Times*. London: Phoenix Sports Books, 1956.

Bellin, Steven. "Tricking the Muse by Taking Out the Trash." In *Conversations with Rita Dove*, edited by Earl G. Ingersoll, 121–35. Jackson: University Press of Mississippi, 2003.

Benét, Stephen Vincent. *John Brown's Body*. New York: Rinehart, 1928.

Benjamin, Rick. "Mixed-Up Medium: Kevin Young's Turn-of-the-Century American Triptych." In *American Poets in the 21st Century: The New Poetics*, edited by Claudia Rankine and Lisa Sewell, 193–209. Middletown: Wesleyan University Press, 2007.

Bennett, Lerone, Jr. *The Negro Mood and Other Essays*. Chicago: Johnson Publishing, 1964.

Berlin, Ira. *Many Thousands Gone: The First Two Centuries of Slavery in North America*. Cambridge, MA: Belknap Press, 1998.

Berlin, Ira, and Leslie S. Rowland, eds. *Families and Freedom: A Documentary History of African-American Kinship in the Civil War Era*. New York: New Press, 1997.

Bingham, Remica L. "Interview with Natasha Trethewey." In *Conversations with Natasha Trethewey*, edited by Joan Wylie Hall, 61–76. Jackson: University Press of Mississippi, 2013.

Birdsong, Destiny O. "'Memories that are(n't) mine': Matrilineal Trauma and Defiant Reinscription in Natasha Trethewey's *Native Guard*." *African American Review* 48, nos. 1–2 (Spring/Summer 2015): 97–110.

Bischofberger, Bruno. "Reflections on and Experiences with Basquiat, Clemente and Warhol." In *Jean-Michel Basquiat*, edited by Géraldine Pfeffer-Lévy, 2:62–67. Paris: Galerie Enrico Navarra, 2010.

Blassingame, John, W. *The Slave Community: Plantation Life in the Antebellum South*. New York: Oxford University Press, 1972.

Boone, N. S. "Resignation to History: The Black Arts Movement and Rita Dove's Political Consciousness." *Obsidian III* 5, no. 1 (Spring-Summer 2004): 66–83.

Brooks, Gwendolyn. *Blacks*. Chicago: Third World Press, 1987.

Brouwer, Joel. Review of *Honorable Amendments* by Michael S. Harper. *Harvard Review* 10 (Spring 1996): 207–8.

Browning, Maria. “Making a Necessity of Memory: Poet Natasha Trethewey Talks about History, Her Work, Her Biracial Identity, and the Violence in Her Past.” *Chapter 16*, March 16, 2015. https://chapter16.org/making-a-necessity-of-memory.

Buckley, William F., Jr. “‘The Southern Imagination’: An Interview with Eudora Welty and Walker Percy.” In *Conversations with Eudora Welty*, edited by Peggy Whitman Prenshaw, 92–114. Jackson: University Press of Mississippi, 1984.

Burns, Ken, dir. *Unforgivable Blackness: The Rise and Fall of Jack Johnson.* Arlington, VA: WETA and Florentine Films, 2004. Film.

Butler, Octavia. *Kindred*. Boston: Beacon, 1979.

Byerman, Keith E. *Seizing the Word: History, Art, and Self in the Work of W. E. B. Du Bois*. Athens: University of Georgia Press, 1994.

Cade, Toni. *The Black Woman: An Anthology*. New York: Signet, 1970.

Cavalieri, Grace. “Brushed by an Angel’s Wings.” In *Conversations with Rita Dove*, edited by Earl G. Ingersoll, 136–47. Jackson: University Press of Mississippi, 2003.

Cedar Grove Mansion Inn and Restaurant. Website and marketing by L. E. T. Group. July 7, 2017. Cedargroveinn.com.

Cha-Jua, Sundiata Keita, and Clarence Lang. “The ‘Long Movement’ as Vampire: Temporal and Spatial Fallacies in Recent Black Freedom Studies.” *Journal of African American History* 92, no. 2 (Spring 2007): 265–88.

“Champion. Ohio Girl, Champion Speller Defeats All Opponents, ‘Voluble’ Is Winning Word.” *Negro Star*, May 15, 1936, 1.

Chang, Jennifer. “The Public Life of Poetry: An Interview with Natasha Trethewey.” *Los Angeles Review of Books*, June 11, 2013. https://lareviewofbooks.org/article/the-public-life-of-poetry-an-interview-with-natasha-trethewey.

Chase-Riboud, Barbara. *Hottentot Venus: A Novel*. New York: Doubleday, 2003.

Chesley, Mabel Norris. “Spelling Bee a Big Event.” *Daytona Beach Morning Journal*, November 1, 1975, 3B.

Church, L. Teresa, Lenard D. Moore, and Evie Shockley. “Incident in the Lives of Three African American Poets, Written by Themselves.” *African American Review* 38, no. 2 (Summer 2004): 281–88.

Cimprich, John. “The Fort Pillow Massacre: Assessing the Evidence.” In *Black Soldiers in Blue: African American Troops in the Civil War Era*, edited by John David Smith, 150–68. Chapel Hill: University of North Carolina Press, 2002.

“Civil Rights Turmoil in Verse: Retelling Medgar Evers’ Story.” NPR. December 26, 2013. https://www.npr.org/2013/12/26/256869886/poetry-uncovers-legacy-of-medgar-evers-50-years-later.

Clark, Norris B. “Michael S. Harper (18 March 1938–).” In *Afro-American Poets Since 1955*, edited by Trudier Harris-Lopez and Thadious M. Davis, vol. 41, *Dictionary of Literary Biography Main Series*, 152–66. Farmington Hills, MI: Gale, 1985.

Clemons, Walter. “Meeting Miss Welty.” In *Conversations with Eudora Welty*, edited by Peggy Whitman Prenshaw, 30–34. Jackson: University Press of Mississippi, 1984.

Clifton, Lucille. *The Collected Poems*. Rochester: BOA Editions, 2012.

Collins, Florence M. “Best Speller Stumbles over Word Nemesis.” *The Afro American*, May 30, 1936, n.p.

Crais, Clifton, and Pamela Scully. *Sara Baartman and the Hottentot Venus: A Ghost Story and a Biography*. Princeton, NJ: Princeton University Press, 2009.

Davis, Charles T. "Robert Hayden's Use of History. In *Modern Black Poets: A Collection of Critical Essays*, edited by Donald B. Gibson, 96–111. Englewood Cliffs, NJ: Prentice-Hall, 1973.

Davis, Miles. *Jack Johnson*. 30th Street Studio, New York. Columbia Records, 1971. Album.

Davis, Thadious M. "Enfoldments: Natasha Trethewey's Racial-Spatial Phototexting." *Southern Quarterly* 50, no. 4 (Summer 2013): 37–54.

———. *Southscapes: Geographies of Race, Region, and Literature*. Chapel Hill: University of North Carolina Press, 2011.

De Cenzo, Giorgia. "Natasha Trethewey: The Native Guard of Southern History." *South Atlantic Review* 73, no. 1 (Winter 2008): 20–49.

Debo, Annette. "Ophelia Speaks: Resurrecting Still Lives in Natasha Trethewey's *Bellocq's Ophelia*." *African American Review* 42, no. 2 (Summer 2008): 201–14.

———. "Reflecting Violence in the Warpland: Gwendolyn Brooks's *Riot*." *African American Review* 39, nos. 1–2 (Spring/Summer 2005): 143–52.

Delaney, Ted, and Phillip Wayne Rhodes. *Free Blacks of Lynchburg, Virginia 1805–1865*. Lynchburg, VA: Warwick House, 2001.

DeLaughter, Bobby. *Never Too Late: A Prosecutor's Story of Justice in the Medgar Evers Case*. New York: Scribner, 2001.

Derricotte, Toi. Introduction to *Gathering Ground: Celebrating Cave Canem's First Decade*, edited by Toi Derricotte, Cornelius Eady, and Camille T. Dungy, 4–6. Ann Arbor: University of Michigan Press, 2006.

DeVries, Lisa. "Because of Blood: Natasha Trethewey's Historical Memory—Interview." In *Conversations with Natasha Trethewey*, edited by Joan Wylie Hall, 106–12. Jackson: University Press of Mississippi, 2013.

Dew, Charles B. "The Slavery Experience." In *Interpreting Southern History: Historiographical Essays in Honor of Sanford W. Higginbotham*, edited by John B. Boles and Evelyn Thomas Nolen, 120–61. Baton Rouge: Louisiana State University Press, 1987.

Dick, Bruce Allen, and Forrest Gray Yerman. "'Still Chasing These Words': A Conversation with Frank X Walker." *Appalachian Journal* 38, no. 4 (Summer 2011): 408–22.

Diemer, Andrew K., *The Politics of Black Citizenship: Free African Americans in the Mid-Atlantic Borderland, 1817–1863*. Athens: University of Georgia Press, 2016.

Dillhunt, CX, and Drew Dillhunt. "Frank X Walker." *Verse Wisconsin Online* 110 (October 2012). http://www.versewisconsin.org/Issue110/prose/walker.html.

Dodd, Elizabeth. "The Great Rainbowed Swamp: History as Moral Ecology in the Poetry of Michael S. Harper." *ISLE* 7, no. 1 (Winter 2000): 131–45.

Dove, Rita. Foreword to *Wheels of Fortune: The Story of Rubber in Akron*, by Steve Love and David Giffels. vii–viii. Akron: University of Akron Press, 1998.

———. *Grace Notes*. New York: Norton, 1989.

———. *Museum*. Pittsburgh: Carnegie Mellon University Press, 1983.

———. "Poet's Choice." *Washington Post*, September 24, 2000. https://www.washingtonpost.com/archive/entertainment/books/2000/09/24/poets-choice/3572bc22-ead8-4bcf-93d0-619b97a7ce03.

———. *Thomas and Beulah*. Pittsburgh: Carnegie Mellon University Press, 1986.

Du Bois, W. E. B. "Criteria of Negro Art." *The Crisis* 32 (October 1926): 290–97.

———. *John Brown*. Edited by Henry Louis Gates, Jr. New York: Oxford University Press, 2007.

———. *The Philadelphia Negro: A Social Study*, edited by Henry Louis Gates Jr. with an introduction by Laurence Bobo. New York: Oxford University Press, 2007.

———. "The Prize Fighter." *The Crisis*, August 1914, 181.

Dunbar, Erica Armstrong. *A Fragile Freedom: African American Women and Emancipation in the Antebellum City*. New Haven, CT: Yale University Press, 2008.

Dungy, Camille T. *Black Nature: Four Centuries of African American Nature Poetry*. Athens: University of Georgia Press, 2009.

———. "A Brief History of Near and Actual Losses." *VQR* (Summer 2014): 175–81.

———. *Guidebook to Relative Strangers*. New York: Norton, 2017.

———. "In Others' Voices: The Millennial Poets and Personae." *Black Issues Book Review* 8, no. 2 (March-April 2006): 16–17.

———. "Interview with Rita Dove." *Callaloo* 28, no. 4 (2005): 1027–40.

———. "A Shade North of Ordinary." *New England Review* 36, no. 2 (2015): 157–67.

———. *Suck on the Marrow*. Pasadena, CA: Red Hen Press, 2010.

———. "Unwelcome in My Country, Unwelcome in My Church." Literary Hub, Grove Atlantic and Electric Literature. January 24, 2017. https://lithub.com/unwelcome-in-my-country-unwelcome-in-my-church/.

Dungy, Camille T., and Adrian Matejka. "Full of Many Stars: Pushing Past (and Pushing the Past into) the Heliocentric Poem." In *Tracking/Teaching: On Documentary Poetics*, edited by Joseph Harrington, 17–45. Buffalo, NY: Essay Press, 2015. https://www.essaypress.org/wp-content/uploads/2015/04/harringtonltspread1.pdf.

Eady, Cornelius. Introduction to *Gathering Ground: Celebrating Cave Canem's First Decade*, edited by Toi Derricotte, Cornelius Eady, and Camille T. Dungy, 1–4. Ann Arbor: University of Michigan Press, 2006.

Edwards, Frank, Hedwig Lee, and Michael Esposito. "Risk of Being Killed by Police Use of Force in the United States by Age, Race-Ethnicity, and Sex." *Proceedings of the National Academy of Sciences of the United States* 116, no. 34 (2019): 16793–98.

Ellison, Ralph. "An American Dilemma: A Review." In *Shadow and Act*, 303–27. New York: Random House, 1964.

Evers, Myrlie. *For Us, the Living*. New York: Doubleday, 1967.

Evers-Williams, Myrlie. *Watch Me Fly: What I Learned on the Way to Becoming the Woman I Was Meant to Be*. Boston: Little, Brown, 1999.

Farr, Finis. "Jack and the Game." *Sports Illustrated*, June 22, 1959. http://www.si.com/vault/1959/06/22/607143/jack-and-the-game.

Faulkner, William. *Absalom, Absalom!* New York: Modern Library, 1993. First published 1936 by Random House (New York).

Fetrow, Fred M. "'Middle Passage': Robert Hayden's Anti-Epic." *CLA Journal* 22 (1979): 304–18.

———. "Portraits and Personae: Characterization in the Poetry of Robert Hayden." In *Black American Poets between Worlds, 1940–1960*, edited by R. Baxter Miller, 43–76. Knoxville: University of Tennessee Press, 1986.

Foner, Eric. *Gateway to Freedom: The Hidden History of the Underground Railroad*. New York: Norton, 2015.

———. *Who Owns History?: Rethinking the Past in a Changing World*. New York: Farrar, Straus, and Giroux, 2002.

Freeman, Jean Todd. "An Interview with Eudora Welty." In *Conversations with Eudora Welty*, edited by Peggy Whitman Prenshaw, 172–99. Jackson: University Press of Mississippi, 1984.

Friedlander, Benjamin. "Robert Hayden's Epic of Community." *MELUS* 23, no. 3 (September 1998): 129–43.

Gabbin, Joanne V., and Lauren K. Alleyne, eds. *Furious Flower: Seeding the Future of African American Poetry*. Evanston, IL: Northwestern University Press, 2020.

Gablik, Suzi. "Report from New York: The Graffiti Question." *Art in America*, October 1982: 33–39.

Gallagher, Catherine, and Stephen Greenblatt. *Practicing New Historicism*. Chicago: University of Chicago Press, 2000.

Gay, Georgia Lee. *Whatever Happened to MacNolia Cox?* Baltimore: Publish America, 2008.

Geldzahler, Henry. "Interview with Jean-Michel Basquiat." In *Making It New: Essays, Interviews, and Talks*, 197–205. New York: Harcourt Brace, 1996.

Gilman, Sander L. "Black Bodies, White Bodies: Toward an Iconography of Female Sexuality in Late Nineteenth-Century Art, Medicine, and Literature." *Critical Inquiry* 12, no. 1 (Autumn 1985): 204–42.

Gilman, Sander L. "Black Bodies, White Bodies: Toward an Iconography of Female Sexuality in Late Nineteenth-Century Art, Medicine, and Literature." In *"Race," Writing, and Difference*, edited by Henry Louis Gates Jr., 223–61. Chicago: University of Chicago Press, 1985.

Gilyard, Keith. "*To Repel Ghosts*: Five Sides in B Minor." *African American Review* 36, no. 3 (Fall 2002): 510–12.

Goad, Jill. "Throwaway Bodies in the Poetry of Natasha Trethewey." *South: A Scholarly Journal* 48, no. 2 (Spring 2016): 265–82.

Goodman, James. Editorial. *Rethinking History* 23, no. 1 (2019): 1.

Gordon-Chipembere, Natasha. "Claiming Sarah Baartman: The Politics of Representing Black Women in the Twenty-First Century." In *Expressions of the Body: Representations in African Text and Image*, edited by Charlotte Parker, 297–312. Oxford: Peter Lang, 2009.

Gould, Stephen Jay. "The Hottentot Venus." *Natural History* 91, no. 010 (October 1982): 20–27.

———. *The Mismeasure of Man*. New York: Norton, 1981.

Graw, Isabelle. "Interview." In *Basquiat*, edited by Luca Marenzi, 67. Milan: Charta, 1999.

Gross, Terry. "Poet Laureate: 'Poetry's Always a Kind of Faith.'" *Fresh Air*, produced by NPR. June 8, 2012. https://www.wuwm.com/2012–06–08/poet-laureate-poetrys-always-a-kind-of-faith.

———. "Poet Natasha Trethewey, Hymning the Native Guard." *Fresh Air*, produced by NPR. July 16, 2007. https://freshairarchive.org/segments/poet-natasha-trethewey-hymning-native-guard.

Grossman, Lionel. "History and Literature: Reproduction or Signification." In *The Writing of History: Literary Form and Historical Understanding*, edited by Robert H. Canary and Henry Kozicki, 3–39. Madison: University of Wisconsin Press, 1978.

Gutkind, Lee, and Hattie Fletcher, eds. *Keep It Real: Everything You Need to Know about Researching and Writing Creative Nonfiction*. New York: Norton, 2008.

Gwin, Minrose. *Remembering Medgar Evers: Writing the Long Civil Rights Movement*. Athens: University of Georgia Press, 2013.

Hackett, Pat. Introduction to *The Andy Warhol Diaries*, edited by Pat Hackett, 9–19. New York: Warner, 1989.

Hall, Jacquelyn Dowd. "The Long Civil Rights Movement and the Political Uses of the Past." *Journal of American History* 91 (March 2005): 1233–63.

Hall, Joan Wylie. "'The Larger Stage of These United States': Creativity Conversation with Natasha Trethewey and Rosemary Magee." *Southern Quarterly* 50, no. 4 (Summer 2013): 17–28.

Haney, David. "A Conversation with Natasha Trethewey." In *Conversations with Natasha Trethewey*, edited by Joan Wylie Hall, 18–32. Jackson: University Press of Mississippi, 2013.

Harding, Vincent. "Beyond Chaos: Black History and the Search for the New Land." *Amistad 1* (1970): 267–92.

Harper, Michael S. *Dear John, Dear Coltrane*. Pittsburgh: University of Pittsburgh Press, 1970.

———. *Debridement*. New York: Doubleday, 1973.

———. "Every Shut-Eye Ain't Asleep / Every Good-Bye Ain't Gone." *Obsidian/Black Literature in Review* 8, no. 1 (Spring 1981): 9–15.

———. *Healing Song for the Inner Ear*. Urbana: University of Illinois Press, 1983.

———. *History Is Your Own Heartbeat*. Urbana: University of Illinois Press, 1972.

———. *Images of Kin: New and Selected Poems*. Urbana: University of Illinois Press, 1977.

———. "Remembering Robert Hayden." *Michigan Quarterly Review* 21 (Winter 1982): 182–86.

Harper, Michael S., and Aldon Lynn Nielsen. "Conversation." In *The Furious Flowering of African American Poetry*, edited by Joanne V. Gabbi, 77–96. Charlottesville: University of Virginia Press, 1999.

Harper, Michael S., and Anthony Walton, eds. *Every Shut Eye Ain't Asleep: An Anthology of Poetry by African Americans since 1945*. Boston: Little, Brown, 1994.

———. *The Vintage Book of African American Poetry*. New York: Vintage, 2000.

Harris, Robert L., Jr. "Coming of Age: The Transformation of Afro-American Historiography." *Journal of Negro History* 67, no. 2 (Summer 1982): 107–21.

Harrison, Suzan. "'It's Still a Free Country': Constructing Race, Identity, and History in Eudora Welty's 'Where Is the Voice Coming From?'" *Mississippi Quarterly* 50, no. 4 (Fall 1997): 631–46.

Hayden, Robert. *American Journal*. Taunton: Effendi Press, 1978.

———. *A Ballad of Remembrance*. London: Paul Breman, 1962.

———. *Collected Poems*, edited by Frederick Glaysher. New York: Liveright, 1985.

———. *Collected Prose*, edited by Frederick Glaysher. Ann Arbor: University of Michigan Press, 1984.

Hayden, Robert, and Michael Harper. "Robert Hayden and Michael Harper: A Literary Friendship." *Callaloo* 17, no. 4 (Autumn 1994): 980–1016.

Hebdige, Dick. "Welcome to the Terrordome: Jean-Michel Basquiat and the 'Dark' Side of Hybridity." In *Jean-Michel Basquiat*, edited by Richard Marshall, 60–70. New York: Whitney Museum of American Art, 1992.

Hellman, Lillian. *Pentimento: A Book of Portraits*. Boston: Little, Brown, 1973.

Henninger, Katherine R., "What Remains: Race, Nation, and the Adult Child in the Poetry of Natasha Trethewey." *Southern Quarterly* 50, no. 4 (Summer 2013): 55–74.

Hewitt, Lawrence Lee. "An Ironic Route to Glory: Louisiana's Native Guards at Port Hudson." In *Black Soldiers in Blue: African American Troops in the Civil War Era*, edited by John David Smith, 78–106. Chapel Hill: University of North Carolina Press, 2002.

Hills, Patricia. *Painting Harlem Modern: The Art of Jacob Lawrence*. Berkeley: University of California Press, 2009.

Hirsch, Edward. "Mean to Be Free." *The Nation*, December 21, 1985, 685–86.

Hoban, Phoebe. *Basquiat: A Quick Killing in Art*. New York: Viking, 1998.

Hobson, Janell. *Venus in the Dark: Blackness and Beauty in Popular Culture*. New York: Routledge, 2005.

Hollandsworth, James G., Jr. *The Louisiana Native Guards: The Black Military Experience During the Civil War*. Baton Rouge: Louisiana State University Press, 1995.

Holmes, Rachel. *African Queen: The Real Life of the Hottentot Venus*. New York: Random House, 2007.

Holt, Thomas C. "African-American History." In *The New American History*, edited by Eric Foner, 211–31. Philadelphia: Temple University Press, 1990.

hooks, bell. *Black Looks: Race and Representation*. Boston: South End Press, 1992.

Hoppenthaler, John. "Interview with Michael S. Harper." *Connotation Press: An Online Artifact*. https://www.connotationpress.com/a-poetry-congeries-with-john-hoppenthaler/december-2009/233-michael-s-harper-poetry.

Howard, W. Scott. "Resistance, Sacrifice, and Historicity in the Elegies of Robert Hayden." In *Reading the Middle Generation Anew: Culture, Community, and Form in Twentieth-Century American Poetry*, edited by Eric Haralson, 133–52. Iowa City: University of Iowa Press, 2006.

Hughes, Langston. *The Collected Poems of Langston Hughes*, edited by Arnold Rampersad and David Roessel. New York: Vintage, 1994.

———. Foreword to *Poems from Black Africa*, 11–15. Bloomington: Indiana University Press, 1963.

Ingersoll, Earl G. "Not the Shouted Slogan but the Whisper for Help." In *Conversations with Rita Dove*, edited by Earl G. Ingersoll,180–93. Jackson: University Press of Mississippi, 2003.

"An Interview with A. Van Jordan." *Nashville Review*, December 1, 2014. https://as.vanderbilt.edu/nashvillereview/archives/9559.

Jackson, Lawrence. *Ralph Ellison: Emergence of Genius*. New York: Wiley, 2002.

Jackson, Major. "The Historical Poem." *American Poet* 35 (2008): 3–6.

———. *Roll Deep*. New York: Norton, 2015.

Jean-Michel Basquiat, edited by Géraldine Pfeffer-Lévy, 3 vols. Paris: Galerie Enrico Navarra, 2010.

Jones, Meta DuEwa. "Renovating New Rhythms in the Present-Future of Black Poetry and Music." In *Furious Flower: Seeding the Future of African American Poetry*, edited by Joanne V. Gabbin and Lauren K. Alleyne, 213–30. Evanston, IL: Northwestern University Press, 2020.

Jordan, A. Van. *M-A-C-N-O-L-I-A*. New York: Norton, 2004.

Kaplan, Sara. "Interview: Natasha Trethewey on Facts, Photographs, and Loss." In *Conversations with Natasha Trethewey*, edited by Joan Wylie Hall, 37–44. Jackson: University Press of Mississippi, 2013.

Kaplan, Sidney. "The Miscegenation Issue in the Election of 1864." *Journal of Negro History* 34, no. 3 (1949): 274–343.

Keller, Lynn. *Forms of Expansion: Recent Long Poems by Women*. Chicago: University of Chicago Press, 1997.

Kim, Jee Eun. "'His Story Intersecting with My Own': Miscegenation as History in Natasha Trethewey's *Native Guard*." *Valley Voices: A Literary Review* 12, no. 2 (Fall 2012): 91–95.

Klarman, Michael J. *Brown v. Board of Education and the Civil Rights Movement*. New York: Oxford University Press, 2007.

Kuehl, Linda. "The Art of Fiction XLVII: Eudora Welty." In *Conversations with Eudora Welty*, edited by Peggy Whitman Prenshaw, 74–91. Jackson: University Press of Mississippi, 1984.

Kutzinski, Vera M. "Changing Permanences: Historical and Literary Revisionism in Robert Hayden's 'Middle Passage.'" *Callaloo* 26, no. 1 (Winter 1986): 171–83.

Lambert, Raphaël. "The Slave Trade as Memory and History: James A. Emanuel's 'The Middle Passage Blues' and Robert Hayden's 'Middle Passage.'" *African American Review* 47, nos. 2–3 (Summer/Fall 2014): 327–38.

Lansana, Quraysh Ali. *They Shall Run: Harriet Tubman Poems*. Chicago: Third World, 2004.

Lehman, David. "Politics." *Poetry* 123, no. 3 (December 1973): 173–80.

LeMahieu, Michael. "Robert Lowell, Perpetual War, and the Legacy of Civil War Elegy." *College Literature* 43, no. 1 (Winter 2016): 91–120.

Leonard, Keith D. *Fettered Genius: The African American Bardic Poet from Slavery to Civil Rights*. Charlottesville: University of Virginia Press, 2006.

Lindner, April. "Eloquent Silences: Lyric Solutions to the Problem of the Biographical Narrative." In *The Contemporary Narrative Poem: Critical Crosscurrents*, edited by Steven P. Schneider, 102–22. Iowa City: University of Iowa Press, 2012.

Loewen, James W. *Lies My Teacher Told Me: Everything Your American History Textbook Got Wrong*. New York: Simon and Schuster, 1995.

London, Jack. *Jack London Reports: War Correspondence, Sports Articles, and Miscellaneous Writings*, edited by King Hendricks and Irving Shepard. New York: Doubleday, 1970.

Loughborough, Mary Ann Webster. *My Cave Life in Vicksburg: With Letters of Trial and Travel; by a Lady*. New York: D. Appleton, 1864.

Love, Steve, and David Giffels. *Wheels of Fortune: The Story of Rubber in Akron*. Akron, OH: University of Akron Press, 1998.

LoVerde-Dropp, JoAnn. "An Interview with Frank X Walker." *Poetry Matters: Poetry Book Reviews and Interviews*. June 30, 2014. http://readwritepoetry.blogspot.com/2014/06/an-interview-with-frank-x-walker.html.

Lynch, Bohun [John Gilbert]. *Knuckles and Gloves*. New York: Henry Holt, 1923.

Maguire, James. *American Bee: The National Spelling Bee and the Culture of Word Nerds*. New York: Rodale, 2006.

Marrs, Suzanne. *Eudora Welty: A Biography*. New York: Mariner Books, 2006.

Martin, Dawn Lundy. *a gathering of matter a matter of gathering*. Athens: University of Georgia Press, 2007.

Massengill, Reed. *Portrait of a Racist: The Man Who Killed Medgar Evers?* New York: St. Martin's, 1994.

McClain, Shirla Robinso. "The Contributions of Blacks in Akron: 1825–1975." PhD diss., University of Akron, 1975.

McGuigan, Cathleen. "New Art, New Money." *New York Times Magazine*, February 10, 1985. https://www.nytimes.com/1985/02/10/magazine/new-art-new-money.html.

McGuire, Danielle L. *At the Dark End of the Street: Black Women, Rape, and Resistance: A New History of the Civil Rights Movement from Rosa Parks to the Rise of Black Power*. New York: Vintage, 2010.

McHaney, Pearl Amelia. "An Interview with Natasha Trethewey." In *Conversations with Natasha Trethewey*, edited by Joan Wylie Hall, 45–60. Jackson: University Press of Mississippi, 2013.

———. "Natasha Trethewey's Triptych: The Bodies of History in *Bellocq's Ophelia, Native Guard,* and *Thrall*. *Southern Quarterly* 50, no. 4 (Summer 2013): 153–72.

McKee, Marc. "A Conversation with Natasha Trethewey." In *Conversations with Natasha Trethewey*, edited by Joan Wylie Hall, 136–49. Jackson: University Press of Mississippi, 2013.

McKibbin, Molly Littlewood. "Southern Patriarchy and the Figure of the White Woman in Gwendolyn Brooks's 'A Bronzeville Mother Loiters in Mississippi. Meanwhile, a Mississippi Mother Burns Bacon.'" *African American Review* 44, no. 4 (Winter 2011): 667–85.

McRae, Elizabeth Gillespie. *Mothers and the Making of Massive Resistance*. New York: Oxford University Press, 2018.

Medina, Tony. "Persona Non Grata." In *Furious Flower: Seeding the Future of African American Poetry*, edited by Joanne V. Gabbin and Lauren K. Alleyne, 360–64. Evanston, IL: Northwestern University Press, 2020.

Mendi + Keith Obadike. *Big House/Disclosure*. 1913 Press, 2008.

Mlinko, Ange. Review of *Native Guard* by Natasha Trethewey. *Poetry* 191, no. 1 (October 2007): 59–61.

Montrose, Louis A. "Professing the Renaissance: The Poetics and Politics of Culture." In *The New Historicism*, edited by H. Aram Veeser, 15–36. New York: Routledge, 1989.

Morrison, Toni. *Beloved*. New York: Plume, 1987.

———. "The Site of Memory." In *Inventing the Truth: The Art and Craft of Memoir*, edited by William Zinsser, 101–24. Boston: Houghton Mifflin, 1987.

Morrison, Toni, and Robert B. Stepto. "'Intimate Things in Place': A Conversation with Toni Morrison." *Massachusetts Review* 18, no. 3 (Autumn 1977): 473–89.

Moyer, Bill. "Poet Laureate Rita Dove." Billmoyer.com. August 21, 2015. https://billmoyers.com/content/poet-laureate-rita-dove.

Mullen, Harryette. Introduction to *Gathering Ground: Celebrating Cave Canem's First Decade*, edited by Toi Derricotte, Cornelius Eady, and Camille T. Dungy, 7–10. Ann Arbor: University of Michigan Press, 2006.

Murphy, Paul V. *The Rebuke of History: The Southern Agrarians and American Conservative Thought*. Chapel Hill: University of North Carolina Press, 2001.

Nash, Gary B. *Forging Freedom: The Formation of Philadelphia's Black Community 1720–1840*. Cambridge, MA: Harvard University Press, 1988.

Nelson, Marilyn. *Carver: A Life in Poems*. Asheville, NC: Front Street, 2001.

Nesbett, Peter T., and Michelle Dubois. *Jacob Lawrence: Paintings, Drawings, and Murals (1935–1999) A Catalogue Raisonné*. Seattle: University of Washington Press, 2000.

"New Plays in Manhattan: Ziegfeld Follies of 1936." *Time*, February 10, 1936, 47.

New Standard Dictionary of the English Language. Funk and Wagnalls, 1935. s.v. "nemesis."

Newton, Michael. *The Ku Klux Klan: History, Organization, Language, Influence and Activities of America's most Notorious Secret Society*. Jefferson, NC: McFarland, 2007.

Nielsen, Aldon Lynn. *Writing between the Lines: Race and Intertextuality*. Athens: University of Georgia Press, 1994.

Nisco, Maria Cristina. "Dark Histories, Bright Revisions: Writing the Black Female Body." *Nebula* 3, no. 1 (April 2006): 65–72.

Novick, Peter. *That Noble Dream: The "Objectivity Question" and the American Historical Profession*. New York: Cambridge University Press, 1998.

Painter, Nell Irvin. "Remembering Herbert Gutman." *Labor History* 29, no. 3 (Summer 1988): 336–43.

Parks, Suzan-Lori. *Venus*. New York: Theatre Communications Group, 1996.

Pereira, Malin. *Into a Light Both Brilliant and Unseen: Conversations with Contemporary Black Poets*. Athens: University of Georgia Press, 2010.

———. "Re-reading Trethewey through Mixed Race Studies." *Southern Quarterly* 50, no. 4 (Summer 2013): 123–52.

Phillip, Christine. "An Interview with Elizabeth Alexander." *Callaloo* 19, no. 2 (Spring 1996): 493–507.

Pinto, Samantha. *Difficult Diasporas: The Transnational Feminist Aesthetic of the Black Atlantic*. New York: New York University Press, 2013.

Plante, Jessica. "An Interview with A. Van Jordan." *storySouth* 36 (Fall 2013). http://storysouth.com/stories/an-interview-with-a-van-jordan/.

Potter, Vilma Raskin. "A Remembrance for Robert Hayden: 1913–1980." *MELUS* 8, no. 1 (March 1981): 51–55.

Price, Mark J. "A Way with Words." *Akron Beacon Journal* 21 (May 2000). https://www.beaconjournal.com/story/news/2021/07/11/1936-akron-spelling-champ-blazed-trail-2021-national-winner/7932212002/.

Quarles, Benjamin. *Black Mosaic: Essays in Afro-American History and Historiography*. Amherst: University of Massachusetts Press, 1988.

Queen, Khadijah. "Natasha Trethewey's Palimpsestic Poetics." In *North American Women Poets in the 21st Century: Beyond Lyric and Language*, edited by Lisa Sewell and Kazim Ali, 311–33. Middletown, CT: Wesleyan University Press, 2020.

Rambsy, Howard, II. "Catching Holy Ghosts: The Diverse Manifestations of Black Persona Poetry," *African American Review* 42, nos. 3–4 (Fall-Winter 2008): 549–64.

Ramsey, William M. "Terrance Hayes and Natasha Trethewey: Contemporary Black Chronicles of the Imagined South." *Southern Literary Journal* 44, no. 2 (Spring 2012): 122–35.

Randall, James, and Michael S. Harper. "An Interview with Michael S. Harper." *Ploughshares* 7, no. 1 (1981): 10–27.

Ratiner, Steven. "A Chorus of Voices." In *Conversations with Rita Dove*, edited by Earl G. Ingersoll, 103–20. Jackson: University Press of Mississippi, 2003.

Rawick, George P. *From Sundown to Sunup: The Making of the Black Community*. Westport, CT: Greenwood, 1972.

Regosin, Elizabeth A., and Donald R. Shaffer, *Voices of Emancipation: Understanding Slavery, the Civil War, and Reconstruction through the U.S. Pension Bureau Files*. New York: New York University Press, 2008.

Reiner, Ron, dir. *Ghosts of Mississippi*. Castle Rock Entertainment, 1996. Film.

Reynolds, David S. *John Brown, Abolitionist*. New York: Knopf, 2005.

Righelato, Pat. "Rita Dove and the Art of History." *Callaloo* 31, no. 3 (Summer 2008): 760–75.

———. *Understanding Rita Dove*. Columbia: University of South Carolina Press, 2006.

Romain, Michael. "The Tragedy of MacNolia Cox." *Journal of Oak Park and River Forest*, May 20, 2015. https://www.oakpark.com/2015/05/20/the-tragedy-of-macnolia-cox/.

Ronda, Bruce A. *Reading the Old Man: John Brown in American Culture*. Knoxville: University of Tennessee Press, 2008.

Rooks, Noliwe M. "The Beginnings of Black Studies." *Chronicle of Higher Education* 52, no. 23 (2006). https://www.chronicle.com/article/the-beginnings-of-black-studies/.

Rosenthal, Emerson. "The Exclusive Story behind Warhol and Basquiat's Boxing Photos." *Vice Magazine*. July 7, 2015. https://www.vice.com/en/article/ez5aaw/the-exclusive-story-behind-warhol-and-basquiats-boxing-photos.

Rowell, Charles H., ed. *Angles of Ascent: A Norton Anthology of Contemporary African American Poetry*. New York: Norton, 2013.

Rowell, Charles H. "'Down Don't Worry Me': An Interview with Michael S. Harper." *Callaloo* 13, no. 4 (Autumn 1990): 780–800.

———. "Inscriptive Restorations: An Interview with Natasha Trethewey." *Callaloo* 27, no. 4 (2004): 1022–34.

———. "An Interview with Kevin Young." *Callaloo* 21, no. 2 (Winter 1998): 43–54.

———. "Interview with Rita Dove: Part 2." *Callaloo* 31, no. 3 (Summer 2008): 715–26.

———. "'The Poem Is Smarter Than the Poet': An Interview with A. Van Jordan." *Callaloo* 27, no. 4 (Autumn 2004): 908–19.

Royals, Tom, and John Little. "A Conversation with Eudora Welty." In *Conversations with Eudora Welty*, edited by Peggy Whitman Prenshaw, 252–67. Jackson: University Press of Mississippi, 1984.

Ruggles, Jeffrey. *The Unboxing of Henry Brown*. Richmond: Library of Virginia, 2003.

Sagan, Carl. *Broca's Brain: Reflections on the Romance of Science*. New York: Random House, 1974.

Samuels, David. "The Call of Stories." *Lingua Franca* (May/June 1995): 35–43.

Saul, Scott. "Triple-Conscious Brothers in the Vein: Reading Michael S. Harper through John Brown and W. E. B. Du Bois." *Journal of Ethnic American Literature* 6 (2016): 61–83.

Schnabel, Julian, dir. *Basquiat*. Miramax Films, 1996. Film.

Schneider, Steven. "Coming Home: An Interview with Rita Dove." *Iowa Review* 19, no. 3 (Fall 1989): 112–23.

———. "Writing for Those Moments of Discovery." In *Conversations with Rita Dove*, edited by Earl G. Ingersoll, 62–73. Jackson: University Press of Mississippi, 2003.

Schomburg, Arthur A., "The Negro Digs Up His Past." In *The New Negro*, edited by Alain Locke, 231–37. New York: Atheneum, 1992. First published 1925.

Schwalm, Leslie A. "Ar'n't I a Woman? Rethinking the History of Women, Gender, and Slavery." Unpublished paper. Annual Meeting of Southern Historical Association. 2003.

Schwartz, Claire. "An Interview with Toi Derricotte." *Transition* 124 (2017): 157–75.

———. "'Moving toward What I Don't Know': An Interview with Tracy K. Smith." *Iowa Review* 46, no. 2 (Fall 2016): 173–92.

———. "Natasha Trethewey: Language and Ruthlessness." *Oxford American*, January 8, 2016. http://www.oxfordamerican.org/item/745-natasha-trethewey-language-and-ruthlessness.

Schwartz, Marie Jenkins. *Birthing a Slave: Motherhood and Medicine in the Antebellum South*. Cambridge, MA: Harvard University Press, 2006.

Sellar, Tom. "Making History: Suzan-Lori Parks: The Shape of the Past." In *Suzan-Lori Parks in Person: Interviews and Commentaries*, edited by Philip C. Kolin and Harvey Young, 49–54. New York: Routledge, 2014.

Shockley, Evie. "The Black Arts Movement and Black Aesthetics." In *Cambridge Companion to Modern American Poetry*, edited by Walter Kalaidjian, 180–95. Cambridge: Cambridge UP, 2015.

———. "Going Overboard: African American Poetic Innovation and the Middle Passage." *Contemporary Literature* 52, no. 4 (Winter 2011): 791–817.

———. *the new black*. Middletown, CT: Wesleyan University Press, 2011.

———. *Renegade Poetics: Black Aesthetics and Formal Innovation in African American Poetry*. Iowa City: University of Iowa Press, 2011.

Silverstein, Jake. "Writing a Poem." *Texas Monthly* 36, no. 6 (June 2008): 30.

Smith, Tracy K. "Back to Earth: Tracy K. Smith on Her New Poetry Project." April 19, 2013. Minneapolis: Graywolf Press. https://www.graywolfpress.org/back-earth-tracy-k-smith. Accessed Nov. 29, 2016.

———. "I Will Tell You the Truth about This, I Will Tell You All about It." In *Lines in Long Array: A Civil War Commemoration*, edited by David C. Ward and Frank H. Goodyear III, 68–82. Washington, DC: National Portrait Gallery, 2013.

———. *Wade in the Water*. Minneapolis: Graywolf Press, 2018.

Solomon, Deborah. "Native Daughter." *New York Times Magazine*, May 13, 2007, 15.

"Spelling Her Way to Success." *Ebony*, October 1998, 144–46.

Steffen, Therese. *Crossing Color: Transcultural Space and Place in Rita Dove's Poetry, Fiction, and Drama*. Oxford: Oxford University Press, 2001.

Steinman, Lisa M. "Dialogues between History and Dream." *Michigan Quarterly Review* 26, no. 2 (1987): 428–38.

Stepto, Robert B. "Michael Harper's Extended Tree: John Coltrane and Sterling Brown." In *Twayne Companion to Contemporary Literature in English*, edited by R. H. W. Dillard and Amanda Cockrell, 1:423–37. New York: Twayne, 2002.

Strange, Sharan. "Dark Room Collective: Essay." *Mosaic Magazine*, May 12, 2013. https://mosaicmagazine.org/dark-room-collective-essay/.

Sublette, Ned, and Constance. *The American Slave Coast: A History of the Slave-Breeding Industry*. Chicago: Lawrence Hill Books, 2016.

Switala, William J. *Underground Railroad in Pennsylvania*. Mechanicsburg, PA: Stackpole, 2001.

Taleb-Khyar, Mohamed B. "Gifts to Be Earned." In *Conversations with Rita Dove*, edited by Earl G. Ingersoll, 74–87. Jackson: University Press of Mississippi, 2003.

Tate, Greg. "Nobody Loves a Genius Child." In *Flyboy in the Buttermilk: Essays on Contemporary America*, 231–44. New York: Simon & Schuster, 1992.

Teresi, Christian. "An Interview with Natasha Trethewey." In *Conversations with Natasha Trethewey*, edited by Joan Wylie Hall, 112–25. Jackson: University Press of Mississippi, 2013.

Thomas, Lorenzo. *Extraordinary Measures: Afrocentric Modernism and Twentieth-Century American Poetry*. Tuscaloosa: University of Alabama Press, 2000.

Thoreau, Henry D. *Walden: A Fully Annotated Edition*. New Haven, CT: Yale University Press, 2004.

Treseler, Heather. "Office Hours: A Memoir and an Interview with Michael S. Harper." *Iowa Review* 39, no. 3 (Winter 2009): 100–123.

Trethewey, Eric. "Connections and Correspondences." *Antioch Review* 66, no. 4 (Fall 2008): 682–94.

———. "Walking Home." *Southern Review* 39, no. 1 (2003): 198–208.
Trethewey, Natasha. *Bellocq's Ophelia*. Saint Paul, MN: Graywolf Press, 2002.
———. *Domestic Work*. Saint Paul, MN: Graywolf Press, 2000.
———. "The Far, Deep Things of Dreamland: An Interview with Elizabeth Alexander." *Poets & Writers* 11.01.01 (November/December 2001). https://www.pw.org/content/far_deep_things_dreamland_interview_elizabeth_alexander.
———. *Memorial Drive: A Daughter's Memoir*. New York: Harper Collins, 2020.
———. *Native Guard*. New York: Houghton Mifflin, 2006.
———. Natasha Trethewey Papers. Stuart A. Rose Manuscript, Archives, and Rare Book Library, Emory University, Atlanta,.
———. "On Whitman, Civil War Memory, and My South." *Virginia Quarterly Review* 81, no. 2 (Spring 2005): 50–57.
———. "The Quarrel with Ourselves: Robert Penn Warren's 'World of Action and Liability.'" *AWP* (March/April 2015). https://www.awpwriter.org/magazine_media/writers_chronicle_view/3684/the_quarrel_with_ourselves_robert_penn_warrens_world_of_action_and_liability.
———. *Thrall*. Boston: Houghton Mifflin, 2012.
———. "'Why I Write': Poetry, History, and Social Justice." *Waccamaw* 12 (Fall 2010). https://waccamawjournal.com/archive/.
T'Shaka, Oba. "Africana Studies Department History: San Francisco State University." *Journal of Pan African Studies* 5, no. 7 (October 2012): 13–32.
Turner, Daniel Cross. "Southern Crossings: An Interview with Natasha Trethewey." *Waccamaw* 6 (Fall 2010). https://waccamawjournal.com/archive/.
———. *Southern Crossings: Poetry, Memory, and the Transcultural South*. Knoxville: University of Tennessee Press, 2012.
Tyson, Timothy B. *The Blood of Emmett Till*. New York: Simon and Schuster, 2017.
Vendler, Helen. "In the Zoo of the New." *New York Review of Books*, October 23, 1986, 47–52.
"Vigilant Committee of Philadelphia Records." 1839–1844 (Collection 1221). Historical Society of Pennsylvania. http://www2.hsp.org/collections/manuscripts/v/VCPAm3375.html.
Walker, Frank X. *Buffalo Dance: The Journey of York*. Lexington: University Press of Kentucky, 2004.
———. *Turn Me Loose: The Unghosting of Medgar Evers*. Athens: University of Georgia Press, 2013.
Wallace, Patricia. "Divided Loyalties: Literal and Literary in the Poetry of Lorna Dee Cervantes, Cathy Song and Rita Dove." *MELUS* 18, no. 3 (Autumn 1993): 3–19.
Walsh, William. "The World Has to Fall Away: An Interview with Rita Dove." *Georgia Review* (Spring 2016). https://thegeorgiareview.com/posts/the-world-has-to-fall-away-an-interview-with-rita-dove/.
Warhol, Andy. *The Andy Warhol Diaries*. Edited by Pat Hackett. New York: Warner, 1989.
Warren, Nagueyalti. "History, Memory, and Nostalgia in the Works of Natasha Trethewey." *Southern Quarterly* 50, no. 4 (Summer 2013): 75–98.
Warren, Robert Penn. *Audubon: A Vision*. New York: Random House, 1969.

———. "The Briar Patch." In *I'll Take My Stand: The South and the Agrarian Tradition, by Twelve Southerners*, 246–64. New York: Harper Torchbooks, 1962. First published 1930 by Harper and Bros. (New York).

———. *Segregation: The Inner Conflict in the South*. New York: Random House, 1956.

———. *Who Speaks for the Negro?* New York: Random House, 1965.

Weaver, C. P., ed. *Thank God My Regiment an African One: The Civil War Diary of Colonel Nathan W. Daniels*. Baton Rouge: Louisiana State University Press, 1998.

Webster's Second International Dictionary of the English Language. Merriam, 1934. s.v. "nemesis."

Welty, Eudora. *The Collected Stories of Eudora Welty*. New York: Harcourt Brace Jovanovich, 1980.

Werbanowska, Marta. "Reclaiming the Commodified Body: The Stories of Saartjie Baartman and Josephine Baker in the Poetry of Elizabeth Alexander." *Ethos: A Digital Review of Arts, Humanities, and Public Ethics* 1, no. 1 (2014): 18–35.

Wheat, Ellen Harkins. *Jacob Lawrence American Painter*. Seattle: University of Washington Press, 1986.

White, Deborah Gray. "My History in History." In *Telling Histories: Black Women Historians in the Ivory Tower*, edited by Deborah Gray White, 85–100. Chapel Hill: University of North Carolina Press, 2008.

White, Hayden. "The Historical Text as Literary Artifact." *Tropics of Discourse: Essays in Cultural Criticism,* 81–100. Baltimore: Johns Hopkins University Press, 1978.

———. *The Practical Past*. Evanston, IL: Northwestern University Press, 2014.

Wiggins, William H., Jr. "Jack Johnson as Bad Nigger: The Folklore of His Life." *The Black Scholar* 2, no. 5 (January 1971): 34–46.

Wiley, Bell Irvin, and Hirst D. Milhollen. *They Who Fought Here*. New York: Macmillan, 1959.

Williams, Michael Vinson. *Medgar Evers: Mississippi Martyr*. Fayetteville: University of Arkansas Press, 2013.

Williams, Pontheolla T. *Robert Hayden: A Critical Analysis of His Poetry*. Urbana: University of Illinois Press, 1987.

Williams, Wilburn, Jr. "Covenant of Timelessness and Time: Symbolism and History in Robert Hayden's *Angle of Ascent*." In *Chant of Saints*, edited by Michael S. Harper and Robert B. Stepto, 66–84. Urbana: University of Illinois Press, 1979.

Willis, Deborah. Introduction to *Black Venus 2010: They Called Her "Hottentot*," edited by Deborah Willis, 3–11. Philadelphia: Temple University Press, 2010.

Wilson, Carol. *Freedom at Risk: The Kidnapping of Free Blacks in America, 1780–1865*. Lexington: University Press of Kentucky, 1994.

Winch, Julie. *Between Slavery and Freedom: Free People of Color in America from Settlement to the Civil War*. Lanham: Bowman and Littlefield, 2014.

Wood, Eben. "The Private Lives of System: Rukeyser, Hayden, Middle Passage." *Modernism/modernity* 17, no. 1 (January 2010): 201–22.

WPA Guide to Ohio: The Buckeye State. Federal Writers' Project. 1940. San Antonio: Trinity University Press, 2013.
Wright, Richard. "The Ethics of Living Jim Crow." In *Uncle Tom's Children*, 1–15. New York: Harper, 1938.
Yau, John. "Street Song: The Art of Jean-Michel Basquiat and the Poetry of Kevin Young." In *The Passionate Spectator: Essays on Art and Poetry*, 87–101. Ann Arbor: University of Michigan Press, 2006.
Yetman, Norman R., "Ex-Slave Interviews and the Historiography of Slavery." *American Quarterly* 36, no. 2 (Summer 1984): 181–210.
Young, Kevin. *Brown: Poems*. New York: Knopf, 2018.
———, ed. Introduction to *Giant Steps: The New Generation of African American Writers*, 1–12. New York: Perennial, 2000.
———. *The Grey Album: On the Blackness of Blackness*. Minneapolis: Graywolf, 2012.
———. Preface to *Blue Laws: Selected and Uncollected Poems 1995–2015*. New York: Knopf, 2016.
———. *To Repel Ghosts*. South Royalton: Zoland Books, 2001.
———. *To Repel Ghosts: The Remix*. New York: Knopf, 2005.
Zinn, Howard. *The Politics of History*. Chicago: University of Press, 1970.

INDEX